D1408914

RELIGION: A Sociological View

ELIZABETH K. NOTTINGHAM

RELIGION:
A Sociological View

RANDOM HOUSE — NEW YORK

ISBN: 0-394-31021-7
Library of Congress Catalog Card Number: 75-122976

Manufactured in the United States of America by The Kingsport Press, Inc., Kingsport, Tenn.

First Edition
9 8 7 6 5 4 3

Based on *Religion and Society*, by Elizabeth K. Nottingham. Copyright 1954 by Doubleday and Co., Inc.
Design by J. M. Wall

To
Charles H. Page

PREFACE

Religion: A Sociological View was originally undertaken as a revision of my earlier *Religion and Society*. As the work progressed, however, it became clear that the new material outbalanced the old, and the present much longer book, which includes a more extended treatment of the role of religion in non-Western societies and a theoretical Appendix, called for a new title. Much of the framework of the earlier book, however, has been retained, and the book is still concerned with the varying roles religion has played in societies of differing types. But today events move too quickly for the mind to completely grasp their significance, and in the process of writing I began to realize that a new type of society, which I have called a Model Four society, is currently emerging. Some of its characteristics I was able to glimpse rather clearly, though unfortunately, since my insight into the shifting contemporary scene fails to equal my hindsight, I was not able to delineate it in its entirety.

The increasing rapidity of social and religious change in recent years poses some bewildering and fascinating problems for the sociology of religion. Conventional distinctions, for instance, between the concepts of the "religious" and the "secular" are becoming blurred. Sociologically oriented theologians, such as Harvey Cox, see the "religious" as being meaningful only within the "secular" milieu, which Cox views chiefly as that of the changing metropolis. On the other hand, some sociologists, notably J. Milton Yinger, regard the term "secularization" as itself a misnomer and claim that much behavior that has been termed "secularized" represents, in fact, *religious change*. It is not clear, however, whether all changes in a secular direction can fairly be thus described, but the question does arise as to the continued usefulness of the dichotomy between the religious and the secular.

It has been customary, nevertheless, to regard modern Western societies as "secular"; indeed, their powerfully organized institutions, political, economic, and military, do appear to be largely independent of religious influences. Yet even in contemporary electronically mechanized society undercurrents of religious ferment can be discerned. This ferment is little in evidence, according to recent research findings, among conventionally orthodox members of established churches. Among the denominationally unaffiliated, however, particularly among students and other young people, among members of small religious and quasi-religious movements and fringe groups, as well as among some dissident members of the churches, the winds of change are blowing. Furthermore, since the Second Vatican Council, Ecumenism no longer denotes a mainly top-level attempt at organizational mergers of divided bodies of Christians. It has developed into a largely informal movement of lower clergy and laity reaching out to men and women of good will. This outreach is extended to those who profess any and all of the religions of the world as well as to some who make no formal profession of faith.

It may be that from some combination of these elements that the new shape of religion will emerge. It may possibly be successful in permeating, to a greater extent than religion does now, the spirit of a new society; or it may languish and die in a period of political repression and warfare. The picture is still unclear. Traditional religious organizations are in disarray, and instant communication via satellite is making the world a village in which time-honored religious divisions are becoming increasingly pointless.

I am sadly aware that in this present work these new horizons are as seen but through a glass darkly. It is my hope that a rising generation of sociologists will be able to give depth and precision to insights that are now largely tentative and hypothetical. In this task they will need to cooperate with theologians, anthropologists, and depth psychologists; for sociologists can no longer maintain an olympian aloofness from their subject matter or from its related disciplines.

It remains for me to thank those who have helped to make this book possible. Especial thanks are due to my former students at Queens College, whose comments and queries contributed to my sociological education and stimulated my explorations. I wish to make special acknowledgments to Joan McGuire and Marie-Helene Laraque who read parts of the manuscript while in preparation. Dr. Laile E. Bartlett and Dr. Paul Clasper also read several chapters and made numerous helpful suggestions. I must also mention with gratitude the Fulbright Exchange Program that enabled me to spend a year in Burma and so gain some understanding of the social impact of a non-Western religion, namely Theravada Buddhism. To my former research assistant, Sao Htun Hmat Win (now Research Director of the Institute for Advanced Buddhistic Studies in Rangoon, Burma), I am indebted not only for the collection of much Burmese material but also for help in interpreting it. To Susan Rothstein and other members of the Random House editorial staff go my grateful thanks for their meticulous and patient work in the final editing of the manuscript.

But for the constant encouragement and inspiration of my friend, fellow sociologist and consultant editor, Charles H. Page, this book would probably never have been finished. I take particular satisfaction in dedicating it, with affection, to him.

Elizabeth K. Nottingham
Berkeley, California

CONTENTS

RELIGION: A Sociological View

1

A Sociological View
of Religion

THE SOCIOLOGIST'S
CONCERN WITH RELIGION

Because of the richness and variety of its subject matter, the field of religion is a difficult one for the exercise of sociological discrimination. For many the main interest in religion is personal and individualistic; and in thinking about it, some are apt to focus on the more intellectual and emotional aspects of ethics and belief. Like William James, they are concerned with the "feelings, acts and experiences of individual men in their solitude . . . in relation to whatsoever they consider the divine."[1] But in his definition of religion James left out precisely those universal, societal, and institutional aspects of religion that most directly concern the sociologist. The sociologist's interest is not that of the philosopher, theologian, or individual psychologist. He is interested in religion as a universal function of human societies. His concern is with religion as an aspect of group behavior and with the roles religion has played through the ages, and still plays, in furthering and hampering the survival of human groups. The less individual and the more universal, the less unusual and the more repetitive the behavior under observation, the more useful it is to the sociologist.

The sociologist, in addition, is committed to the attempt to study religion objectively, from the viewpoint of a social scientist. This aim may present a problem to the student. Indeed, some scholars assert that the difficulties are almost insuperable, and an even greater number of religionists claim that a cool, "scientific" study of religion, even were it possible, would be undesirable.

Religion is, for many people, so much an affair of the heart, so often inexplicable even to themselves, so colored by their own special feeling for the particular beliefs and ceremonies that have become sacred to them through long association, that it is difficult for them to assume an objective, scientific stance. In Western society, for example, religion for many is closely bound up with certain cherished ideals: a belief in one God, in Jesus Christ His Son, and in the ultimate worth and lofty destiny of man. Although readers smile at Fielding's Parson Thwakum and his naive identification of "religion" with the religion of "the Church of England,"[2] they, too, in more subtle guise, may half-consciously slip into the error of accepting as their model of religion the one they know best, thus limiting their concept of religion in general to their own particular experience. Yet religion in a broad sense cannot be equated with any one set of practices and ideals.

It has been said that the question of the desirability of an objective study of religion is even more controversial than the question of its possibility.[3] Since religion is based on faith, it is feared that an objective study may weaken faith and dissolve religious allegiance. It is perhaps understandable that many religionists fear that too cool a scrutiny may diminish the value of what they hold dear or tarnish their feelings toward it. The worshiper is—must be—constrained by loyalty, faith, and awe. The obligation of the student is to truth; yet in the pursuit of truth he is surely required to control and use, rather than divest himself of, all feeling and emotion. Although the capacity to combine the attitudes of the student and of the worshiper may at times be difficult to maintain, it is the contention here that it is within the compass of a single individual. Even though it would be impossible to demonstrate that the analysis of religion by science is universally beneficial, it can be argued that the long-run consequences of scientific study are beneficial, whereas a continuance of ignorance and bias is in the long run harmful.[4]

On the other hand, the sociologist, as an empiricist, may become nonscientific in his very zeal for science, as J. Milton Yinger has aptly pointed out, by claiming that "all that is important about religion is available to the objective observer." [5] Sociology, as a science, inevitably abstracts relevant aspects from concrete reality. Hence it would be arrogant for sociologists to claim that their propositions concerning religion, however objectively derived, exhaust the meaning of religion. Fortunately sociologists today are more modest in their claims than they were even twenty-five years ago, and this modesty has greatly facilitated the social-scientific study of the field.

Nonreligionists also encounter problems in maintaining scientific objectivity. They may find it difficult to give sufficient weight to phenomena that they judge to have no ultimate objective validity, to be no more than stupendous projections of the human imagination. Thus it is unlikely that either religionists or nonreligionists can examine the part played by religion in society without ethnocentrism and without bias.

These are real problems. Nevertheless, scholars who hold the most diverse opinions about the empirical—that is, the experimentally or experientially verifiable reality of "things unseen"— are increasingly in agreement about the real and practical significance of nonempirical (nonverifiable) things in social life. They do not misunderstand the nature of the truths or the techniques established by the natural sciences, but they are also aware (as are many natural scientists) that the truths of natural science are not the only truths men live by. Indeed, science as conceived by many is not merely a bundle of techniques, of means adapted to ends, but a faith—a faith in the eventual power of human reason to understand and control the universe.

It was stated at the outset that the sociology student must practice discrimination in singling out for study those aspects of religion with which his discipline is properly concerned. This should not be understood to imply that the sociologist of religion should so narrow his perspective that he fails to cultivate a sensitive awareness of contributions made by related disciplines. Some of the most important of these other disciplines are psychology, anthropology, philosophy, and theology.

As pointed out earlier, the central concern of the sociologist differs from that of the psychologist. Yet the sociologist's understanding of religion as a phenomenon, and of religious motivation in particular, is greatly enhanced by the work of psychologists such as William James, Gordon W. Allport, and Sigmund Freud. Furthermore, the work of anthropologists such as Bronislaw Malinowski and A. R. Radcliffe-Brown has afforded to sociologists of religion notable insights, many of which will be utilized in this volume. Even theology, whether or not it is regarded as a science, ought not to be treated with indifference. The sociologist is not required to pass judgment on the truth or the falsity of particular theological systems; nevertheless, insofar as theological systems are belief systems that significantly influence social behavior, they supply the sociologist with important data that he cannot afford to ignore. Theologians such as Paul Tillich, Rheinhold Niebuhr, and Martin Buber have been deeply influential in stimulating sociological thinking in regard to religion's social role. Indeed, only an emasculated sociology of religion would result from shutting out these interdisciplinary influences.

THE PROBLEM OF DEFINITION

The famous German sociologist Max Weber began his *Sociology of Religion* with the statement, "To define 'religion,' to say what it *IS,* is not possible at the start of a presentation such as this. Definition can be attempted, if at all, only at the conclusion of the study." [6] There is a profound sense in which this statement is true. Some scholars focus too heavily on this matter of definition; they busy themselves interminably with playing off one man's definition against another's, only to discover that they have been engaged in nothing more substantial than a game of words. Nevertheless, it is the contention here, as it was of the French sociologist Émile Durkheim, that there is some value in preliminary definitions if—as Durkheim's were—they are based on familiarity with a wide range of relevant empirical material [7] and if, furthermore, they are viewed in the light of suggestive hypotheses, subject to subsequent modification, rather than as rigid and unchangeable prescriptions.

Some of the divergences that characterize the many existing definitions of religion may well be confusing. But if it is clearly understood that different people have different purposes in mind when they attempt to define phenomena, some of this confusion may disappear. One group of writers may attempt to define a given phenomenon in terms of what they think it should be. Such definitions are likely to be of little value to the social scientist. Another group may limit their definition to data derived from a particular manifestation of a given phenomenon, and such definitions also have strictly limited usefulness for social scientists. A third group may attempt to build their definitions after making a study of many concrete manifestations of a given phenomenon and distilling that which they have in common.[8] The definitions formulated by this third group are most likely to be of interest to the sociologist. And although there is no unanimity among social scientists in the field of religion with respect even to this third type of definition, there exists among such scholars today a considerable body of implicit agreement.

The problem, then, that confronts the sociologist is that of finding a definition of religion suitable for his particular purposes, namely, one sufficiently specific to furnish a useful tool for understanding particular forms of religious life and yet broad enough to be applicable to the religious behavior of "all sorts and conditions of men." [9]

Why is so broad a concept necessary? Such a definition is desirable since religious behavior of one sort or another appears to be universal among human beings. Although some recent writers have contested the imputation of universality to religion,[10] it is the opinion here that it may for practical purposes be assumed. The earliest relics of Neanderthal man show evidences of activities that some scholars have interpreted as religious. No modern ethnologist has yet discovered a human group without traces of behavior that may be similarly described. Difficult as this universality may be to explain, its existence finds substantial support in the researches of both historians and anthropologists. The manifestations of this religious behavior, however, may vary enormously and are, in addition, so intricately interwoven with other important aspects of man's behavior that it is difficult to disengage the specifically religious element.

RELIGION AND THE CONDITION OF MAN

It is clear that no single definition of religion can satisfy everybody. For one thing, religion in its almost unimaginable variety calls for description rather than definition. It is a phenomenon so much "in the round" that it yields reluctantly to attempts at scientific abstraction. Religion is associated with man's attempts to plumb the depths of meaning both in himself and in the universe. It has given rise to the most spacious products of his imagination, and it has been used to justify the extremest cruelty of man to man. It can conjure up moods of sublime exaltation, and also images of dread and terror. Although preoccupied with the reality of a world that cannot be seen, religion has been involved with the most mundane details of daily life. It has been used to blaze new trails into the heart of the unknown, and utopias have been founded in its name; yet it has also served to shackle men to outworn customs or beliefs. Worship in common—the sharing of the symbols of religion —has united human groups in the closest ties known to man; yet religious differences have accounted for some of the fiercest group antagonisms. Religious worship has been adorned with all the exuberance of the arts, but it has also flourished under conditions of the barest austerity. Religion has provided men with symbols whereby they may express the inexpressible; yet the essence of the religious experience forever eludes expression. The thought of God has served to encourage men in the tasks of every day, to reconcile them to an unkind fate, or again, to "take arms against a sea of troubles, and by opposing end them." [11]

Paradox is at the heart of religion, for as men have sought to

8

plumb the mystery of things, they have necessarily attempted to understand and reconcile the great polarities in the universe and in themselves: good and evil, love and loathing, worship and dread, god and devil.

What does all this mean for the student of society? What bearing does it have on his attempts to understand religion's social role? Although the sociologist's main interest is in religion as *behavior*, he can never be indifferent to religion as a total experience. The foregoing discussion therefore implies, at the very least, that the basis of religion in human society is as complex as are human conditions themselves, and that the nature of religion can be understood only in relation to the total predicament of man. It would be convenient, but a falsification of all available evidence, if man's religious propensity could be traced to some definable instinct; for in that way its universality would be established beyond question, and in addition, we would possess important clues as to religion's essential nature. However, man's religion cannot be derived from any one of the endowments that he shares with other animals.[12] Nor can it be thought of as stemming from any one aspect of his distinctively human attributes. However significant for religion the long period of dependency of the human young on their parents may be, neither God nor gods can be explained as simply a massive projection, or projections, of parental images.[13] There is rather general agreement among scholars that no such simple explanations are adequate.

The great nineteenth-century interpreters of religion, the founding fathers of the social-scientific approach, were aware for the most part that man's seemingly inveterate tendency toward religion could not be accounted for on overly simple instinctual grounds. They attempted, however, to deduce from their conception of man's total dilemma some universal motivations for religious behavior. Although most of their theories have since been either discarded or modified and are, strictly speaking, more relevant to the field of social psychology than to sociology proper, they have nevertheless afforded to sociologists many valuable insights.

Among nineteenth-century thinkers, who were greatly preoccupied with evolutionary theories, there was a general assumption that if the origins of religion could be unearthed, the essentials of religion itself and the dynamics of man's impulse to express himself religiously would thereby be discovered. It was further assumed that all human societies passed through a series of evolutionary stages and that by studying the religions of primitive peoples, scholars were in fact studying earlier—and comparable—manifestations of contemporary religion. Since it was commonly believed at that time that all human societies passed through a totemic stage, it was not surprising that several eminent scholars attempted to lay bare religion's origins by analyzing the role of religion in totemic societies.[14]

Although most of the assumptions shared by these nineteenth-century scholars are no longer accepted today and although their attempts to define religion in terms of its origins have now been largely abandoned, it is worthwhile for students to acquaint themselves with some of their ideas.[15] In this chapter, however, a very brief mention of some of their major emphases must suffice.

Once man is assumed to be a rational being, it may be further assumed that his reason would prompt him to inquire into his nature and destiny. E. B. Tylor, the first anthropologist to give us a well-thought-out history of religions from the beginnings up to the time of the great Egyptian and Sumerian civilizations, conceived of religion as the outcome of man's intellectual curiosity. According to Tylor, early man was led by his dream experiences to infer the existence of spiritual beings, including that of his own spiritual entity, his soul.[16] This emphasis on man's reason and curiosity would appear to be part, but not all, of the cause underlying man's drive toward religion. Indeed, Tylor has been criticized by other scholars for having overstressed the rationalistic aspects of religion and for having grounded the urge toward religious behavior too exclusively in intellectual factors. Nevertheless, Tylor did not ignore man's fears—fear of apparitions that he encountered in dreams, fear of death, fear of spirits, and fear of the unknown.

The British sociologist Herbert Spencer regarded fear—especially the fear of early man due to his ignorance of science and hence powerlessness in the face of the terrors of the natural world—as a main factor in religion's origin. Indeed, the attribution of man's religious drive to fear is very old indeed. The Roman writer Petronius considered the gods themselves to be creations of human fears.

In marked contrast to Tylor, both Durkheim and Freud emphasized the deeply emotional basis of man's religious urge. For Durkheim the crucial emotional component was the product of a particular kind of social event, namely, the periodical tribal gathering, or *corrobbori*, that punctuated the humdrum daily lives of "primitive" Australian totem worshipers and aroused in them a veritable mass frenzy of excitement. The contrast between their ordinary daily lives and the effervescence engendered by the *corrobbori* created a feeling in the tribesmen of being transported to another realm, the realm of the *sacred* (as Durkheim saw it) as opposed to the *secular,* or *profane,* world of their everyday lives.[17] For Durkheim the *corrobbori* was the crucial event necessary to the emergence of this idea of the sacred, for in his view the notion of two separate and distinct worlds of experience—the *sacred* and the *profane*—was essential to the development of religion.

Freud saw man's religious drive as grounded in man's racial heritage of crime and guilt. Reasoning by analogy from data collected in psychoanalytical sessions with patients who had displayed mixed feelings of hate and love toward their actual parents, Freud inferred that a great Primal Crime had taken place in the childhood of the race. The primal father was murdered by his sons for the sake of the women whom—in what was then believed to be the primate fashion—he kept under his sole control. This act of aggression against paternal authority was followed by anguished remorse on the part of the sons, whose feelings of tenderness toward the father then reasserted themselves over the feelings of hatred that had so recently resulted in the murder. The sons then banded together to carry out the wishes of the father by restraining their aggressive impulses and by denying themselves the liberated women. Thus the primal father—Freud's prototype of deity—became more powerful dead than alive.[18] Hence, according to Freud, religion—and, indeed, civilization itself—arose from the sublimation, triggered by anxiety and guilt, of man's powerful drives of aggression and sex. Few scholars today accept Freud's reconstruction of religion's genesis, nor must we do so in order to appreciate some of Freud's insights as to the paramount role played by anxiety and guilt in the development of religion.

In brief and oversimple fashion we have indicated some of the very diverse human situations coupled with their intellectual and emotional components that such thinkers as Tylor, Spencer, Durkheim, and Freud have seen as having played important parts in the emergence of religion. No one of these writers has made the final statement about the origin of religion, nor is it likely that a final statement will ever be made. The point here is that the very diversity of their views speaks eloquently about the complexity of the sources of religion in human nature and society. This very complexity, the fact that it can never be "written off" as "nothing but" intellectual curiosity, fear, crowd excitement, or projected guilt, is essential to an appreciation of religion's multifaceted nature.

Furthermore, all the writers mentioned above, with the possible exception of Freud, viewed man's religious behavior as almost entirely reactive and took little account of his creative capacities in the religious sphere. For man alone among the animals is capable of symbolic language and abstract thought. Not only does man act and react under the spur of fear, excitement, and anxiety, but he also innovates and anticipates action and uses his creative imagination to express his yearnings and his hopes. In addition, we find him not only experiencing but also reflecting on his experiences and struggling to make "sensible" interpretations of them. Most important, man's existential plight is such that in no period of human history up to the present have men had the empirical knowledge and power completely to control their destiny. There has always been a gap between their powers of rational control and their survival needs. The existence of this gap has, humanly speaking, helped to activate and maintain man's interest in a superempirical realm. All that we have said so far concerning the emergence of religion is implicit in the statement that religion, *from the point of view of the sociologist,* is a product of culture, an outgrowth of man's activity as a culture-bearing creature. From this standpoint, then, religion may be regarded as a cultural tool by means of which man has been able to accommodate himself to his experiences in his total environment, which includes himself, his fellow group members, the world of nature, and that which is felt by him to transcend them all.

THE NATURE OF THE RELIGIOUS REALM

There is rather general agreement among scholars that it is this last element in man's total environment—the direction of human thought, feeling, and action to things that man feels are beyond his ordinary everyday experiences—that constitutes the very core of religion. It follows, therefore, that religion is essentially a matter of *experience* in relation to a specifically religious "realm," although the experience may vary in the degree of its intensity and in the totality of a given individual's commitment and response. Furthermore, the nature and "contents" of the religious realm have been variously viewed by scholars. These various scholarly conceptions are not characterized by "either or" differences; they may be seen rather as shading into one another, as graduated positions on a continuum, ranging from relatively exclusive to more broadly inclusive definitions.

For a number of thinkers this specifically religious realm is the beyond of the *supernatural,* the dwelling place of a personal God or at the very least of godlike beings and spirits. For them a religion without a supernatural would be no religion at all. Arthur Darby Nock, the Harvard historian of religion, stated this view succinctly: "Religion is what men do, say and think—in that order—concerning the supernatural." [19] Other thinkers are less specific in attributing "contents" to the religious realm.

They may, like Paul Tillich, characterize it more vaguely as comprising the area of "man's ultimate concern," [20] or, like Rudolf Otto, as the "Holy." [21] For Durkheim, on the other hand, the religious realm was coterminous with what he has called the *sacred*, a category not to be defined in terms of specific "contents" but rather in terms of particular *attitudes* in regard to an almost infinite variety of beings and objects. As compared to the first group of thinkers, then, Durkheim takes a very broad view of what constitutes religion.

It will be apparent shortly that the description of religion given here as a social phenomenon leans heavily on Durkheim. The fact that it does so, however, should not be understood as passing judgment on the existence or nonexistence of God, gods, or the supernatural. Durkheim's broad category of the sacred includes the supernatural but also includes much else. Furthermore, Durkheim's formulations are designed to furnish sociologists not with articles of belief but rather with conceptual tools for the analysis of socioreligious behavior. Although no formulation is acceptable that is at variance with concrete realities, the sociological question is not whether or not the supernatural exists, or whether religion ought or ought not to include the supernatural, but rather how *useful* is so broad a concept for purposes of sociological analysis. Some scholars may find Durkheim's concepts too broad. Others, while not rejecting them out of hand, may prefer a narrower concept for a particular piece of research. The choice of the concept used commonly reflects the scholar's judgment about the most appropriate tool for the sociological task in hand.

In the description that follows, Durkheim's broad conception of religion and view of the *sacred* are used mainly to help the student become aware of certain aspects of religion and religious behavior that may previously have escaped his notice and to provide a basis for the interpretation of what he has been thus enabled to observe. Durkheim regarded religion, not as an indivisible unity, but rather as a more or less complex system of interrelated parts.[22] In Durkheim's view, which follows here, the *sacred* (seen by him as religion's core) is closely related to the subsystems of *belief* and *ritual*, which in turn depend for maintenance on another subsystem—namely, the supporting attitudes of a *community of worshipers.* More recently Joachim Wach has characterized the subsystems, or parts, in somewhat different terms but with essentially the same meaning; namely as the *theoretical, practical,* and *sociological* expressions of mankind in response to religious "reality." These interrelated parts of the religious system are considered in more detail below.[23]

THE RELIGIOUS SYSTEM: THE MEANING OF THE SACRED

What, then, is the sacred? It is easier by far to recognize than to define. The sacred is concerned with the wonderful and terrible mystery of things. In all known societies there exists a distinction between the holy and the ordinary or, as often phrased, the sacred and the secular, or profane. Yet there is hardly a thing in heaven or on earth that has not been regarded by some people as sacred. The Hindus revere the Sacred Cow, the Moslems the Black Stone of the Kabah, the Christians the Cross upon the altar, the Jews the Ark of the Covenant, and many preliterate peoples their totems (animals or plants believed to symbolize the mythical primal ancestor of the tribe). The sacred objects just listed are tangible, concrete. But the sacred has also an unseen, intangible aspect. Sacred beings and entities of all kinds—gods, spirits, angels, devils, and ghosts—are revered as awesome or holy; the Person of the Risen Christ, the Virgin Mary and the Saints, Zeus and the whole Greek pantheon, entire cosmologies of Buddhas and bodhisattvas, Allah and Mohammed His Prophet are sacred to their respective votaries and are revered in ceremonials and enshrined in systems of belief.

What common element can be found in this almost infinite variety of sacred objects and entities that we may characterize as the sacred itself? If we merely consider the objects and entities in and of themselves, no answer is possible. It is not the things themselves but the nature of the attitudes and the sentiments ✗

reinforcing them that is the hallmark of the sacred. Sacredness consists, then, of emotionally supported mental attitudes. Awe itself, the most apparent sacred emotion, is a compound of worship and dread. Awe polarizes the attraction of love and the repulsion of danger. Most emphatically it is not an everyday or secular emotion but rather a feeling that separates the object or objects to which it is directed from the sphere of ordinary concerns. The sacred, then, can be best seen as that which is set apart from the utilitarian concerns of everyday living by the attitude of respect in which it is held and by the fact that it cannot be understood by the exercise of the empirical common sense sufficient for such ordinary concerns.

Sacred objects, it should be stressed, are not materially different from ordinary objects. To the uninitiated the Sacred Cow of the Hindus appears to be like any other cow, or the Holy Cross of the Christians like any other two pieces of transfixed wood. Again, it is the attitude of the worshipers that makes the crucial difference. The sacred entities or beings, which are intangible and invisible and whose existence thus cannot be demonstrated experimentally, may well seem to the uninitiated to be nonexistent. Yet the awe in which they are held by their worshipers is real emotion. Not only does this awe invest its objects with their sacred characters, but it also makes it possible for these "imaginary" entities to exist in the minds of their worshipers. Moreover, such entities, however imaginary, have observable (empirical) consequences.

Closely allied to the sacred, or the holy, is the unholy, which includes whatever under particular circumstances is thought to desecrate the holy. It is precisely to avoid this possibility of contamination that the sacred is hedged about with prohibitions or taboos. Sacred objects should not be touched or eaten or even closely approached except on special occasions or by specially authorized persons; the name of the sacred being should not be spoken, or if it is, then in no ordinary voice or language. Orthodox Jews, for instance, believe that death awaits the non-Levite who defiles the Ark of the Covenant with his touch; the devout Catholic approaches only to a certain distance from the altar on which the consecrated Host lies.

Furthermore, the use of ancient rather than contemporary language for dealing with sacred things is a characteristic of Eastern as well as Western religions. Hindus and Buddhists make use of Sanskrit, Pali, and Ancient Chinese. Even today Orthodox Jews and Roman Catholics celebrate the sacred name and the sacred mysteries in a special religious language. In the Roman Catholic Church, however, in recent years, as a result of the Second Vatican Council, certain parts of the Mass are recited not in Latin but in the vernacular.

BELIEFS AND PRACTICES

It is not enough, however, that sacred objects and entities merely "exist"; their existence must be continually renewed and kept alive in the minds of the worshiping group. Beliefs (that is, creeds and myths) and practices (that is, ceremonies and rituals) contribute to this end. Religious belief not only assumes the existence of sacred objects and beings, but repetition of beliefs strengthens and reaffirms faith. Beliefs also attempt to explain the nature and origin of sacred objects and beings and to provide, so to speak, a guide to the unseen world. Beliefs may be elaborated into theologies and cosmologies. The theologies may be complicated, highly articulate, and intellectualized, such as the Nicene Creed; and the cosmologies may be vast and intricate structures, such as the Hindu cycles of existence or the heaven, purgatory, and inferno in Dante's Christian vision. Or again, they may be simpler and less articulate, such as the beliefs of some preliterate peoples in myths and charms.

Beliefs not only describe and explain sacred beings and the unseen world—God and the angels, Shiva and Krishna, Jupiter and Mars, heaven and hell—but most important they tell how this unseen world is meaningfully related to the actual human world. Belief explains how the tangible realities of the bread and wine in the Eucharist are mystically connected with the sacred Body and Blood of the invisible, risen Christ. But whether the belief refers "to the invisible things beyond the senses or to the sacred objects within plain view . . . it is belief based upon faith rather than upon evidence; it is in Biblical language the substance of things hoped for, the evidence of things not seen."[24]

In thinking about religion Westerners have perhaps tended to put too much stress on belief in its more intellectual aspects,[25] on disputes about theologies and creeds, which have been so important in Western religious history. For a sociological understanding of religion in general, however, ritual, or ceremonialism, may well be more important. Ritual is the active, observable side of religious behavior. It can include any kind of behavior: wearing special clothing, sacrificing life and produce, reciting formulas, maintaining silence, singing, chanting, praying, praising, feasting, fasting, dancing, wailing, washing, reading.[26] Ritual's sacred nature then, depends not on the intrinsic character of the sacred objects, but depends rather on the mental and emotional attitudes held by the group toward the ritual and the social and cultural context within which it is performed. The same behavior—eating, for example —may be secular in one context, as when one has breakfast, but sacred in another, as when one partakes of the Host in the celebration of the Mass or shares in the Passover meal. Ritual, in other words, defines the context within which sacred behavior takes place. Ritual also assigns roles to the participants. Through regular recurrence and meticulous repetition it channels emotion and so enhances the emotion-evoking power of the symbols used. It is especially effective when people are gathered together, for they stimulate one another. Thus an important function of ritual is to fortify faith in the unseen world and to afford a symbolic means of expression for religious emotion.

SYMBOLISM

Since the essence of religious emotion is viewed as inexpressible, all attempts to express it are approximations and therefore symbolic.[27] Yet as a means of making the unseen world of sacred objects and beings live in the minds and hearts of the worshipers, symbolism, although less exact than more intellectualized modes of expression, has a peculiar potency of its own. Because symbols have a power to evoke feelings and associations over and above mere verbal formulation of the things they are believed to symbolize, throughout history they have been (and still remain) among the most powerful stimulants of human sentiment. Hence it is not hard to understand that the sharing of common symbols is a particularly effective way of cementing the unity of a group of worshipers[28] It is precisely because the referents of symbols elude overprecise intellectual definitions that their unifying force is the more potent; for intellectual definitions make for hair-splitting and divisiveness. Symbols may be shared on the basis of not-too-closely-defined feeling.

THE COMMUNITY OF WORSHIPERS

Everything said so far has implied that the sharing of beliefs and practices by a social group, a group of worshipers, is essential to religion. Only as this sharing takes place can the beliefs and practices be kept alive. The group may be a tribe of Australian aborigines celebrating a totem rite, an assembly of Holy Rollers at a testimonial meeting, a Presbyterian congregation listening devoutly to a sermon, or a quiet gathering of the Religious Society of Friends. The specific form of the rite makes little matter—what does matter is the common sharing.

Human groups who share their beliefs and practices thereby become a moral community, or as Durkheim put it, they constitute a "church."[29] The very process of sharing symbolic rites and beliefs strengthens a group's sense of its own identity, accentuates its "we feeling." This was notably the case among the Australian preliterates who furnished the material for Durkheim's studies, for in sharing the totem meal the worshipers partook of the name of the totem animal and of its very life. But in less direct and dramatic form this strengthening of group identity is a result of all shared worship. Among Moslems the common observance of the hours of public prayer both designates and unites the brotherhood of believers. For many Christians, too, the sharing of a sacramental meal both symbolizes and reaffirms the communion of the faithful.

MORAL VALUES

The sharing of belief and ritual implies that the relationship of the group members to the sacred is in some way intimately connected with the group's moral values. This implicit connection is made apparent in the abstention of certain groups of worshipers from particular foods or in the preservation of some particular animal. In Gandhi's opinion the cult of the cow was the one religious value held in common by the entire Hindu world. The cow is, then, a sacred object for the Hindus, and their abstention from eating its flesh is a moral value derived from the fact; the cult of the cow serves to unite Hindu worshipers and to distinguish them from beef-eating and non-pork-eating Moslems and Jews. The Jewish dietary laws, assumed to have been enjoined by Yahweh himself, are a classic example of the moral values of a given group being directly traceable to a belief in an immediate divine decree, with the continued observance of those laws acting as a most powerful cement of a moral community. In the two cases just cited the connection between the shared moral values of the group and the commands of God or gods in the unseen world is exceedingly clear. The fact is that upon careful analysis many distinctive customs of any particular group are likely to be revealed as stemming from that group's conception of its relation to the sacred; in other words, the customs probably have a religious origin.

This connection between a people's conception of the sacred and its moral values may be illustrated in another way. The kind of relationships that a particular group believes to exist among the sacred beings in the unseen world, and also between these beings and man, is often regarded as the ideal pattern of human relationships that should exist in society itself. For instance, a sheep-herding people may picture their God as the Good Shepherd, and thus for them the devotion of the good shepherd to his sheep becomes at once the prototype of their God's relationship to them, his worshipers, and also an ideal model for their own relationships to one another. Or, again, as with the early Hebrews or the followers of Mohammed, the God may be the prototype of the fierce tribal patriarch who will brook no rival; or, as in Mahayana Buddhism, the heavens may be peopled with benevolent bodhisattvas, the celestial embodiments of magnanimous princes. In these cases the implications for human conduct are apparent. The important issue here is not whether man creates his gods in his own image but rather the correspondence between the moral values imputed to the inhabitants of the unseen world and those of their human worshipers. The moral values attributed to the unseen provide a sacred sanction for those of the objective human world.

This interdependency of the moral values of the respective worlds of sacred and human beings is especially significant when the relationships among the former are thought of as kinship relationships. Many religions conceive of the unseen as being peopled by families of sacred beings—families that exemplify widely differing ideals of family life. The example of a sacred family best known in the Western world is that described in the Christian Gospels. There are many ways in which the moral values associated with this Holy Family have given a sacred sanction to the values of family life in Western society at large. Equally important for the moral values of Western communities has been the Christian conception of God as the Father of all mankind. This ideal of God as the Father and the group of worshipers as his children carries with it the implication that all worshipers are, in God, related to one another and ought to behave toward one another as brothers. In addition, all human authority ought to be patterned on that of a loving father, and justice should be tempered with mercy.

We must, however, qualify this statement concerning the religious derivation of moral values. Although religion and morals are closely interwoven (particularly in the kind of societies that

Durkheim was writing about), it should not be assumed that in all societies is the entire moral code derived directly from religion and sanctioned by it. Indeed, insofar as societies are more complex and more secularized, the religious derivation of moral codes is likely to be less clear and less direct. Robert M. MacIver and Charles H. Page have made an important distinction between religiously sanctioned moral codes and those that are sanctioned by purely human (or secular) considerations. They have pointed out that those who profess no religion have their own moral codes and that amorality is very rare. A code of morals is religious, they claim, when its source is presented as divine authority and its sanction is the supernatural. A moral code is secular when it promulgates standards that directly derive their sufficient justification from the human interpretation of good and evil. However, many moral codes that at the present time appear to be secular were originally sanctioned on religious grounds, even though their religious origins may have been forgotten.[30] If, furthermore, one adopts Durkheim's very broad interpretation of the sacred—which, in the final analysis, is based on society itself as its ultimate point of reference and sanction—as the focal point of all religious action, the distinction between religiously derived and humanly derived moral codes becomes less clear.

A SUMMARY STATEMENT

We have seen the essential elements that comprise the idea of the sacred, the emotionally charged attitudes associated with the sacred, the beliefs and practices that both express and reinforce these attitudes, and, finally, the sharing of these beliefs and practices by the group of worshipers who represent a community marked by common moral values.[31]

The definition of religion given here has emphasized the aspects that, from the point of view of sociology, are regarded as essential. It has been pointed out continually that this definition is applicable to an exceedingly wide and varied range of

RELIGION: A SOCIOLOGICAL VIEW

phenomena. Also indicated have been common elements among religions that might seem, at first glance, very far removed from one another.

Yet it is possible that, in the opinion of some readers, what is for them the very spirit and essence of religion has been omitted. Some of these omissions and inadequacies are inherent in any attempt to understand anything so exceedingly complex as religion in terms of the approach of any single discipline. Such an attempt is worthwhile, however, if it helps us to become aware of certain aspects of religion and religious behavior that may have been undetected and if it also provides us with a basis for the interpretation of what we have been thus enabled to observe.

If, as he went along, the reader has been comparing his own religious experiences with the definition given here, he has probably found many similarities. He probably recognized rather readily certain tenets of his church as beliefs and appreciated the sacred character of such of them as his church deems inappropriate to subject to empirical or scientific proof. Similarly, the reader is likely to have thought of some rituals or practices that he considers as set apart by an attitude of special respect from everyday affairs. He might have recognized, too, that the creeds and rituals characteristic of his particular religious community are known and felt emotionally, in a kind of expressive shorthand, by means of symbols. Among such symbols and symbolic acts are the cross on the Christian altar and the lighting of the candles in an Orthodox Jewish home on Friday night. These symbols are capable of invoking in the minds of the worshipers almost instantaneously a whole network of memories and sentiments. Such associations activate and intensify the shared loyalties of the group members and make them more keenly aware of the ways in which they differ from other groups.

It is likely that the reader will also have been conscious of some of the constraints, their relative strength depending on his personal convictions and the religious community under consideration, upon the members to live up to the moral values stressed by the particular church. Whatever these moral values may be —and they concern a wide range of activities—by observing the emphasis that a religious group places on particular values and stresses through its ministers, priests, rabbis, and parents from one generation to the next, the reader will understand how adherence to such values serves to weld the group of worshipers into a moral community.

It would not be surprising, however, if the reader finds it difficult to come to grips with the interpretation given to the term "sacred." If, as claimed here, the sacred is vital to religion, he may wish to know, for example, whether this concept of the sacred includes the supernatural or not, or whether the sacred is identical with the supernatural, or, further, whether religion can exist without a supernatural basis. If such questions have occurred to the reader, he will have put his finger on some of the most controversial issues among students of religion.

The sacred, as defined earlier, includes the supernatural but is not identical with it. Since sacredness inheres in the attitudes of the worshipers, the referents of the attitudes may be objects and entities in this world (regarded in a special way) or objects and entities in the supernatural world. The supernatural, in contrast to the sacred, may be thought of as comprising only other-worldly objects and entities that are assumed to transcend the empirically known world.

The term "supernatural" is sometimes understood in different ways. To some the supernatural appears mainly as a contradiction of nature or, indeed, as a violation of nature. Here, however, the interpretation of the term has been limited to that which is regarded as above and beyond the natural world and not necessarily in contradiction with it. In most Christian and Jewish denominations and in most of the great spiritual religions of the world, the supernatural in this sense is the main object of religious attitudes. Natural objects as symbols, however, are also regarded in a sacred way. In the supernatural world God and heaven are sacred; in the natural world there are sacred books and candles, which symbolize the sacred.

Deeper problems become apparent, however, if a further question is raised: Is a religion really a religion if the objects and entities regarded by its votaries as sacred consist *only* of natural,

24

this-worldly objects and entities? In other words, suppose the supernatural point of reference for attitudes of respect and awe associated with the sacred is entirely lacking? And what kind of religions are possible if attitudes of reverence and respect are bestowed only on this-worldly objects and beings? These questions, especially today, are not merely academic.

SUPERNATURAL AND SECULAR RELIGIONS

The traditional world religions of Buddhism,[32] Judaism, Christianity, Hinduism, and Islam, with their emphasis on sacred, other-worldly values, are all religions of the supernatural. There are, however, powerful movements in the modern world that do not emphasize supernaturalism and yet possess most of the other characteristics of religions. These movements have their beliefs and rituals, their symbolism, their groups of devoted adherents, bound together by shared moral values. We refer, of course, to the great world movements of nationalism, socialism, fascism, and communism. The "sacred" focus of these movements, if sacred attitudes may be thought to obtain at all, is on human life in this world, on particular national communities, or on theories regarding the conduct of human societies. Since they do not have supernatural values, should such movements be excluded from the category of religions? Some students who hold that the supernatural is the essence of religion would say they should. Since the more inclusive category of the sacred is accepted here, as it is by a number of other sociologists of religion, such movements are classified in this book as nonsupernatural, or secular, religions.

Consider the case of communism. Communist theory professes a materialistic view of society and, indeed, of the universe. Far from regarding supernatural entities with respect and awe, the Communist regime in Soviet Russia until fairly recently severely restricted the practice of supernatural religion and directly inculcated atheism and scientific materialism. There is no basis for a supernatural religion here. But if the question of whether or not communists regard certain phenomena as sacred is asked, the answer given must be different. There are things they regard with an attitude of much more than everyday respect, entities that at least some of them view with awe rather than with rational common sense.

There would be nothing sacred about communism if communists were concerned only with achieving practical ends by using the practical means appropriate to such achievement. But communism is also a faith, a faith in the Marxian dialectic as something that will work itself out and produce a classless society— a kind of heaven on earth, supposedly—independently of or even in spite of the political and economic means used. Many communists have worked and suffered and died for this faith. Viewed in this way, as a faith in an unverifiable historical principle, communism is a religion, although not a supernatural one. Regarded solely from the standpoint of a political power structure, of course, there is nothing distinctively religious about communism.

Consider nationalism in a similar way. A national group organized for purposes of protection and the good life is not in itself a sacred phenomenon. Nationalism takes on a sacred aspect, however, when a mystical attitude toward the nation as an entity takes the place of a common-sense regard for the well-being of the members for whom the group was organized.

It may seem to some a remarkable fact that despite the decline in the hold of supernatural religions on many people in recent times throughout the world, religious attitudes still persist. These attitudes, however, can be readily redirected to nonsupernatural values—the nation, the state, or man-made, so-called scientific theories such as Marxism, for it would appear that religion as well as nature abhors a vacuum.*

But although important insights as to the nature of religion's relationship to society may be gained by viewing such phenom-

---

* It is also noteworthy that in spite of the official sanction given to communism (a secular religion), the older religions of the supernatural (for example, Orthodox Christianity and Judaism) still persist in Russia.

ena as nationalism and communism through Durkheimian spectacles, the main concern here is with the "religious" religions—that is, the religions of the supernatural—rather than with the secular ones. The inclusion of the latter in the purview would enlarge the field to be surveyed far beyond the capacity to cover it here. For the purposes of this book, however, it seems worthwhile to point out both the prevalence and the dynamic character of these secular religions as an eloquent testimony to that universality of religion among mankind mentioned at the outset.

REFERENCES

1. William James, *The Varieties of Religious Experience* (New York: Modern Library, 1937), pp. 31–32.
2. Henry Fielding, *The History of Tom Jones* (New York: Modern Library, 1931), p. 84. The full quotation is as follows: "When I mention religion I mean the Christian religion; and not only the Christian religion but the Protestant religion; and not only the Protestant religion but the Church of England."
3. J. Milton Yinger, *Religion, Society and the Individual* (New York: Macmillan, 1957), p. 4.
4. *Ibid.*, p. 5.
5. *Ibid.*, p. 4.
6. Max Weber, *The Sociology of Religion*, trans. Ephraim Fischoff (Boston: Beacon Press, 1963), p. 1.
7. Émile Durkheim, *The Elementary Forms of the Religious Life*, trans. Joseph Ward Swain (New York: Collier, 1961), p. 38.
8. *Ibid.* "Leaving aside all conceptions of religion in general, let us consider the various religions in their concrete reality and attempt to disengage that which they have in common; for religion cannot be defined except by the characteristics which are found wherever religion itself is found."
9. It is, of course, quite common for a given sociologist arbitrarily to limit the concept of religion that he proposes to utilize for a particular study. He does not thereby necessarily limit his own conception of religion as a total phenomenon. See Hervé Carrier, *The Sociology of Religious Belonging* (New York: Herder & Herder, 1965), pp. 46–49.
10. See, for example, Werner Cohn, "Is Religion Universal?" *Journal for the Scientific Study of Religion*, 2, no. 1 (1962), 23–33. For

an opposing viewpoint see Joachim Wach, *Types of Religious Experience: Christian and Non-Christian* (Chicago: University of Chicago Press, 1951), pp. 30–47 and 237–241.

11. William Shakespeare, *Hamlet*, Act 3, Sc. 1, 1. 70.

12. See Ruth Benedict, "Religion" in Franz Boas (ed.), *General Anthropology* (New York: Heath, 1938), pp. 627–665.

13. See Sigmund Freud, *The Future of an Illusion* (Garden City, N.Y.: Doubleday, Anchor Book, 1964), *passim*. In this provocative study of the nature and possible future of religion, Freud inclines to the view that deities are human projections of parental images.

14. Émile Durkheim's *Elementary Forms of the Religious Life* and Sigmund Freud's *Totem and Taboo* (see reference note 18) are both notable attempts to trace religion's origin to totemism.

15. There are, however, some recent signs of renewed interest in evolutionary theories and even in origins. See the *American Sociological Review*, 29 (June 1964), especially the articles by Talcott Parsons and Robert N. Bellah on evolutionary theory. See also Guy E. Swanson, *The Birth of the Gods: The Origin of Primitive Beliefs* (Ann Arbor: University of Michigan Press, 1960), for a modern approach to the problem of origins.

16. E. B. Tylor, *Religion in Primitive Cultures,* Vol. 2 of *Primitive Culture* (1873; reprint ed., New York: Harper Torchbook, 1958), Chapter 2, especially pp. 24–25.

17. Durkheim, *op. cit.,* pp. 245–251.

18. Sigmund Freud, *Totem and Taboo* (1913; reprint ed., New York: Norton, 1952). *Totem and Taboo* and *The Future of an Illusion* are the two main works in which Freud expounded his views on the origin and nature of religion. The former, in particular, has been much criticized. However, if it is regarded (as the anthropologist A. L. Kroeber once suggested) not as a factual account of religion's beginnings, but rather as a "Just So Story," it supplies many revealing insights. It remains in doubt whether Freud regarded the totemic origin of religion in the Primal Crime as hypothesis or history.

19. Arthur Darby Nock. From notes taken on his lectures at Harvard University.

20. Paul Tillich, *Systematic Theology,* Vol. 1 (Chicago: University of Chicago Press, 1951), pp. 12–14.

21. Rudolf Otto, *The Idea of the Holy,* trans. John W. Harvey (New York: Oxford University Press, 1923), Chapter 5 and *passim*.

22. Durkheim, *op. cit.,* p. 51.

23. Wach, *op. cit.,* Chapter 2, especially pp. 34–47.

24. Kingsley Davis, *Human Society* (New York: Macmillan, 1949),

RELIGION: A SOCIOLOGICAL VIEW

p. 534. Davis's chapter on religion and its institutions is still one of the best treatments of religion in any general sociological text.

25. See Ernest Benz, "On Understanding Non-Christian Religions" in Mircea Eliade and Joseph M. Kitagawa (eds.), *History of Religions: Essays in Methodology* (Chicago: University of Chicago Press, 1959), pp. 120–130. Reprinted in Louis Schneider (ed.), *Religion, Culture, and Society: A Reader in the Sociology of Religion* (New York: John Wiley, 1964), pp. 3–9. Benz's illuminating article shows how this rather typical Western habit of "intellectualizing" can impede our understanding of non-Western religions.

26. Davis, *op. cit.*, p. 534.

27. See Talcott Parsons, *The Social System* (Glencoe, Ill.: Free Press, 1951), Chapter 9, especially pp. 394–399, where Parsons characterizes religious ritual systems as special types of expressive symbolism.

28. See Peter L. Berger, *The Sacred Canopy* (Garden City, N.Y.: Doubleday, 1967). Berger has substituted for the Durkheimian conception of the "community of worshippers" that of a "community of plausibility"; that is, a group that continues to ascribe reality—or "facticity," to use Berger's term—to a certain set of beliefs.

29. Durkheim, *op. cit.*, pp. 43–44. Durkheim uses the term "church" in a generic sense. He is not here concerned to distinguish between churches, synagogues, mosques, and the like.

30. See Robert M. MacIver and Charles H. Page, *Society: An Introductory Analysis* (New York: Holt, Rinehart and Winston, 1949), pp. 168–174. MacIver and Page present a useful chart (p. 319) showing the dominant types of interrelationships between major types of moral codes and their sanctions—both religious and secular.

31. Durkheim, *op. cit.*, p. 62.

32. Early Buddhism may be regarded as an exception, in that it disavowed all concern with a Creator God, or with the "soul." Indeed, Durkheim (*op. cit.*, pp. 45–48) cites Early Buddhism as a prime example of a religion that does *not* emphasize the supernatural but that *does* emphasize *sacred things*—in this case the Four Noble Truths. Later Mahayana Buddhism, however, reintroduced the concepts of deity and the supernatural, although Theravada (or Southern) Buddhism has to this day no concept of a Creator God.

2
Religion and Types of Society

FUNCTIONAL AND STRUCTURAL ASPECTS OF RELIGION

There are two basic, although complementary ways, in which religion may be viewed by sociologists. On one hand sociologists may examine its *structure* concerning themselves with its component parts and their articulation, as done for the most part in Chapter 1. As noted, most scholars examining the structure of religion agree in pointing out three main interrelated contributory systems that are present wherever religion as a fully developed phenomenon is found: first, an *intellectual* system, or system of beliefs; second, an *action* system, or system of rites and ceremonies; and third, a *communal*, or social interaction, system, a system of group organization. Both of the first two systems are of necessity symbolic; and, as already seen, the content of all three systems may vary within wide limits.

On the other hand, sociologists may conceptualize religion in terms of its *functions*, and in that case the concern is with what religion *does*, with what it contributes—if anything—to the survival and maintenance of human societies and groups. This concern of sociologists, also mentioned at the outset, has been the particular preoccupation of a group of anthropologists and sociologists known as *functionalists*.[1] This approach, which has contributed much to our understanding of religion as a social phenomenon, is not to be thought of as unconcerned with structure; indeed, *structural functionalism* would, as Talcott Parsons maintains, be a better name for it.[2]

During recent years, however, the structural-functional approach has been under considerable attack,[3] in part because some of its opponents have not understood all its implications (in fact, structural functionalists themselves do not all agree) and in part also because some supporters have made overenthusiastic claims for it. In Chapter 3 we will discuss the theoretical position of the functionalists and will attempt some assessment of the strengths and weaknesses of this point of view. The opinion here is that many of the discussions about the social functions of religion have little value because the discussants stage their disputes in a historical vacuum and thus frequently talk past one another. It must surely be apparent that a particular religious structure cannot be rightly understood as functioning in society in general, but rather in a particular type of society. However, because functionalist theory was initially developed chiefly by anthropologists, there has been a tendency, even among sociologists, to make large claims about the social functions of religion in general, with scant regard for the historical context, on the basis of functions that have been observed by anthropologists in their studies of primitive societies. When the historical context is considered, the functions of religion vary, depending on the particular society examined; they may be seen as furthering solidarity or as increasing conflict, as being a conservative force or as having a revolutionary impact, and so on.

Since the particular society does affect the interpretation of religious functions, this chapter presents models of three basic types of society and the role of religion and religious institutions in each type.[4] It will become apparent that the structural as well as the functional aspects of religion—for instance, the character of the religious symbol system, the type of ritual action, and the form of religious organization—will tend to be modified in consonance with changes in society as a whole. In bringing about these changes, moreover, religion itself changes. In short, religion and society must be regarded as mutually interactive.

WHY USE SOCIETAL MODELS?

Societal models * are useful because of their availability as yardsticks against which the reader may compare the concrete characteristics of the societies he encounters either at first hand or in the pages of books. It is obviously impossible to describe every society in concrete detail. Nor can we here depict the many subtle shadings of difference among the models we have chosen to present. In fact, in each case certain features are purposely exaggerated to bring out clearly the "profiles" of the model. The descriptions are of necessity oversimplified.

Model One is a type of society in which religious values predominate, Model Three a type of society in which secular values are in the ascendant, and Model Two a combination of religious and secular values.[5] These three models are not intended, however, to represent inevitable stages in historical development, although many, but by no means all, societies have passed through or are passing through these or similar stages. Yet approximations to these types of societies have existed in historical times and may also be found today—sometimes in uneasy proximity—in our rapidly shrinking world.

The reader will observe that in addition to describing the organizational features of these societal models and the structure of the religious system associated with each of them, we have given particular stress to the concomitant variations in the functions of religion.

---

* The term "model" is used here in a general descriptive sense and not in the precise mathematical sense in which it is sometimes used.

MODEL ONE: PRELITERATE SOCIETIES AND RELIGIOUS VALUES

Our first model represents societies that are typically small, isolated, and preliterate.[6] They have a low level of technical development and relatively little division of labor or elaboration of social classes. The family is their most important institution, and specialization of the organization of government and economic life is rudimentary. The rate of social change is slow.

Intellectual systems of belief and myth are likely to be rather compact and undifferentiated; that is, men do not typically conceive of their objects of religious veneration as being essentially different or far removed from themselves. Their most potent religious symbols are commonly mythical figures such as tribal ancestors or culture heroes, who may be symbolized under a variety of forms.[7] The individual and his society are seen as merged in a natural-divine cosmos.

Religious action systems, therefore, are commonly directed to bringing about an *identification* between the worshiping group and that which they worship. A totem feast, in which the totem animal, in some sense symbolic of the tribe, is killed and eaten is an extreme and vivid example of the *participation mystique,* which is a common goal of religious action in such societies.

Religious organization, as such, is likely to be rudimentary or even nonexistent apart from the total organization of the society. Every member of the society, by virtue of his membership, shares in the religion of the group. Religious organization itself constitutes not so much a separate institution as an aspect of the total activities of the group. Religion pervades other group activities, whether economic, political, familial, or recreational. For example, the Trobriand Islanders, those South Sea Islanders made known to us through the famous researches of the anthropologist Bronislaw Malinowski, build their canoes and plant their gardens (economic and technical operations) as part and parcel of their performance of the magical and religious rituals that traditionally accompany these jobs.[8]

The major functions of religion in such a society and its role in relation to the group and its members are usually readily apparent. Since this type of society is small enough for most of its customs to be known, at least by hearsay, to all its members, it follows that religion can very forcibly place its imprint on the value system of the society. Coupled with magic, it is also an important means of dealing with many situations of stress. Furthermore, in the relatively undeveloped state of the other institutions, that is, except the family, religion is likely to provide the principal focus for the integration and cohesion of the society as a whole. Religious values often, although not invariably, promote conservatism and militate against change; this is an important reason why the hand of tradition is heavy in such societies. Again, because of the absence of rival interests and the fusion of religion with almost all aspects of social life, religion exercises a dominantly cohesive, stabilizing influence. As one anthropologist has put it, "In such a society life is a one-possibility thing." [9] Consequently, life in preliterate societies affords little leverage for religion to bring about social change.

For the individual, religion puts its stamp on the entire socialization process. Socialization is marked by religious rituals at birth, puberty, marriage, and other crucial times in the life cycle.[10] Personality organization is closely related to religious values, which are handed on directly to the developing individual by family and community. In the absence of a variety of possibly competing personality models, especially secular models, religion stands unrivaled as an integrating focus for the personality patterning of individuals in societies of this type.[11]

The mode of life characteristic of our first model has been studied by anthropologists for many years. Anthropologists have enormously helped sociologists in the latter's investigation of religion in relatively simple societies where the bones, so to say, of social structure are less obscured by complex develop-

RELIGION: A SOCIOLOGICAL VIEW

ments. Anthropologists have also drawn our attention to continuing aspects of religion's functions in more complex societies, functions that otherwise would probably have been overlooked. Nonetheless, more complex social conditions are associated with important modifications in the role played by religion. These modifications are revealed in considering societies subsumed under our Model Two.

MODEL TWO: CHANGING PREINDUSTRIAL SOCIETIES

Model Two societies are less isolated, change more rapidly, are larger and more expansive in both area and population, and are marked by a higher degree of technological development than are Model One societies. Considerable division of labor, distinctiveness and diversity of social classes,[12] and some degree of literacy are common features. Agriculture and hand industries are the chief means of support of a mainly village economy, with a few urban trading centers. The institutions of government and economic life are becoming specialized and distinct. Although there is more overlapping of governmental, economic, religious, familial, and recreational activities than in modern industrialized societies (Model Three), sharper lines are drawn between the occasions on which people go to work, go to play, or go to worship than, say, among the Trobrianders. This second societal model is illustrated concretely by the societies in which the great historical religions—Buddhism, prophetic Judaism, Christianity, and Islam—emerged and matured.

The intellectual and symbol systems of these historical religions differ greatly among themselves, but all share an important emphasis on *transcendentalism* that distinguishes them from the religions most typical of Model One societies.[13] These symbol systems portray a dualistic universe, emphasizing the contrast between life in this world and life in another specifically "religious" realm. This religious realm is viewed as man's true dwelling, and the goal of *salvation,* or entrance into this realm—whether described as heaven, enlightenment, or release—becomes the central religious quest.

The religious action system in such societies is concerned above all else with action necessary for obtaining salvation. To act religiously in a way that gains salvation becomes, in principle, the obligation of every human being. Man himself is no longer thought of mainly as a member of a particular tribe, or the devotee of a particular deity, but as an individual in a more universal sense, namely, as a human being capable of salvation. Man is also seen, however, as a being with serious flaws in his nature, and the attainment of salvation is therefore a difficult and responsible task demanding discipline and self-denial. Man is called upon to deny himself this-worldly pleasures and pursuits that might militate against his quest for an other-worldly salvation. Hence the historic religions tend to devalue the actual empirical world and to consider the most efficacious kind of religious action to be asceticism and withdrawal from worldly affairs.[14] To be sure, this denial and devaluation of the world may take a wide variety of forms, as Max Weber has pointed out.[15] Yet in one form or another Christianity, Buddhism, and Islam have each, at important periods in their history, inculcated one or more such forms of world-rejection.* World-rejection, let it be said, does not of necessity involve solitude, nor does the earnest seeker after salvation invariably abjure all contact with other humans. Hermits and other religious solitaries come close to doing this, but paradoxically (although almost inevitably) the preferred form of religious world-rejection has been carried on in like-minded groups organized under some form of monastic rule.

Religious organization is commonly of two kinds. A closely regulated quasimonastic organization of the religious elite exists side by side with a looser and more comprehensive kind of or-

---

* World-rejection, common at various periods in the histories of Buddhism, Christianity, and Islam, is much rarer in the history of Judaism. But even Jews had their withdrawing sects, such as the Essenes, and also some prophets who sought solitary places.

ganization for the vast majority who, from necessity or choice, remain involved in worldly affairs. Religiously, however, the latter are considered somewhat inferior to the former, who more nearly embody the religious ideal.* However, the religious organization as a whole comprises both monks (and priests) and laity, who are essential for the former's support.

In Model Two societies, then, this double-barreled organization, regarded as a whole, is a relatively separate and distinct part of the societal structure. It commonly aims at including at least as lay members all the inhabitants of a given political territory, but it usually possesses a formal, hierarchical organization of its own professional personnel.

The functions of religions in the Model Two type of society are more complex and contradictory than those in Model One societies. Religion still gives meaning and cohesion to the society's value system, but it also functions as an important stimulus to societal conflict both within societies and between them. For in these Model Two societies, the religious spheres and the secular spheres, although they continue to overlap at certain points, are becoming progressively more distinct from one another. Furthermore, the emerging institution of government is developing rapidly and consequently becoming a potential rival of the religious organization—the church—as a focus for the cohesion, integration, and stabilization of the society. Hence the possibility of internal institutional clashes is increasingly present. Of course, government in such societies is not always sufficiently secularized to be able to dispense with a religious legitimation for its authority. The Holy Roman Emperors of the medieval West, for example, tried to ensure this legitimation by being anointed by the Popes. Nevertheless, the possibility of church-state tension, and even of outright conflict, is ever

---

* This bipartite form of religious organization is very clearly seen in Buddhism, particularly in the Theravada Buddhism of Southeast Asia. The community of monks (Sangha) is clearly set off religiously from that of the laity, and monks are considered more favorably situated than are the laity for the attainment of salvation (Nirvana). The laity are thought to improve their own chances of salvation largely through the material support they render to the monks.

present in Model Two societies. Conflicts of interest between religious and political organization are likely to be acute particularly in the later stages of their development, as each organization develops its own hierarchical structure and rationale and tends to make, each on its own level, a total claim on the loyalty of the individual members. Such conflicts of interest are complicated by the fact that although the ecclesiastical organization is typically regarded, at any rate officially, as "other-worldly," or even "world-denying," nevertheless religious organizations very commonly fall heir to money, lands, and buildings, and their functionaries play political roles. These worldly properties, moreover, are generally regarded by their religious owners as exempt from the payment of taxes and other "this-worldly" services to political governments. The massive church-state struggles in which medieval and early modern Christian and Islamic countries were involved are such religious-political conflicts.

The history of Model Two societies also is replete with examples of total societies locked in struggle, in large part because of religious rivalries. Model Two societies are typically expanding societies. Hence the coupling of religious organization (claiming to be the repository of a universal ethic) with the political power structure provides a setting in which attempts to spread the religion become fused with efforts to extend political domination. In medieval times, for example, the missionary drive of Islam to extend its religious beliefs westward, and of Christianity to spread its faith eastward, were also aspects of a political struggle for empire between two great rival civilizations. Such religious-political clashes may be regarded as integrative insofar as they helped to weld together the respective societies involved. From this point of view, indeed, the Crusades may be said to have helped to integrate Western Christendom.[16] But on the larger stage the bloody wars between Christianity and Islam are important examples of religion's disruptive and destructive tendencies; and even within Christendom itself it may be argued that the Crusades unleashed disintegrating forces at least as potent as those that they harnessed.

In Model Two societies, however, religion is not only a possible source of division and strife; it may also play a creative and innovating role. In contrast to the situation in Model One societies, religion is not merely an aspect and hence an implicit endorsement of custom but rather constitutes to some extent a rival system of sanctioned behavior. In these societies religion is not only of local application but is assumed to be universal; and in addition, it is thought of as representing ethical values "higher" than the everyday standards of ordinary social life. The excoriation of the prevailing customs of Israel and Judah by the Hebrew prophets Amos and Hosea because they fell short of religious standards furnishes a dramatic example of this disparity between religious ethic and social custom as conceived in societies of this type.

Furthermore, as such societies become increasingly complex, the dominant classes of an earlier period begin to yield before the challenge of rising classes representing a newly emergent political and economic order, while at the same time significant changes in the formulation of the religious ethic are likely to occur. These ethical innovations may themselves be important factors in helping to bring about the economic and social transformation under discussion, as Max Weber has argued in *The Protestant Ethic and the Spirit of Capitalism.*[17] Such innovations may be temporarily disintegrating, but in the long run they often contribute to the integration of a different type of society, as will be illustrated shortly.

In spite of these and other striking examples of the disruptive and innovative role played by religion in these Model Two societies (an aspect of religion's role that has sometimes been overlooked by sociologists), the important part played by religion in conserving traditional values should not be forgotten. The tendency for religion to become merged in social tradition still remains.

As far as the individual is concerned, in Model Two societies religious values continue to furnish the main focus for the integration of his behavior and the formation of his self-image. The fact that most of the members of the society are also members of a single dominant religious organization, which as a rule also controls the tools of literacy and education, lessens the likelihood of internal psychic conflicts on religious grounds. In addition, the sacred sanction given by the church to the system of statuses and vocations current in the society makes it possible for the individual to accept his social station with a minimum of internal conflict.* With the passage of time in such a society, however, both the increase of literacy and contact with other cultures may encourage religious heresy and skepticism. Societies of this type have produced a Jesus of Nazareth, a Gautama Buddha, and a Mohammed, as well as an Arius, an Averroes, and an Abelard among their dissenters.

Our description of this second model of society necessarily has been formulated in dynamic terms. The process of change that marks this type becomes increasingly apparent as such societies evolve. Not only do economic and technological developments play an indispensable part in breaking the "cake of custom," but internal developments within religion itself, in its beliefs, practices, and social organization, also contribute importantly to this end. An even greater acceleration of the tempo of change characterizes Model Three societies.

MODEL THREE: INDUSTRIAL-SECULAR SOCIETIES

Unlike our first two models, which were constructed from anthropological and historical materials drawn from almost every part of the world, our third model is based exclusively on the social and cultural situation in the modern West. Today the Model Three societal pattern is being rapidly diffused on a global scale (and inevitably contains a number of subtypes that our typology cannot adequately account for), but its point of origin is Western Christendom. Hence the model here presented is derived from a study of the Western world and is ad-

---

* Here, it may be surmised, is an important source of Riesman's "inner-directed" (or gyroscopically governed) character type.

mittedly somewhat slanted toward urban society in the United States. The latter, however, because of its high degree of secularism, may be regarded as one of the nearest approximations to our model.

These societies are highly dynamic. Technology increasingly affects all aspects of life, having an impact most immediately on adjustments to the physical universe, but just as significantly on human relationships. The influence of science and technology has important consequences also for religion. This influence is one reason why members of these societies become more and more accustomed to apply methods of empirical common sense (and science) and efficiency to more and more human concerns. Thus the sphere of the secular is being continually enlarged, often at the expense of that of the sacred. In large part this secularizing trend accounts for the fact that religious beliefs and practices are confined to smaller and more specialized segments of the life of the society and its members.

To keep pace with this trend and in order to retain their influence, the churches themselves engage in a growing number of secular activities. In spite of the efforts of some churches to compete with secular institutions, the trend continues to relegate religion to limited times and places. In this respect the contrast with Model One societies, in which religion is an aspect of most social activity, is vivid.

The religious symbol system of Model Three societies, in part because of the secularizing tendencies just mentioned and in part because of the pluralistic nature of religious organization, is exceedingly difficult to pin down. In fact, no single universally accepted system of religious symbolism exists. Insofar as the various religious organizations are able to commend their officially sanctioned symbol systems to their membership, a plurality of symbol systems may be said to coexist simultaneously. Furthermore, many individuals, even organizational members, feel at liberty to interpret freely—or even repudiate—the traditional symbol systems handed down by hierarchical or other religious authority. Although this freedom of interpretation varies among memberships of different religious bodies, there exists a

growing awareness among the religiously affiliated and nonaffiliated alike that symbols *are* symbols and that man in the last analysis is responsible for the choice of his symbolism.[18]   Among the
perhaps 95 percent of Americans who claim to believe in God
(as reported several years ago),[19] many reinterpret religious symbols in a fashion so thorough-going that even liberal theologians
and religionists are sometimes left aghast.   In the world view
that has emerged from the tremendous intellectual advances and
upheavals of the last two centuries, there is little or no room for
the "duplex" religious symbol system that characterized the historic religions of Model Two societies.   Indeed, the notion of a
dichotomy between a transcendent religious realm and a devalued earthly realm is increasingly repugnant to members of
Model Three societies.   Although conservative orthodox religionists still hold to the older "dualistic" world view, the major thrust
of modern religious thought is toward the reinterpretation of
religious faith and its symbolization to bring them into some
kind of harmony with twentieth-century science and the economic and political conditions of the twentieth-century world.[20]

Religious action systems in the twentieth-century context
increasingly emphasize action *within* the present world, action
that Harvey Cox has aptly called "the sacralization of the secular."[21]   Even the monastic orders, traditionally, for the most
part, aloof from the world, are increasingly concerned with
teaching, medicine, and other forms of social service.   More and
more priests and nuns, both Roman Catholic and Episcopal, are
seeking professional and technical training at secular universities in order better to fulfill their religious duties in this world.[22]
The Second Vatican Council has stressed the need for social
relevance in respect to the Church's contemporary activities.
Members of the Catholic Church in America in some areas play
an active role in relation to the Negro's struggle for civil and
other human rights.   Nuns as well as priests have on occasion
marched in civil rights demonstrations, side by side with representatives of the clergy and laity of many different faiths.   Even
the contemplative orders, such as the Trappists (as the writings
of Thomas Merton attest) reach out, through the mass media, to

help the ordinary laymen to interpret and handle their everyday "this-worldly" problems in a religious manner.

Protestants and Jews, to be sure, have been traditionally more involved with the world and have stressed more than have Catholics the *religious* significance of action within one's profession or occupation. Today Protestant, Catholic, and Jewish religious organizations are likely to have special departments for social action and social justice, as well as numerous elaborately organized philanthropic activities. Some religious bodies focus their activities on the "inner city" and maintain special services for immigrants and others who have to struggle with the extremely difficult living conditions in these areas.

Perhaps even more significantly, middle-class Americans of all faiths are becoming increasingly concerned with the ethical problems inherent in their own business, professional, political, and family activities. Some churches sponsor forums, lectures, and discussions (sometimes following a sermon) in which their members may become aware of these ethical issues, express their concern, and possibly devise ways of resolving them.

The foregoing remarks should emphatically *not* be taken to imply that in existing Model Three societies "religion" has already infiltrated every area of living. Not only does religion for many individuals continue to be a "duplex" compartmentalized affair, but numerous others have abandoned the "duplex" concept only to organize their lives within an exclusively secular context. What has been said above, however, does point to a growing feeling among religiously involved individuals that if religion is to exist at all, it must prove itself in some kind of this-worldly action.

Standards for such this-worldly religious action are likely to be difficult to formulate in a complex society that changes so rapidly that the automatic application of norms handed down from former days no longer suffices. While the individual may look to religion to aid him in his search for *personal* maturity and social relevance, those responsible for the welfare of the nations of the world must seek in every available quarter for action patterns that may help to ensure world peace and human survival. In Model Three societies religious organizations and, more particularly, concerned clergy and laity within such organizations, are actively (and sometimes militantly) involved in the search for peace. But in a world society possessed of the weapons of self-destruction, religious action in general, if it is to be socially relevant in *this* world, cannot be confined to religious organizations per se, but the religiously involved must work through secular organizations to achieve their "religious" objectives.

Religious organization in industrial societies is, as noted above, both divided and pluralistic. Membership is on a voluntary basis, at least in principle. No single dominant church claims, even theoretically, the allegiance of all members of the society, as in the case of Model Two societies. With few exceptions no official tie exists between religious organizations and the secular government. In some societies of this type, such as France and the United States, such relationships are legally repudiated; and in countries like England, where there is an official state church, the latter's relation with the government has become attenuated and modified. In general there are a number of competing religious organizations, large and small, with many members of the society either nonaffiliated or what are termed "paper members" of churches. In the United States in 1964 there were some 258 religious bodies with approximately 63.4 percent of the population enrolled.[23] Hence, 36 percent of the population—a very low proportion compared to that in European countries—are nonaffiliated.[24]

Furthermore, both among those enrolled and those not enrolled in religious organizations, the "privatization" of religion appears to be becoming ever more common.[25] It has been suggested, half seriously perhaps, that one might be tempted to see in Thomas Paine's "My mind is my church" or Thomas Jefferson's "I am a sect myself" the typical expression of religious organization in the near future.[26] Nevertheless, it seems unlikely that religious organization will quickly disappear, although the function it performs may be to a decreasing extent distinctively religious.

The functions of religion in Model Three societies are profoundly affected by the changing characteristics of religion just discussed. Religious divisions combined with the growth of secularism greatly weaken religion's integrating function, and even its divisive power is somewhat blunted. Toleration of religious differences, typical of this kind of society, is partly the outcome of indifference in the face of the growing dominance of the secular value system; religious organizations themselves are not immune to this secularizing influence. Furthermore, some 36 percent of the inhabitants of the United States appear to be able to survive and maintain themselves without affiliating themselves with any kind of religious organization—a fact that raises serious questions concerning religion's function.

Religious beliefs and practices, however, may serve an integrating function within the various organizations themselves. This is particularly likely to be the case when the membership of such groups is largely drawn from class or ethnic minorities within the larger society. Here they serve a purpose as centers of "belongingness" for groups deprived or discriminated against in an increasingly depersonalized social order.

Assessing the extent of the integrative and value-forming functions of religion and striking a balance between this and its disintegrative potential is difficult. Against the weakened influence of religious organizations may be set the fact that the religious values of an earlier day persist in the society in more or less attenuated form as part of its basic tradition. In this form the values continue to contribute, to an extent extremely difficult to measure, to the cohesion of the society. Evidence of this is the frequency, especially in times of stress, of public appeals to this common heritage of religious tradition. Presidents open their inaugurals with prayer, and in times of war or national danger the help of God is solemnly and publicly invoked.

On the other hand, the state and the economic order between them have taken over important functions performed by religion in Model One and Model Two societies. For example, the secular sanctions of political law and economic supply and demand to a large extent underwrite the system of social obligations without which societies cannot persist. It is possible, moreover, that Model Three societies may be able to maintain themselves with a looser and somewhat different kind of integration than either of the previous models discussed. Hence, How secular can one get? becomes a vital question. Can the secular institutions do the minimum integrative job essential for society without borrowing back, as it were, some of the sacred values previously abandoned?

Will Herberg has supplied us with important clues that may suggest an answer to this question. He sees the "religions of America"—whether Protestant, Catholic, or Jewish—as providing the spiritual underpinnings for the "American Way of Life," a moral and democratic way of life that thus becomes invested with a sacred aura. Meanwhile, the institutionalized religions become instrumental to the preservation of national values, which are themselves increasingly regarded as ultimate.[27]

In certain other Model Three societies, to a greater extent than in the United States, governments have attempted to reinvest themselves with a sacred aura. Fascist and communist governments in particular (although not exclusively) have surrounded themselves with a panoply of quasisacred ritual and claim the total allegiance of the members of a particular society, not on the common-sense secular grounds of public services efficiently performed but rather on some quasireligious ground.[28] Fascist governments, for example, have on occasion claimed that the state, as represented by the government in question, is a sacred end in itself. Such an example gives point to our earlier inquiry, How secular can one get? But the answer remains unclear.

The pursuit of economic power may also take on a quasisacred tinge. In many popular descriptions of the economic arrangements of modern societies, it seems at times that *monetary* values are substituted for *moral* values without either the reader or the writer being clearly aware of the difference between the two.

Religion and the Individual

The personalities of relatively few individuals in modern industrial societies are shaped solely, or even mainly, in accordance with religious values. The weakness of religious values as an integrating focus, of course, is due in part to the diversity of the value systems of various religious organizations that at times contend for the individual's loyalty. But the chief rival of all religious value systems is the increasingly dominant system of secular values. The latter are clustered around nationalism, science, economic and occupational matters, and status-striving. In view of these facts, achievement of personality integration is a more difficult and more self-conscious feat than in societies subsumed under Models One and Two.

In bringing up their children, however, perhaps the majority of American parents continue to act as if they regard traditional religious values, or a somewhat modified version of them, as a necessary background for the building of acceptable character. Parents who have themselves long ceased to attend church nevertheless often feel that their children should be taught the elements of a religious faith in Sunday or Sabbath school. A residuum of fear seems to exist among elders that unless they ensure a minimum of religious instruction for their children, the rising generation may not acquire the moral fitness to maintain, as adults, those values that the elders still feel, perhaps inarticulately, to be necessary for the welfare of society. Therefore many parents, whether they themselves are "religious" or not, persist in sending their children to parochial schools. For in the United States, where the public school not only takes over much of the socialization job once performed in the family but is also legally separated from all organized religion, a considerable number of people who may themselves be members of no church feel that it is neither safe nor fitting for children to be educated in an atmosphere in which the name of God is perhaps never mentioned, no prayer is uttered, and no sacred book is read. Thus the practice of many a moral maxim, which adults often disregard in their own behavior, is enjoined by the same adults on children and young people. Such practices not only widen the communication gap between the generations but also contribute to personality conflicts among members of the high school and college generation. The latter are taking the parental generation to task for failing to practice what they preach, either in person or by proxy. Today the possibilities for conflict are accentuated by the acclaim given by some members of the college generation to Oriental and American Indian religions. Although these religions are often imperfectly understood, they appeal to a certain segment of "hippie" youth precisely because from their viewpoint, they are unconventional and espouse a philosophy that appears to be refreshingly different from the conventional and "hypocritical" religion of their parents.*

There are several prevalent types of adjustment to the problem of personality integration in modern industrial societies. First, the individual's personality may be integrated almost exclusively on the basis of the values of the particular religious organization to which he belongs. This type of integration is probably rare today. Second, the individual may frequently achieve a working personality integration by a process of compartmentalization. He may combine a more or less conventional acceptance of so-called Sabbath or Sunday religion with a workaday orientation to secular values. Thus potentially conflicting maxims, such as "Love thy neighbor as thyself" and "Business is business" or "All's fair in love and war," are not permitted to come into open conflict. Under stress, however, this

---

* The above statement should *not* be taken as implying that *all* current interest in Oriental and other "foreign" religions is superficial and motivated mainly by rebelliousness against the older generation. On the contrary, there exists today much serious study of non-Christian religions by both older and younger individuals. The existence, at Harvard University, of a graduate *Center for the Study of World Religions* is evidence of this fact. Furthermore, a superficial interest in a non-Christian religion, initially triggered by rebelliousness, may well give place to a deep and genuine interest in, and possibly practice of, the religion for its own sake. Oriental religions in particular may exercise a strong appeal because they have largely retained a contemplative component that Western Christianity, especially in its Protestant branches, has almost entirely lost.

compartmentalized system may break down, as the case histories of many mental patients attest. In the third type of adjustment some individuals may come to adopt, perhaps after a struggle or perhaps by default, an integration of their personalities in terms of secular values alone. This mode of adjustment is also rather common, but it too may break down in stress situations, such as those involved in warfare. Finally, some people, probably a minority, outstanding among whom were Albert Schweitzer and Alfred North Whitehead, achieve integration in terms of ultimate religious values, which they reinterpret and reevaluate in the light of modern philosophy and science. By means of this reinterpretation they bring religious values into what for them (and for the writer) is a meaningful relationship with the secular values of modern industrialized societies.

THE INTERMIXTURE OF TYPES OF SOCIETY IN THE MODERN WORLD

The attempt to use the three types of society as aids in understanding the functions of religion in actual societies does pose a difficulty. No one of these types exists unmixed in any of the great national societies of the modern world. For instance, Model Three societies, the most dynamic in the world today, are continually impinging their science, technology, and secular values on the more religiously oriented Model Two societies and on the few remaining representatives of Model One society. In comparison, the absence of rapid communication in medieval and early modern times meant that our own Western world experienced a period of relative isolation of several centuries during which took place the transition from a society approximating Model Two to one more nearly approaching Model Three. Even so, the accompanying changes in the role of religion in the society did not take place without prolonged and widespread social disintegration and disruption.

Today the great agricultural societies of the world, the contemporary counterparts of Model Two, are connected, whether their members desire it or not, in a worldwide network of rapid communications. Even their agricultural economies have become more and more dependent on world conditions of trade. Moreover, the kind of social life that has developed in the ports and other urban centers in direct contact with the industrialized West does not differ greatly from that of the secularized societies designated as Model Three. Hence the functions of religion in Calcutta, Bombay, Hong Kong, or Singapore are in many respects comparable to those it exercises in London, Paris, or New York. Yet in the thousands of agricultural villages that make up the greater part of such societies, the sacred values of an earlier day remain dominant. Nevertheless, the radio and movies penetrate into all but the most remote of such villages, and modern technology is being applied to ancient methods of agriculture. In Model Two societies religious observances and sacred values are intermeshed with traditional agricultural methods and are tied in with long-established patterns of social obligations and relationships. Therefore, technological innovations in agriculture, such as the introduction of "miracle rice" (a very high yield rice) in certain Asian countries recently, cannot fail ultimately to affect the sacred values themselves. When this happens, the social functions of religion in these societies will also be modified.

Even in the predominantly industrialized United States there still remain some relatively isolated rural areas, subsocieties within the larger society, where the role played by religion is often quite similar to the prevailing situation in Model Two societies. In such areas religion may still serve in part to define the position of social ranks in local communities and to preserve traditional values, as, for instance, in the Deep South, in the Kentucky Mountains, or in some of the open farm country in the West. But even in these remote and poverty-stricken areas, religious values are constantly being challenged by those of the current mass media, with its enticing commercials backed up by enterprising salesmen. The very poor may not be able to buy these tempting products, but at least they learn of their existence and to a decreasing extent are turning to religion as a substitute for material deprivation. The "Poor People's March" on Washington under religious leadership provides a striking illustration of how the dwellers in hitherto neglected and obscure rural communities are turning to political—that is, secular—action.

In spite of the changes just mentioned, religion does play a different part in remote rural areas than in metropolitan New York, Chicago, or Los Angeles. Yet even these metropolitan cities themselves, our closest approximation to Model Three societies, contain many individuals who have migrated either from rural areas in the United States or from peasant societies in southern and eastern Europe, Asia, or the Caribbean. The values of the older immigrants from such peasant societies frequently approximate those of Model Two societies. Such new immigrants to our great cities, mostly Negroes and Puerto Ricans, are often completely bewildered by the values that prevail, even among "religious" people, in American urban communities. For the expectations of such people concerning the role religion ought to play in social life are likely to be very different from those of most of their urban neighbors.

The existence of these smaller subsocieties, with their divergent conceptions of religion's role, within our larger urban societies gives rise to conflicts and discrepancies, both within the social order and within individual personalities. Some understanding of these conflicts and discrepancies, especially insofar as they result from the close and sometimes enforced contact between societies of different types, is essential for an intelligent grasp of the role of religion in the world today.

REFERENCES

1. Some of the most important functionalists among anthropologists are A. R. Radcliffe-Brown, Bronislaw Malinowski, and Clyde Kluckhohn. Among sociologists may be reckoned Émile Durkheim—a forerunner of this school, although he did not label himself as such—and, among contemporaries, Talcott Parsons, Robert K. Merton, and William J. Goode.

2. Talcott Parsons, *The Social System* (Glencoe, Ill.: Free Press, 1951), pp. 19–22.

3. See, for example, Allan Eister, "Religious Institutions in Complex Societies," *American Sociological Review*, 22 (August 1957), 387–391.

4. For a typology that uses five rather than three models, see Robert Bellah, "Religious Evolution," *American Sociological Review*, 29 (June 1964), 358–374. Bellah constructs a *primitive* model and also a model for *archaic* religion. (The latter would include the religion of the ancient Greeks, for instance.) In addition, he differentiates between "early modern" and "modern" religious models. Otherwise, the typology employed by Bellah, although much more fully worked out in regard to religious symbolization, is somewhat similar to that which we have used. We are much indebted to Bellah's article for our characterization of the various religious symbol systems. The entire article is well worth reading for its stimulating insights.

5. See Logan Wilson and William L. Kolb, *Sociological Analysis* (New York: Harcourt, Brace, 1949), pp. 344–349, for a similar distinction.

6. Compare Robert Redfield, "The Folk Society," *American Journal of Sociology*, 52 (January 1947), 293–308.

7. See Bellah, *op. cit.*, pp. 362–363.

8. See Bronislaw Malinowski, *Magic, Science, and Religion* (Glencoe, Ill.: Free Press, 1948; reprint ed., Garden City, N.Y.: Doubleday, Anchor Book, 1954), pp. 27–28.

9. W. E. H. Stanner, quoted in Bellah, *op. cit.*, p. 364.

10. See Malinowski, *op. cit.*, pp. 37–41.

11. See David Riesman *et al.*, *The Lonely Crowd* (New Haven: Yale University Press, 1950; reprint ed., Garden City, N.Y.: Doubleday, Anchor Book, 1954), Chapter 1. Model One societies especially, perhaps, give rise to the "tradition-directed" character type described by Riesman in his provocative sociological essay. However, modern anthropological research into so-called primitive societies has revealed a great deal of variation of which earlier writers, such as Malinowski (and Durkheim) were not aware. Thus Model One societies subsume numerous subtypes.

12. See Bellah, *op. cit.*, pp. 367–368. Bellah sees a shift from a two-class system to a four-class system as typically accompanying the change from Model One to Model Two societies. The four classes he mentions are a political-military elite, a religious-cultural elite, a rural lower-status group (peasants), and an urban lower-status group (small merchants and artisans).

13. *Ibid.*, p. 366.

14. *Ibid.*, p. 367.

15. See Max Weber, "Religious Rejections of the World and Their Directions" in *From Max Weber: Essays in Sociology,* trans. and ed. Hans H. Gerth and C. Wright Mills (New York: Oxford University Press, Galaxy Book, 1958), pp. 323–359.

16. See Arnold Toynbee, *The World and the West* (New York: Oxford University Press, 1953), *passim.*

17. See Max Weber, *The Protestant Ethic and the Spirit of Capitalism,* trans. Talcott Parsons (New York: Scribner, Students' Edition, 1958). This classic study should be read by all students of the sociology of religion. We are not concerned at this point to take sides in the much-debated question about the priority of economic as opposed to religious factors.

18. Bellah, *op. cit.,* p. 373. It may be mentioned that some modern men and women are actively engaged in inventing new symbolic forms, both liturgical and creedal, which they deem more in harmony with the modern age. See, for example, C. J. McNaspy, S.J., "The Quest for Community," *America,* August 19, 1967, pp. 174–175.

19. See Will Herberg, *Protestant, Catholic, Jew* (Garden City, N.Y.: Doubleday, Anchor Book, 1960), p. 72. Herberg quoted from the Gallup poll, *Public Opinion News Service,* December 18, 1954. Charles Y. Glock and Rodney Stark in their *Religion and Society in Tension* (Chicago: Rand McNally, 1965), p. 25, claim, on the basis of various recent polls, that between 95 and 97 percent of Americans acknowledge a belief in God. Such figures, however, as Glock and Stark point out, leave open the important question of the *saliency* of the belief for the individuals concerned.

20. Bellah, *op. cit.,* p. 370: "How the specifically religious bodies are to adjust their time-honored practices of worship and devotion to modern conditions is of growing concern in religious circles. Such diverse movements as the liturgical revival, pastoral psychology, and renewed emphasis on social action are all efforts to meet the present need." The Second Vatican Council, and particularly Pope John XXIII's opening speech on "updating" *(aggiornamento),* which has been called upon to legitimate much current liturgical and other experimentation in liberal Catholic circles, is a prominent example of the concern mentioned above.

21. See Harvey Cox, *The Secular City* (New York: Macmillan, 1965), *passim,* for a trenchant statement of this position.

22. See Sister M. Charles Borromeo, C.S.C. (ed.), *The New Nuns* (New York: New American Library, 1967); also, Harvey Cox, "The

New Breed," *Daedalus* (Winter 1967), 135–150, in which Cox characterizes a new type of Protestant clergy.

23. See *Year Book of the American Churches* (New York: National Council of the Churches of Christ in the U.S.A., 1964), p. 252.

24. The nonaffiliated—that is, the religious "nones"—are, as Glenn M. Vernon has aptly pointed out, an insufficiently analyzed residual category that is by no means uniform. See his unpublished paper, "The Religious 'Nones': A Neglected Category," *Journal for the Scientific Study of Religion,* 7 (Fall 1968), 219–229.

25. See Thomas Luckman, "On Religion in Modern Society," *Journal for the Scientific Study of Religion,* 2, no. 2 (Spring 1963), 159–161, and also, *The Invisible Religion: The Problem of Religion in Modern Society* (New York: Macmillan, 1967), by the same author.

26. Bellah, *op. cit.,* p. 373.

27. Herberg, *op. cit.,* pp. 74–90. There are, of course, great differences of opinion as to the extent to which individuals and entire religious organizations view religious faiths as instrumental to American national values. Herberg himself, it should be noted, merely describes what he takes to be the *de facto* situation. Personally, as a believing Jew, he deplores the conclusions that as a sociologist he draws from his observations of American society.

28. Recent reports from Russia, for example, appear to indicate that the secular religion of Communism does not suffice for a number of individuals and that there is an increase in overt and covert Jewish and Christian religious observance. See *The New York Times,* October 5, 1967, p. 1.

3
Religion and the Functional Approach

INTRODUCTION

Readers of Chapter 2 should not be surprised to find that there is no single mode of theoretical approach that is universally applicable to the sociological study of the many-faceted relationships between religion and society. In that chapter we discussed the interaction of religions and societies and the changes each undergoes in the process. The variations in both the religions and the societies there described render it unlikely that any one simple theory as to the relationships between the two will be completely adequate. Theoretical approaches and formulations useful for the study of Model One societies may have to be considerably modified, or even discarded, when studying Model Two and Model Three societies.

Nevertheless, as students of sociology our main concern with religion, as we pointed out at the start, is with its functions in human societies. The term "function," as also noted, refers to the contribution of religion, or of any other social institution, to the maintenance of human societies. Sociologists are, of course, also interested in analyzing different types of religious organization, in various types of leadership and followership, and in the interconnections between religious institutions and the other institutions of society. They are also interested in certain features of religious organization peculiar to the American scene and in a more general way in understanding and accounting for some of the consistencies and similarities between the religious culture and the broader culture of particular societies. All of these aspects of religion will be discussed in this volume. They are, however, subsidiary to the basic problem of religion's societal functions, which is the concern of this chapter.

Our object in first presenting schematic characterizations, or models, of the changing nature of religion and its interactions with different types of societies was to furnish conceptual and substantive background for a more detailed and critical analysis of the functional approach to the study of religion.

STRUCTURAL FUNCTIONALISM

Throughout this book the structural-functional approach is emphasized, not because it is the only or even the earliest theoretical approach to the study of religious phenomena that has been, and is, utilized by sociologists, but because, in our view, it is the most illuminating and comprehensive. It differs from some of the other theoretical approaches to be mentioned later (such as the positivistic, historical, typological, evolutionary, and comparative approaches) in that it is, potentially at any rate, a "total" approach to the study of the interrelationships between religion and society.[1]

Viewed in this broader sense, the structural-functional approach is not a special theory within the discipline of sociology. Structural functionalism originated, to be sure, as a special theoretical orientation, in large part as a protest against the ethnocentric judgments of certain anthropologists and sociologists and also as a move away from a purely descriptive concern with social and cultural phenomena. Today, however, sociology has freed itself from a preoccupation with subjective evaluations of "strange" religious beliefs and practices and no longer is concerned merely with raw empirical data. Structural-functional analysis does encounter difficulties in its practical implementation, but then so does sociological theory in general. Kingsley Davis has argued persuasively that the difficulties that each encounters are so similar that sociologists would be well advised to "bury" structural functionalism as a special kind of theory and to drop the rather cumbersome terminology that is connected with it.[2] There is much to be said for Davis's point of view. However, since the use of the structural-functional approach is still a matter for discussion by contemporary sociologists, some of its main assumptions and some of the problems inherent in its application will be considered here.

RELIGION AND SOCIETY'S MINIMAL NEEDS: CONSENSUS AND CONTROL

The structural-functional approach views human societies as self-contained systems (although the degree of self-containment may vary considerably) that maintain themselves within a framework of necessity. The assumption is that social systems must be assured of certain minimal essential elements in order to survive. Religion has commonly, although not invariably, been regarded as one such requirement. The basic needs of the social system, for food, reproduction, protection, and the like, are fulfilled through the interrelationships of its major institutional structures, that is, through the family, government, religion, and other institutions.[3]

At this point, in order to understand the functionalist approach, it is necessary to explore in more detail some of the requirements that are viewed as minimum essential elements for human societies and to explore the nature of the contribution that religion, as is frequently claimed, makes to them. The limits of the context within which functionalists are prepared to consider this question must be made clear at the outset. For the most part they will be satisfied if it can be shown—granting that societies do in fact have certain minimal survival and maintenance needs—that religion functions to fulfill *some* of them, even though there are contradictions and discrepancies in the way it does so. They do not contend that in all societies and under all circumstances religion (or religion alone) performs *all* the functions claimed for it by some anthropologists who have been chiefly concerned with simple societies. With this caution, let us examine the organization of society in order to highlight at least the principal features that are considered essential for maintaining societies.

First, societies depend for their survival on the continued expectancy that their members will discharge certain known and acknowledged obligations. Furthermore, if there were not some common agreement about the nature and extent of these social obligations, as well as adequate rewards and penalties to ensure their fulfillment, human societies would be in danger of falling apart, like plays in which the actors are continually missing their cues.

Hence some degree of common agreement, or *consensus*, about the nature of these crucial obligations, as well as the existence of power sufficient to constrain individuals and groups to fulfill them, is viewed as a minimum requirement for the persistence of the social order. How, then, is such agreement obtained? Again, what constraint is sufficiently strong to induce individuals and groups to forego their short-range self-interests for the sake of society as a whole? *

It is usually claimed that religion has helped in this important task by promoting agreement about the nature and content of social obligations and by providing values that serve to channel the attitudes of a society's members and to define for them the content of these obligations. In this role religion is viewed as helping to create systems of social values that are integrated and coherent. Religion, in short, is seen as having accounted, in large part, for the fact that values in almost all human societies are not a mere hodgepodge but constitute a hierarchy. In this hierarchy, religion, it is argued, defines the ultimate values and hence coordinates, although often unknowingly, into a more or less integrated system diverse values that might otherwise appear unrelated and meaningless. For instance, if God, as an ultimate value, is conceived of as a loving father, the content of this higher

---

* In the long run many of the "self-interests" of the individual are fulfilled by means of the organization of society. We do not intend to assume a sharp dichotomy between the interests of the individual and those of society.

RELIGION: A SOCIOLOGICAL VIEW

value has a direct bearing on the content of intermediate and subordinate values in the entire value hierarchy. Important among the intermediate values are values members of society place upon one another and also upon material objects, such as money or land.*

We can perhaps understand more clearly how religion has helped to bring about that minimal consensus essential for the functioning of societies if we understand how social attitudes are related to social values. When sociologists speak of the attitudes of the members of any society, they use the term "attitudes" to designate *habitual tendencies to act in particular ways toward particular objects.* It is thus the objects—the goals—of social attitudes that are invested with social *values.* Consequently, the values (objects of social attitudes) may refer to concrete things, such as money or land, or to concrete beings, such as a sweetheart or a child. But values may also refer to abstractions, such as some sacred entity or god, or to some customary way of fulfilling social obligations, as, for instance, paying respect to parents, honoring debts, and regulating sexual behavior. Thus the values of a given society inhere in a great variety of phenomena.

Second, most sociologists see good reasons for believing that religion has also played a vital role in supplying the constraining power that underwrites and reinforces custom. In this connection, it should be noted that the attitudes of reverence and respect with which especially binding customs (mores) are regarded are closely akin to the feelings of awe which, as seen earlier, are evoked by the sacred itself. In all societies more or less clear notions of appropriate behavior are found. These ideal standards of behavior, these "oughts," that incorporate social values are often referred to by sociologists as *norms.* The very existence of such norms (important among which are religious norms) tends to shape behavior in conformity with them, for

---

* However, as we shall discuss later, complex societies may generate *conflicting* values not readily subsumed in a "hierarchy." These conflicting values may occasion acute stress to members of such societies. How religion may function to alleviate such situations of stress will be considered in Chapter 4.

most people internalize norms in some measure and when acting in conformity with them are apt to feel that they are merely doing "what comes naturally." But such conformity is even more likely when norms are buttressed by potent rewards and punishments. Social rewards and punishments (or _sanctions_) are implicit in all social norms, if only because most human beings feel rewarded psychologically when they conform to what is expected of them and experience as punishment the informal, as well as "official," censure of their fellows. When norms occur in a sacred frame of reference, however, they are backed by sacred sanctions, and in almost all societies sacred sanctions have a special constraining force since not only human, this-worldly rewards and punishments are involved in this situation but suprahuman, other-worldly prizes and penalties as well.

We may summarize the preceding argument by stating that no society can maintain itself without a certain, although undefinable, minimum of _consensus_ among its members, and that religion, by acting as an agency for value integration and social control, is an important aid in securing this consensus.

THE INFLUENCE OF DURKHEIM ON FUNCTIONALISM

The fact that structural functionalism has heavily stressed the integrative and social-control functions of religion is thus apparent and stems largely from the work of Émile Durkheim. Other sociologists, however, notably Max Weber, have contributed to the functional analysis of religion by emphasizing its creative as well as its conservative potential and also its powerful dynamic for promoting both social conflict and social change. (We shall have more to say about Weber's contribution to our understanding of religion's role later on.) Durkheim's analysis was a precursor of the functionalist approach and furnished, as it does even today, some of our most fundamental insights into religion's societal functions. His work has done more than that of any other single sociologist to throw light on the nature of the interaction between social values and norms and the habitual fulfillment of social and moral obligations by most members of human societies. [To Durkheim the most significant property of the sacred was its capacity to evoke awe; hence its constraining power over human behavior and its consequent reinforcement of the moral values of the worshiping group.] Even though Durkheim's conclusion—namely, that all objects and entities invested by men with sacred quality are fundamentally symbols of the human group itself, thus making society the ultimate object of human worship [4]—has been repugnant to religionists and is also regarded by most sociologists as unacceptable for a variety of reasons, it has nevertheless been influential. Like many great but mistaken hypotheses, this view of Durkheim's has proved vastly stimulating. Even if his view is rejected in the form in which it is stated, it may still suggest important clues concerning the *moral* nature of the constraint that human societies exercise over the behavior of their members. In one of his most famous passages Durkheim wrote:

> Even if society were unable to obtain . . . concessions and sacrifices from us except by a material constraint, it might awaken in us only the idea of a physical force to which we must give way of necessity, instead of that of a moral power such as religions adore. But as a matter of fact, the empire which it holds over our consciences is due much less to the physical supremacy of which it has the privilege than to the moral authority with which it is invested. If we yield to its orders, it is not merely because it is strong enough to triumph over our resistance; it is primarily because it is the object of a venerable respect.[5]

MODIFICATIONS OF THE STRUCTURAL-FUNCTIONAL APPROACH

Concept of Alternative Functions

In large part because of the difficulties in applying the functional approach to complex and highly developed societies, sociologists, and anthropologists as well, have progressively modified their earlier, simpler formulations. For instance, as it became increasingly apparent that a particular need of a given social system was not invariably nor completely met by the same institutional structure, the concept of *alternative functions* was developed in order to allow for shifts in function from one institutional structure to another. For example, although religion, as mentioned earlier, has rather commonly been considered as the principal agent of social control, other institutional structures, such as government and law, frequently may perform that function and may either supplement or supersede religion in carrying out this task. Educational functions too, which were once commonly performed by religious institutions, are in modern societies largely taken over by governments, even though religious institutions may retain such functions in part. Thus the concept of alternative functions has the advantage of giving greater elasticity to the structural-functional approach.

Manifest and Latent Functions

Structural functionalism is often referred to as "action theory." When man acts in conformity with the norms of religious or other institutions, he presumably has certain ends in view, and his actions have certain consequences. However, the consequences of human actions for society may not always be those consciously intended by their performers. Therefore it is important, in attempting to analyze the social functions of religious behavior, to distinguish between what people *intend* to achieve by their behavior and the *unintended* effects of this behavior in social life. If a Tibetan devotee were asked why he repeatedly turned his prayer wheel and chanted "Om padme Om," or if one interrogated a "shouting" Methodist as to the reason for his ebullient enthusiasm, his answer would be very unlikely to show that he had any particular intentions whatsoever in regard to society. The intended effect of the Tibetan's action is to further his attainment of the bliss of Nirvana, and that of the Methodist is to give vent to his happy knowledge that he is saved by God's grace from his sins. They, in common with many other practitioners of religions, are deeply concerned with the attainment of certain states of consciousness. Other avowed objectives of members of various religious groups are connected with life in other worlds, with the gaining of heaven and the avoidance of hell, with the mitigation of the lot of souls in purgatory, and with the securing of one's transmigration into a superior type of being. Still other religious votaries may say that their aim is to bring their spirits into harmony with the universe, to glorify God and perform His will more perfectly, or by prayer to prevail upon the gods to bestow benefits upon human beings.

Robert Merton, making use of concepts found in a variety of disciplines, has labeled the intended consequences of behavior, the *manifest functions* and the unintended consequences, the *latent functions*.[6] This distinction is an important one for, as already shown, the consequences for society of much institutionalized religious behavior are, in fact, often unplanned by the human actors. Furthermore, the intended consequences of religious actions—addressed, as they frequently are, to supernatural beings and invisible forces—are peculiarly difficult to observe or assess. But since much religious activity is performed in a group, its unintended consequences for group organization, to mention only one aspect of religion's social impact, constitute observable aspects of human behavior. Therefore, it is precisely these unintended consequences, these latent functions, that have been a major focus of sociological analysis. It is, however, entirely without prejudice against the conscious intentions of religious practitioners that the functionalist maintains that the unintended consequences of their behavior are often of greater importance for the maintenance of society than are their conscious aims. Indeed, without some conscious intentions the religious behavior would most probably not be performed at all. Hence there would be no consequences, either manifest or latent, and thus little for sociologists to study in this area.

Positive and Negative Functions

Another problem for structural functionalism concerns the evaluation of functions. Some anthropologists, notably A. R. Radcliffe-Brown, among the first to draw attention to the unintended consequences of social actions, were on the whole inclined to view the latent functions of religious institutions as having positive consequences for the societies in question—that is, as making a useful contribution to their survival.[7] However, any existing society must by virtue of its existence have met the survival test. Therefore, if sheer survival were the sole criterion, it follows that almost all consequences of human actions (intended and unintended) must be evaluated as positive. The negative, or *dysfunctional,* aspects of such unintended consequences have therefore frequently been overlooked. If, however, the term "survival" (which was first introduced as an objective criterion) is, so to speak, expanded and taken to mean *survival and maintenance in a reasonable state of societal health,* a new imponderable element is introduced. Who is to judge, in purely objective terms, wherein such societal health consists? There is no easy way to rule out subjective evaluations, although a step in that direction is awareness of the hazards involved. William J. Goode has maintained that many structural-functional theorists (particularly anthropologists) have been overly prone to view the latent functions as positive and have been somewhat blind to their negative aspects. Furthermore, many unintended consequences of religious and other institutionalized actions may be neutral in their influence on society.[8]

STRUCTURAL-FUNCTIONAL ANALYSIS OF DIFFERENT TYPES OF SOCIETY

In Chapter 2 we depicted three societal models and indicated, in a general way, the functions that religion most commonly has performed in each of them. With these models in mind, and with respect to the problems posed by the structural-functional approach that have just been discussed, we may now consider in more precise detail the advantages and disadvantages of this approach.

Model One Societies

Structural-functional analysis, we believe, has been most fruitful in the case of Model One societies. It is not straining the facts too much to treat small isolated societies as more or less self-contained wholes, that is, as closed systems. Since many of the members of these societies live close to the subsistence line, emphasis upon their rather definite, minimal survival needs, and on the rudimentary institutional structures developed to meet such needs, is understandable. The functional necessity for religion is, no doubt, less readily apparent than the necessity for familial and economic institutions, but functionally oriented theorists investigating Model One societies have usually viewed religion and its institutions as essential for social control. Moreover, it is precisely in these Model One societies that other agencies of social control, such as government and law, are little developed. Hence the social-control function of religion may be plausibly viewed as both positive and necessary.

It must not be assumed, however, that all scholars interested in Model One societies have concurred with Durkheim's particular emphasis regarding religion's functions. Bronislaw Malinowski, for instance, took issue with Durkheim for having failed to allow for possible religious innovation (even in simple societies) and for not having recognized sufficiently the role of individual religious specialists, such as Shamans, in bringing about religious change. Malinowski stressed, much more than did Durkheim, religion's functions in mitigating the frustrations and stresses experienced by society's members both individually and collectively and drew attention to religion's supportive and compensatory functions even more than to its conservative or integrative ones. Nevertheless, he was in accord with Durkheim in emphasizing religion's positive contribution to Model One societies.[9] Furthermore, many contemporary anthropologists who have more recently studied a wide variety of simpler peoples tend to emphasize the great variations among them in the functions performed by religions and hence find the generalizations of both Durkheim and Malinowski oversimplified.

Model Two Societies

Model Two societies present a more difficult situation for analysis. These societies, as pointed out in Chapter 2, are typically larger, more complex, more open to outside influences, and hence more subject to change than are Model One societies. The entire institutional structure of such societies is more elaborate and more specialized. Although religion has its own specialized institutional structure, the institutions of government and of law (which have barely emerged in Model One societies) are developed and important in their own right. These latter institutions preempt some of the functions performed by religion in Model One societies without taking them over entirely. Hence the concept of alternative functions is very important in the structural-functional analysis of Model Two societies. It is, however, difficult to assign relative weights to the roles played by religion and government in legitimating the mores, particularly since government itself relies in part on religion for its own legitimation. For the same reason, it is difficult to evaluate the relative efficacy of religious sanctions and punishments and of purely legal ones in securing the necessary minimum of conformity to societal norms. Appraisals of the importance of religion's role are therefore of necessity inexact—a fact that disturbs many modern sociologists.

Furthermore, it cannot be assumed that in Model Two societies religion and its institutions affect all members of the society equally. In Model One societies there are, of course, individual differences with respect to religion's impact. But in Model Two societies the hierarchical structure of the religious institution itself and the distinction commonly made between monks and clergy on the one hand and laity on the other serve to emphasize differences in degree of religious involvement among members of the society. It is therefore more hazardous to make generalizations about religion's impact on Model Two societies.

In Model Two as in Model One societies the absence of highly developed scientific techniques leaves religion with an important function in helping to alleviate situations of stress, particularly those related to health and food supply. But since in addition Model Two societies (especially in the later stages of their development) are typically changing societies, new kinds of stress situations are likely to arise. Massive conflicts, many of them concerned with religion, have in times past (and also in the present) accompanied the transitional stages between Model Two and Model Three societies. Are these conflicts to be regarded as performing positive or negative functions? Sociologists are by no means agreed on this issue. Much depends on whether a short-run or a long-run view is taken. In the short run, because of the stressful and disruptive nature of religious conflict, sociologists have emphasized the negative function of religion in regard to such conflicts. Taking a longer view, however, many sociologists decline to assign to conflict per se (whether or not it stems from religious causes) a purely negative functional significance.[10] It may be the only viable means of effecting needed changes and thereby may produce long-term societal benefits.

In complex societies, moreover, the religion of the society may play an innovative role in one part of the social structure and a conservative role in another.[11] It may be argued that even these simultaneously opposing roles of religion may, in the long run, effect a positive result, for the innovation may prove beneficial while the conservative opposition may prevent even needed changes from being too rapid or too drastic. For instance, during the seventeenth century, the very period, according to Max Weber's analysis, when certain Calvinistic Protestant sects played an *innovating* role in the emergence of modern capitalism, some branches of the Roman Catholic Church were undergoing a *conservative* reaction. But it would be exceedingly difficult to find agreement among scholars as to whether the innovating or conservative religions were performing respectively positive or negative functions for Western European society, or, indeed, whether both, in combination, were playing a positive role.

In summary, it may be stated that, depending on the particular manifestations of religion that are being analyzed, religion may be viewed as performing at one and the same time both integrative and innovative functions. But it should be noted that it has not yet been found possible for either historians or sociologists to eliminate all subjectivity from their positive or negative evaluations of the consequences for society of these diverse aspects of religion's functions.

In Model Two societies, moreover, the *interpretive* functions of religion become more important. Whereas members of Model One societies are usually able to explain and justify inequities in social organization on the basis of custom—"it has been done in this manner for as long as we can remember"—the more complex and, on the whole, less egalitarian social systems characteristic of Model Two societies appear to call for more sophisticated systems of interpretation in order to appear just and right to their members. (The assumption here, of course, is that man is a creature who needs a moral interpretation of his societal environment.) Weber and Talcott Parsons after him have made much of this interpretive function of religion. Such interpretations with respect to Model Two societies, especially in their later stages, tend to be complex, for as the class structure changes and classes proliferate, interpretations of societal meaning that make "moral sense" to an established aristocracy may well be rejected by a rising bourgeoisie, which may be driven to create rival interpretations of society's moral meaning, also legitimated in religious terms. In short, because of the increasing complexity of Model Two societies, functional analyses of religion's role have usually limited their focus to the impact of religion on particular institutions of such societies. Weber's studies of the influence of religion on economic development, notably his *Protestant Ethic and the Spirit of Capitalism,* are important examples of this practice.

The "classical" studies (such as those of Weber) of religion's functions in Model Two societies have generally been concerned with historical societies and have made use of historical materials, cross-checked, in Weber's case, by the use of comparative data. Modern sociologists, however, have shown little inclination to make further studies in the manner of Weber, although an important exception is Robert N. Bellah's sociohistoric investigation of the role of Tokugawa religion in preindustrial Japan—an attempt to find an analogue in Japanese religion for the Protestant Ethic, which would account in part for Japan's successful industrialization after the Meiji restoration in 1880.[12]

Powerful new incentives for the sociological study of religion in Model Two societies, however, exist in our own day. For examples of Model Two societies are not confined to the history of the preindustrial West; they are very much with us in the present. Many, if not most, of the "developing" countries of Asia and Africa today constitute in large part Model Two societies. Most of them are eager to make the transition (first accomplished in the West) from Model Two to Model Three societies. They want to become "modern," and to do so they must industrialize. Hence, considerably increased attention is being paid by social scientists,[13] including sociologists, to the functions of religion in such societies, particularly to an assessment of the impact of traditional religious beliefs and institutions on economic and political development.

Model Three Societies

For the structural functionalist Model Three societies present even more formidable analytic problems than do Model Two societies. Many sociologists today, such as Allan Eister, are disinclined to use the structural-functional approach as a framework for their researches into religion's role in modern industrial societies. They argue that any theoretical approach may be regarded as useful only as long as it provides hypotheses that can be tested empirically by rigorously exact methods.[14] Such sociologists are of the opinion that, as applied to Model Three societies, the structural-functional approach acts as a stumbling block rather than as an aid to the formation of new and fruitful hypotheses.

A number of reasons have been given for taking this position. First, it is claimed that the functional view of modern industrial societies as integrated systems functioning within a framework of necessity is a falsification of the facts. This contention calls into question one of the major concepts of functionalism noted earlier in this section. It is also pointed out that modern industrial societies do in actuality manage to survive and maintain themselves with relatively loose integration and with a very considerable amount of internal conflict and tension. Granted that such is the case, then the "functional necessity" for religion, seen by many functionalists as an aid to social control through its legitimation of norms and their enforcement through religious sanctions, would stand in need of radical revision. Indeed, the entire character of religion's contribution to society would have to be viewed in a different light.

It is further argued that in highly secularized Model Three societies "religion" cannot be regarded as a total entity vis-à-vis another total entity, namely, "society." Religion has not only been considerably weakened, "secularized," and fragmented in such societies but is manifested mainly through a great many organized religious bodies often in competition with one another. Society, too, is comprised of a great variety of occupations, classes, and statuses. Thus "religion" may mean different things and supply different needs for different classes and groups of people. It cannot usefully be regarded as fulfilling functions common to an entire society. This latter contention is powerfully reinforced by the fact (mentioned in Chapter 2) that in Model Three societies it is quite common for many individuals to be unaffiliated with any religious body, while some of the affiliates are members of churches in name only. If, however, it is true that the 36 percent of the individuals in the United States who claim no religious affiliation do indeed maintain themselves no less successfully than their religiously affiliated fellow citizens, how then can it be claimed that "religion" is functionally necessary for the society as a whole? Is it not more to the point to inquire why some individuals and groups seem to need religion, as represented by religious group affiliation, whereas others seemingly do not?

Some sociologists, notably Will Herberg and Robert N. Bellah,[15] have drawn attention to the existence, even in a Model Three society such as the United States, of a national religion (including the religiously unaffiliated) over and above the existence of a multiplicity of religious organizations. Although this distinction between "religion in general" and "organized religion" is highly illuminating, it does not, in and of itself, solve all of the complex analytical problems mentioned above.

A third criticism of any generalized functionally oriented theory as applied to Model Three societies has to do with the extreme variations in the hold that religious beliefs and norms exert over the members of any given religious body. It is evident that the religious beliefs and values of the members can produce an impact on the other institutions of a society only insofar as they are internalized in such a way as to influence overt behavior. Such internalization of religious belief is by no means inevitable, for there is no organic necessity for individuals to "believe" in the same sense that there is an organic imperative that all must eat. Students of religion's role in Model Three societies cannot assume that all members of religious bodies act uniformly in accordance with the codes of such bodies. Therefore, sociologists must devise means to ascertain the degree to which the religious beliefs of the various religious bodies affect the behavior of their members. For this reason general theories regarding the importance of religion for a society as a whole appear to many contemporary sociologists, such as Charles Y. Glock, as immediately less useful than the construction of yardsticks designed to measure existing differences in the degree of religious *commitment*.[16]

Yet another problem concerning religious behavior in modern industrial societies is that a relatively large number of those who perform religious actions, such as worshiping in church or synagogue or participating in ritual prayer at home, are conscious of the positive social functions they hope to further by such means. Indeed, they may even engage in religious rituals for the purpose of attaining social goals. When New York City's subway system carries posters with the injunction, "The family that prays together stays together," it is apparent that functions formerly *latent* have become *manifest* and that desirable social outcomes that were once *unintended* by-products of religious actions have been transformed into *goals*. This modern development raises the interesting question as to whether or not religious behavior directed to social objectives is truly "religious." If families increasingly "pray together" in order to "stay together," do they really pray? Although no satisfactory answer is readily available,* the trends described bear witness to the increasing instrumentalization and secularization of "religion" in Model Three societies. Indeed, in such societies, religious organization frequently performs a variety of functions that are not, in any strict sense, religious at all. Prominent among such functions in the United States is provision of a sense of social and ethnic identification,[17] as well as general recreation such as the sponsorship of bingo games and bridge drives and the promotion of sports, art, and drama. In some Protestant denominations the kitchen is a runner-up in importance to the worship hall and the coffee pot to the chalice. Hence the sociological analyst, in

---

* How, for one's personal satisfaction, one answers this question is likely to depend on how one "defines" religion. Our main concern here is with the implications of this trend for sociological theory and research.

studying various institutions labeled "religious" may not, in point of fact, be studying "religion" at all—particularly if his definition of religion includes a supernatural referent. This secular trend makes it more difficult for the sociologist, whether or not a functionalist, to locate the major focus of his study.

The arguments here are illustrative of the kind of reasoning that has led some contemporary sociologists to question the usefulness of the structural-functional approach, especially as applied to the analysis of religion's role in Model Three societies. Most contemporary researchers, in fact, are inclined to play down general theories and to select some limited problem for study in which they utilize where possible quantifiable data collected to serve their own specific purposes. This tendency to set more limited research objectives and to formulate more modest and testable hypotheses is characteristic today of sociological analysis in general and should not be viewed merely as a rejection of structural functionalism. The sociological analysis of national societies as wholes and the assessment of the functions performed by their various institutional parts, whether economic, political, or religious, is in any case a problematic business. The conclusions of sociologists who have attemped this difficult task are, in the light of our present sociological knowledge and skills, necessarily couched partly in very general or even impressionistic terms. Nevertheless, sociological essays such as Parsons' "Christianity in Modern Industrial Society," Herberg's *Protestant, Catholic, Jew,* and Bellah's "Civil Religion in America," [18] all three of which are structural functionalist in approach, are enormously valuable in affording penetrating insights into the overall interactions of religion and its institutions with modern industrialized societies.

In these essays both Parsons and Herberg view religion not only in terms of religious institutions and religious bodies, but also more broadly as part of national culture. Thus Herberg's conclusion, based partly on well-educated "intuition," that the "American Way of Life" (despite the multiplicity of denominations and creeds) is the real religion of Americans and their most sacred bond of loyalty and solidarity, is entirely consistent with a broad functionalist approach. Indeed, Herberg's thesis may be seen as an extension to modern society of the Durkheimian view; namely, that the most sacred values of the society are symbolic representations of the group itself. The insight afforded by this view into the persistence of tribal religion in modern advanced societies, even in our own, may well be offensive to some individuals but is also illuminating.

In our view, those scholars who have pointed out some of the inadequacies of the structural-functional approach in the study of religion in Model Three societies have performed a useful service, but have failed to provide an adequate substitute. Nevertheless, they have forced sociologists to reappraise current theories in the field. Furthermore, the current upswing of sociological interest in religion and its institutions is in the meantime providing a much larger body of empirical studies (which shall be considered later) on the basis of which more adequate theories may be developed.

REFERENCES

1. See Anthony F. C. Wallace, *Religion: An Anthropological View* (New York: Random House, 1966), pp. 3–51, for a stimulating discussion of theoretical ways in which anthropologists and psychiatrists have approached the study of religion.
2. See Kingsley Davis, "Myth of Functional Analysis," *American Sociological Review,* 24 (December 1959), 757–772.
3. See Allan Eister, "Religious Institutions in Complex Societies," *American Sociological Review,* 22 (August 1957), 387–391, especially 387.
4. Émile Durkheim, *The Elementary Forms of the Religious Life,* trans. Joseph Ward Swain (New York: Collier, 1961), Chapter 7, especially pp. 236–245.
5. *Ibid.,* p. 237.
6. Robert K. Merton, *Social Theory and Social Structure* (Glencoe, Ill.: Free Press, 1957), pp. 61–64. The whole of Chapter 1 of Merton's well-known volume should be read by sociological students of religion.
7. A. R. Radcliffe-Brown, *Structure and Function in Primitive Society* (Glencoe, Ill.: Free Press, 1952), pp. 153–177. Reprinted in Louis

Schneider (ed.), *Religion, Culture, and Society: A Reader in the Sociology of Religion* (New York: John Wiley, 1964), pp. 63–80. This entire excerpt is well worth reading as a statement by an anthropologist of the functionalist viewpoint.

8. William J. Goode, *Religion Among the Primitives* (Glencoe, Ill.: Free Press, 1951), p. 33.

9. Bronislaw Malinowski, *Magic, Science, and Religion* (Glencoe, Ill.: Free Press, 1948; reprint ed., Garden City, N.Y.: Doubleday, Anchor Book, 1954), especially pp. 29–37.

10. Louis Coser, *The Functions of Social Conflict* (Glencoe, Ill.: Free Press, 1956), *passim,* especially pp. 33–38.

11. Wallace, *op. cit.,* p. 78. Wallace sees the concept of "the religion" of a society as one to be used with caution. "It is essentially a summative notion and cannot be taken uncritically to imply that one single unifying, internally coherent, carefully programmed set of rituals and beliefs characterizes the religious behavior of the society or is equally followed by all its members." He sees "the religion" of a society as really "likely to be a loosely related group of cult institutions and other, even less well organized practices and beliefs."

12. Robert N. Bellah, *Tokugawa Religion: The Values of Pre-Industrial Japan* (Glencoe, Ill.: Free Press, 1957).

13. See, for example, Robert N. Bellah (ed.), *Religion and Progress in Modern Asia* (New York: Free Press, 1965).

14. Eister, *op. cit.,* pp. 390–391.

15. See Will Herberg, *Protestant, Catholic, Jew* (Garden City, N.Y.: Doubleday, Anchor Book, 1960), and Robert N. Bellah, "Civil Religion in America," *Daedalus* (Winter 1967), 1–19.

16. Charles Y. Glock and Rodney Stark, *Religion and Society in Tension* (Chicago: Rand McNally, 1965), Chapter 2, especially p. 38.

17. Herberg, *op. cit.,* pp. 49–54. Herberg emphasizes the need of third-generation Americans to obtain some sense of identity to replace their rejection and subsequent loss of ethnic identity.

18. Talcott Parsons in Edward Tiryakian (ed.), *Sociological Theory, Values, and Sociocultural Change* (Glencoe, Ill.: Free Press, 1963), reprinted in Schneider, *op. cit.,* pp. 273–298; Herberg, *op. cit.;* Bellah, "Civil Religion," *op. cit.*

4
Religion and Human Stress

INTRODUCTION

James Michener in *The Bridges of Toko-ri* has brought home to us anew the tragedy of sudden "senseless" death. His hero, Brubacher, a marine jet pilot who perished in Korea, a man who had everything to live for, knowingly risked almost certain death to bomb strategic enemy bridges, even though his commanding officer had given him the chance of refusing the mission. Since this was his second tour of combat duty, Brubacher had already done more than his part to defend his society. His wife, who eagerly awaited his return, had also borne her full share of the sacrifices demanded of women in wartime and therefore had a right to expect some consideration both from her society, and perhaps from fate, in return. Yet her plans and hopes were cruelly frustrated, as are those of so many wives, mothers, and sweethearts throughout the world today.

Brubacher's wife knew how her husband had died. More than most wives, because she had visited her husband at sea and had talked with his commanding officer, she understood intellectually the conditions and hazards of jet plane warfare. She knew, too, that her husband was a brave man who had done his duty; and she also approved intellectually of the United Nations cause for which he had laid down his life. Yet, like all human beings, she was a feeling as well as a thinking creature, and to adjust to her bereavement, she needed something more than "this cold knowledge." [1] Michener does not tell us what this woman did to bear her grief. Whether she took comfort in memories of her husband, in her children, in the understanding of her friends, in the ritualistic expression of sorrow, or in the religious belief that God had both herself and her husband in His keeping and that somehow He would make all things right in the end, we do not know. We do know, however, that in order to come to terms with her sorrow she would need not only factual knowledge but an interpretation of the tragedy that she could accept emotionally as well. Then only could she go on her way, a whole person, to fulfill her part as mother and citizen in society.

Brubacher's wife thus faced a universal problem, a problem that the wives and families of men of many nations who are now fighting in Southeast Asia, Africa, the Middle East, and other parts of the world must also face. Loss of loved ones, especially in situations that leave the bereaved helpless or that appear to them as pointless and unjust, inevitably creates serious stress for the individual. Moreover, the emotional strain and shock may be equally poignant whether death occurs under conditions of war or in the ordinary course of life.

Stress occasioned by bereavement is a crucial example of stress situations that are a perennial part of the human lot. Others, such as those brought about by disease and famine (which will be discussed later) are also recurrent. The perennial and recurrent character of human stress situations, coupled with the rather remarkable constancy of human nature, whether in the Neanderthal age or in today's atomic era, has created a persistent and continuing need for some available means to absorb these events.

THE ROLE OF RELIGION IN STRESS SITUATIONS

In all human societies there are stretches of time when things run smoothly, when social obligations are normally fulfilled, and when men and women play their social roles in reasonable certainty that their fellows will reciprocate. Men know that they can depend on one another, and in the natural as well as in the social world they know in large measure what they can count on.[2] Hence people are able to plan and can look forward to the fruition of their plans. Thus plans are made by parents for the rearing and education of their children, marriages and homes are contemplated, fields and vineyards are tended and harvests anticipated, business and professional activities are marked by planning—and all these plans are made with a reasonable hope of their fulfillment. In short, for the furtherance of such plans there is a tremendous investment of time and energy, both physical and emotional, by human beings everywhere; without this investment of directed energy, human societies could hardly be maintained.

Although there are periods in most societies when people go about their business without particular strain and the means available to them are adequate to attain the goals for which they have been taught to strive, this is by no means always the case. [Indeed, in the life cycle of almost all individuals there are certain events that are fraught with emotionally laden expectations accompanied by considerable anxiety lest these expectations fail to be realized. Birth, coming of age, marriage, and death are among such events, and most societies have developed *rites of passage* not only to give community recognition to such occasions but also to alleviate the anxieties they frequently engender.[3]] There are also crucial situations of stress in the life of all societies when the means available to their members are insufficient to enable them to attain their most cherished goals. Indeed, if human affairs moved along without uncontrollable and unpredictable accidents and strains, the role of religion in human society, if any, would be a very different matter. Without unanticipated events beyond our control, we would be much more likely, as Talcott Parsons has said, to think of the problems of life as mainly practical ones, to be solved by good "horse sense." [4] If this situation existed, moreover, then the development and application of scientific techniques might in fact be expected to produce a utopian world.

We know, however, that tragedy and stress inhere in the very nature of the human situation. There is always a gap, of greater or lesser extent, in all societies between the culturally grooved hopes and expectations of men and their fulfillment. Hence practical scientific techniques, however highly developed, can never be adequate to meet all human situations. Men everywhere must adjust to events that they cannot adequately foresee or control. These adjustments may at times be practical, but they are always emotionally charged. In modern industrial societies scientific techniques are available to relieve many stress situations that cannot be met in this way in other types of society, but emotional frustrations remain. Furthermore, in such societies the extensive development of scientific and technical knowledge has helped to create, indirectly, a number of additional unpredictable and uncontrollable situations. Modern scientific warfare, for example, has possibly added as many frustrations as modern medicine has allayed.

Although it is by no means the whole picture, religion can be thought of as one of the most important means used by man to adjust to situations of stress.

Stress situations may be divided into three main categories.[5] All three concern involvements in which human beings have a great emotional investment in a successful outcome. In the first two cases the outcome is not entirely within human control, and even in the third case the control that can be exercised in a single human life span is narrowly limited. The first category includes situations in which individuals or groups are faced by the loss of other human beings who are important to them. The loss may be final, as in the case of death, or it may be a more conditional loss occasioned by the failure of associates to fulfill expected mutual obligations. Children, for instance, who are the objects of so many hopes, may "repay" their parents with indifference or hostility, betrothals and marriage vows may be broken, business and financial obligations may be dishonored, friendships and national loyalties may be betrayed.

In all of these situations emotional as well as practical frustrations are involved. And since, to quote Parsons once more, human beings cannot just "take it,"[6] means must be found to adjust to both the emotional and the practical aspects of the situation. The example of premature death, with which this chapter began, is perhaps the classic type of situation in this first category.

In the second category of stress situations fall those in which largely uncontrollable and unpredictable natural forces may imperil the vital social concerns of food supply and health. The control of agriculture and the incidence of disease have been important focal points for religious behavior in all societies. The third category comprises conflicting values, stemming from contradictions in a society's social structure and causing on occasion severe mental stress for that society's members. These three types of situations, involving personal loss, the impact of natural wants, and value conflict, are considered at some length in the following pages.

RELIGION AS A MODE OF ADJUSTMENT

The Case of Death

We chose an example of premature death to illustrate the part played by religion as a means of adjustment to frustrations in human relationships because of both the universality of this phenomenon and the extreme frustration and stress it commonly occasions to those who are bereaved.

Death is both unpredictable and ultimately beyond human control. Although all men know that they will die, almost no man knows when death will occur. Currently thousands of young men in the United States, faced by the certainty or probability of being drafted by the military and sent on active duty to Vietnam or elsewhere, are forced to envisage the possibility of an untimely death. "Lord, let me know mine end and the number of my days that I may be certified how long I have to live," said the Hebrew psalmist, giving voice to the most universal of all human uncertainties. No man, save perhaps the suicide, can plan for his death, much less control it. In part because of this uncertainty, religious interpretations of death are found in every society. Although these contain many shadings of belief about life after death, their fundamental feature for social science is not (as they are sometimes interpreted) that they are merely evidences of wishful thinking. Whatever may be considered the ultimate truth about such matters, sociologically viewed, religious beliefs provide a set of "mechanisms" by means of which those about to die and those bereaved are enabled to adjust themselves to the stressful reality.[7]

Talcott Parsons has surmised that in a society in which premature death, through the application of scientific medicine and the elimination of wars and accidents, had been abolished so that everyone could count on living out their "threescore years and ten," the part now played by religion in human affairs might be substantially altered. There is, of course, notwithstanding medical advances such as organ transplants, no immediate prospect of such a society.* But even in this hypothetical case, so great is the emotional investment of each individual in his own life that whenever death comes, it must always, in a sense, be premature. Many of us know individuals who at the age of ninety are full of plans and eager for more life in which their plans may be realized.

Since the frustration of death is unescapable, human beings have always oriented themselves to death by means of both religious belief and ritual. Beliefs about death and afterlife cannot nullify death, of course, but they can help people face it and serve their societies the better while doing so. To combat pilots, and indeed to all those, such as miners and mariners, to whom

---

* Whether or not we would actually delight in such a scientifically controlled and, so to say, machine-made world is, of course, quite another matter. Fictional attempts to portray such a world, as, for instance, Aldous Huxley's well-known *Brave New World*, seem to suggest that many of the values of human personality that we deem most precious would be doomed to extinction. Perhaps the historian Arnold Toynbee had something of the same idea in mind when he claimed that the full potential of the spirit of man can only be evoked as a response to the challenge of the uncontrollable and unpredictable events in human society and that sometimes this very response has made it possible for man eventually to assume a greater measure of control over his human destiny.

the imminence of death is an apparent probability, the need served by these beliefs is perhaps more urgent than it is for the majority of more sheltered folk.

But even more important for human society are what were earlier termed the latent functions of religious beliefs about death and the dead. For these beliefs define for the living the place of the dead in both the suprasocial and the social scheme of things. These definitions not only serve to reassure the living, who may be apprehensive about their relationship to the dead or the intentions of the dead toward themselves, but also have practical social implications.*

For example, the anthropologist Reo Fortune tells us that among the Manus people, who live in the Bismarck Archipelago, the spirits of those who have just died are believed to be actively present in the villages of the living, where they function as a kind of moral policemen, custodians of the village mores. In this capacity the ever-watchful spirits of the recently dead are concerned that the financial obligations, as well as the sexual prohibitions, both of which are central to the Manus system of social values, are strictly observed.[8] Again, Buddhism in the villages of Burma—and in much of Southeast Asia where the belief in rebirth obtains—serves to make of death no more than a stage of life. The aim of the Burmese Buddhist death ritual is not so much to alleviate sorrow as to make sure that the risky transition from one life to the next is safely and smoothly made and that no wandering spirits threaten the peace and safety of the villagers.[9] In Burma every death affords a supreme opportunity for the reaffirmation of the primary Buddhist values of impermanence, suffering, and insubstantiality, and for perpetuating these values in Burmese society. Again, the belief of the Chinese that their dead ancestors continue to exist as sacred beings who thrive on the care and respect rendered to them by a long line of descendants has helped in times past to maintain vital elements in the

---

* It may be argued that the beliefs of some religions about the role of the dead are terrifying rather than reassuring. But even if this is granted, there is at least some reassurance in having the area of terror defined and delimited.

fabric of their society, namely, a veneration for all elders and the strength and cohesion of the greater family, so that Chinese society for thousands of years was notable for its conservatism and stability. In contrast, the creeds of some Christian churches teach that the dead are ever-living and spiritually active members of a "communion of saints" that includes all Christian souls, both "dead" and living. This belief in medieval Christendom constituted a source of strength for the living in their struggle for survival amid the hardships of a turbulent society.

Equally significant for the society is the *ritualization* of death. Whatever meaning death may have for the person most immediately concerned, for those who are bereaved it inevitably entails the severance of a whole network of social relationships and mutual obligations. Although for the religionist this point represents only a small part of what he regards as the truth, from the this-worldly point of view of the sociologist the main social functions performed by the ritualization of death are the rehabilitation of the bereaved and the repairing of the broken web of social relationships. For a wider social community, as well as those immediately bereaved, is affected by the death of an individual, especially an individual holding a responsible position. Therefore the society's temporary breach in its system of mutual obligations must be closed and its normal ways of life continued.

Religious ritual in relation to death, then, serves to reaffirm the social solidarity of the larger social group and to place the latter's support at the disposal of the bereaved. This function of religious ritual has been observed in ancient and modern, primitive and civilized societies. And although the forms of many of these rituals may perhaps seem strange, and at times even laughable, this does not mean that they are mere "errors," soon to be outmoded by the advancement of science. While the forms are likely to be modified, these rituals, if they are to satisfy human needs, can never be based solely on science or common sense.

In fact, some of the older ritual patterns no doubt fulfilled this social function more effectively than certain of our more modern forms. Sociologist Leroy Bowman, in his book *The American*

Funeral, is strongly of the opinion that the modern urban funeral, arranged by funeral directors and taking place in a funeral parlor, is much less effective in rallying community support for the bereaved or in affording a means of catharsis for deeply felt grief than were many of the funeral rites held in Model One or Model Two societies.[10] Popular writers like Jessica Mitford (in her *American Way of Death*)[11] and Evelyn Waugh (in his bestselling book *The Loved One*)[12] have satirized the elaborate and expensive mortuary arts of the funeral directors and the meretricious values to which some of them appeal. "The more costly the casket, the more sincere is the grief of the survivors and the greater the respect paid to the deceased" is perhaps a not too surprising expression of sentiment in a commercial age. Such a claim is in harmony with at least one dominant urban value—namely, that of status striving—although such funeral practices may do little to afford a catharsis for grief or to promote family and community solidarity. However, the conditions of modern urban life are such that many individuals, unlike dwellers in small rural communities, have little firsthand experience of death, either of human beings or of animals. The impulse of urban dwellers living busy lives in crowded conditions is apparently to "sweep death under the rug" as soon as possible and to get back to the business of living. The inexperience of the urban individual in the face of death has the effect of making him willing and relieved to turn to the expert, namely, the funeral director.

Moreover, in contemporary urban societies the nature of orientations toward death and emotional needs concerning bereavement have also undergone considerable change, inevitably leading to modifications of rituals. Indeed, one of the results of the juxtaposition in our modern world of societies of different types (as discussed in Chapter 2) is that individuals accustomed to living in one type of society are, at the time of their bereavement, subjected, even against their will, to death rituals customary in a society of a different type, usually a less "modern" one. In order to carry out the wishes of a member of the older generation, or to respect the feelings of older relatives, a young Jewish urbanite may have to undergo a long period of ritual mourning, or a "modern" Christian may have to acquiesce in a wake where the corpse of the deceased is displayed in an open coffin. Situations such as these are not infrequently acutely distressing to such individuals. To be sure, in some rural communities even today earlier practices are more likely to persist. There community members are still likely to attend traditional funerals in order to demonstrate their standing in and solidarity with local groups as well as to give support to the bereaved.* However, the wakes and wailing ceremonies of peasant societies most clearly reveal this rallying around the survivors.

These wailings and wakes at one time served a more personal function for the bereaved, a function that is now more likely to be performed by individual friends, understanding ministers, or even by psychiatrists, for many of the earlier rites had a quasi-psychiatric function. Although the fact may be difficult to face, considerable ambivalence exists in our emotions concerning the dead. Survivors may resent former actions of the deceased or for reasons either conscious or unconscious they may welcome the death. They may also feel guilty about their own acts of commission or omission with respect to the dead. Either situation is likely to induce some psychic conflict, conflict that may hamper the social participation of the bereaved. Some of the more "primitive" rituals dramatized this internal conflict and, as they served to drain off ambivalent emotions, acted as a catharsis for feelings of guilt as well as of grief. The funeral rites of the Australian Warramunga, for example, in which the participants dramatized self-punitive feelings by acting out extremes of self-mutilation, were in all probability an effective means of allaying self-crippling guilt, even though this method is not one that most persons today would care to emulate.[13]

Lugubrious as they may be, however, death rituals almost always culminate in a positive, affirmative note. For death, like birth, is an integral part of the ongoing life process, a total proc-

---

* Even in big cities political funerals—and gangsters' funerals—may be attended in order to demonstrate solidarity. Funerals of professional people may also be attended for similar reasons.

ess to which we all ultimately contribute. Without death, the eliminator, there could be no continuing life. But even when this positive affirmation is obscure, in many societies the termination of the death rituals, which furnish occasion for the gathering of a group of otherwise scattered individuals, is marked by feasting and circumspect conviviality. Each society has its particular traditions, to be sure, but there are counterparts in many places of the Yorkshireman who said to his friend as he partook of the succulent ham sandwiches customary at funeral "teas," "Eh, lad, Ah've not 'ad such a good time, no, not since my wife's sister was buried!" Although those immediately bereaved are hardly likely to enter fully into this aspect of the occasion, yet their obligation, frequently affirmed by the culture, to provide food and drink for the assembled gathering is a symbolic means by which they affirm even in their grief that the living too must be considered and that in spite of death life must go on.

While in the West the gaiety of such funeral gatherings is usually something less than hilarious—although an Irish wake might prove an exception—the writer has encountered in the Orient some funeral celebrations characterized by overt jocularity. In Burma, for instance, the compound in the house of a deceased villager does not look like a mournful or solemn place. It is gay with gamblers, tea drinkers, and groups of young people serving and ushering.[14] Once, on the occasion of a visit by the author to the household of a Shan * chieftain, she was greeted smilingly by the daughter of the house and asked with every appearance of cheerfulness "to come and be introduced to Daddy." She was somewhat unprepared to find "Daddy" preserved in a glass coffin placed under an elaborate canopy on a dais, with a lively gathering of relatives and friends chatting in the shade of the canopy. The corpse had been lying in state for two weeks, during which watchers were continually present, gaining religious "merit" from this sociable activity. It is also traditional in Burma to celebrate the cremation of a respected member of the Order of Monks (that is, a monk concerning whose chances of a

---

* The Shans live in the Northeast of Burma. They are citizens of Burma but speak a language akin to Thai.

favorable rebirth there could be no possible doubt) with a community-wide festival, somewhat like a fair. The corpse may have been embalmed and thus preserved for three months or more before the ceremony. The preparations for the celebrations will have occupied the entire Buddhist village community for weeks beforehand. Booths and elaborate pavilions, constructed mainly of bamboo and papier maché, will have been erected. Popular music is blared forth by amplifiers, and soft drinks are lavishly supplied. Much party food has been prepared for the ceremonial feeding of deputations of monks as well as for the delectation of the laity. Stylized singing and dancing and games of dominoes and cards go on in various pavilions; pretty young girls in traditional costume place the glass coffin containing the corpse on hangers, after which they swing and rock it, meanwhile singing songs for the safe passage of the deceased to his next birth. The villagers come prepared to spend the day and give every appearance of enjoying the festivities. On the occasion of the cremation of a really prominent monk the celebrations might last for three full days.

We have chosen to discuss at some length these beliefs and rituals surrounding death as an illuminating example of the social and psychological functions performed by religion in the type of situation placed in the first category, the strains and tensions occasioned by death and bereavement. The reader may explore for himself the part played by religion in other stress situations of this order.

Unpredictable Natural Forces

The second category includes situations in which unpredictable and uncontrollable natural forces place human survival in jeopardy. Food is essential to life and health, and the fear of famine is often deep-seated. The success of the harvest is a vital concern all over the earth. The exposure of agricultural products to the uncertainty of weather guarantees an area of precariousness in which human intelligence and skill may fail to obtain the results on which life depends. This situation is most evident in those cultures in which modern technology is least developed and weather conditions are most violent and least predictable, but it is never entirely absent, since man has not yet been able to control nature completely.

The Pueblo Indians of the American Southwest, for example, are skillful in preparing land and planting and cultivating corn; yet harvests are sometimes lacking because rainfall is beyond their control. Similarly, in the West Indies today, where the prosperity of certain areas is almost entirely dependent on the success of the banana crop, a devastating hurricane can destroy the crop at the very time it is coming to fruition. In heavily populated countries like India, where agricultural techniques are still primitive, relatively minor failures in rainfall are likely to be disastrous. Even in regions where technical skill is highly developed, some uncertainty remains. Grasshoppers may batten on Nebraska wheat, or a late frost may decimate the Georgia peach crop.

Agriculture is an important stress situation in which *magic* is a frequently employed means of adjustment. Shortly the precise meaning of magic and its distinction from religion will be discussed. Here we should note that although the ends of magic and religion are not the same, both involve techniques of adjustment to strains brought about by uncertainty. Hence magic, in this context, may be thought of as continuous with religion; in fact, in most agricultural societies magic and religion are closely intertwined. In such societies the rhythm of the seasons and their attendant agricultural activities are characterized by a round of magico-religious observances. Dances and incantations mark the spring planting, and by means of fertility dances and sacrifices the favor of the rain gods is sought or the gods of the swollen rivers are propitiated. Harvest is an occasion for ritual thanksgiving.

Of what use to the society are these magico-religious practices? No man can make crops grow by magic or religion alone. Nor does it seem true that so-called primitive peoples possess such limited mentalities, as the French anthropologist Lucien Lèvy-Bruhl professed to believe,[15] that they are unaware of the es-

RELIGION: A SOCIOLOGICAL VIEW

sential difference between the effects of magico-religious techniques and practical agricultural procedures.*   Malinowski, whose studies of the Trobriand Islanders were cited earlier, illuminated the function of religious magic by showing that the Trobrianders, at any rate, were well aware of this difference. These natives have great respect for such technical know-how as they do possess, but they are also aware of its limitations.   The magico-religious practices that accompany their agriculture and fishing are supplements to, not substitutes for, their practical techniques.   They do not believe that they can make up for their failure to cultivate their gardens efficiently by the use of more and better magic.[16]

More recently, however, sociologist Francis Hsu has questioned Malinowski's contention that simple peoples, or, for that matter, highly developed ones, are invariably able to distinguish so clearly between magico-religious and empirical techniques.   In a study of a Southwest China community during a cholera epidemic shortly after World War II, Hsu found that the villagers used magical, religious, and modern scientific means to combat the disease—with very little discrimination between them.   In fact, scientific techniques were more readily adopted when they were either combined with, or presented under the guise of, magic that was familiar to the people.[17]   Hsu was also of the opinion that in modern industrial societies many essentially "magical" techniques gain a more ready acceptance when "packaged" as science, citing many of the pseudoscientific claims that the advertisers of cosmetic and other products associate with gaining popularity or success in love.   For instance, television advertisements of toothpaste include diagrams that show "scientifically" how it whitens the teeth.   But the implicit claim of the commercial, suggested by pictures of youth and beauty, that the resulting white teeth will capture a sweetheart is surely a "magi-

---

* In this respect they are of one mind with the old Vermont farmer of many a pulpit story. When the minister visited him after church and congratulated him on what the "Lord had wrought" on his recently cleared half acre, the farmer replied laconically, "Yes, but you should have seen it when the Lord had it all to Himself!"

cal" one, however "scientific" the "packaging" may have been. In both the Chinese and the American cases, it would appear that the dominant values of the societies determine in large part the most acceptable kind of packaging to be used.

As a corrective to Lèvy-Bruhl's misleading distinction between the psychological makeup of primitive and of modern peoples, Malinowski's evidence that the Trobrianders did in fact recognize the difference involved in the use of magical and scientific techniques has been of great value. Hsu's study is useful as a reminder that on occasion *neither* primitive nor modern peoples discriminate clearly in their use of scientific-empirical and magico-religious methods. Members of all types of societies, whether they are clear in their minds about the distinction between magical and scientific means or not, use magico-religious techniques to some extent. What, then, are the functions of this religious magic?

Malinowski contended that religious magic reinforces self-confidence in crucial situations of strain in which practical techniques do not suffice to guarantee success.[18] Hence he viewed the incantations and spells employed by the Trobrianders in their gardening and deep-sea fishing—risk-laden activities vital to their survival—as a means of relieving their psychological anxieties through ritualized dramatization. In such situations the use of religious magic or other comparable techniques would appear to be inevitable.[19]

This generalization, however, does not imply that magico-religious techniques invariably have positive social functions. Some modern anthropologists, in opposition to Malinowski, have stressed the negative consequences of magic because in their view magic produces even more anxieties than it alleviates. One of the negative effects of magico-religious practices is the fact that once such means are adopted, there develops a vested interest in their continuance, often blocking the acceptance of more efficient techniques even when they are available. This is a common problem in many so-called backward regions of the world today.

Physical and psychic health is another area in which magico-religious methods are commonly employed, ranging from the spiritual healing authorized by some Christian churches to the practices of witch doctors. Among the Navaho Indians, for example, the main focus of religious behavior is in the area of health and disease. Similarly, for Christian Scientists health in all its aspects is a chief concern of religious activity. Here again religion and magic aid social survival insofar as they "act as a tonic" and help those concerned to tap psychic resources from which they might otherwise be cut off. Yet their use may also hamper a society's well-being if the adoption of scientific methods of tried effectiveness is blocked.

From our discussion so far it should be clear that religion supplies one important method by which man meets situations of stress. Other important means are magic and science. We pointed out earlier that, as a method of adjustment, magic may be thought of as being continuous with religion and that in concrete institutional life magic and religion are frequently intermeshed. We must now differentiate between the two. Magic and religion are alike in that they employ nonempirical means, but they differ significantly in the ends they seek. Religion's goals are oriented to the nonempirical, the other-worldly, the supernatural. Although religion is often concerned with the physical and social welfare of human beings, it always has a transcendental point of reference. This is not true of magic. The ends the practitioner of magic seeks are in the everyday human world.[20]

Furthermore, the religious worshiper, as distinct from the magician or his clients, is constrained by an attitude of awe and reverence toward the sacred ends that he pursues. For him the ends must inhere in the means. The user of magic, on the other hand, is "in business" for practical and arbitrarily chosen results. For him reverence and awe are out of place because he is a manipulator of the supernatural for his own private ends and those of his clients rather than a worshiper of it. To snare a fowl, to net a school of fish, to keep animals from the crops, to heal disease, or to secure the compliance of a lover, he may utter his spells almost casually, in a normal everyday voice, as one who beseeches no favor but expects rather an automatic reaction to correct methods. By means of his special knowledge, which is often very private property, the magician believes that he can control or coerce the supernatural and thereby produce concrete, observable results.

Moreover, the content of magic and of religion differ. Religious systems, particularly in their more elaborate developments, may encompass the whole of life; they may provide a total theory of both the supernatural and human society. The content of magic, on the other hand, constitutes no unified inclusive theory but is likely to be atomistic, something like an old-fashioned book of recipes or a home doctor manual.

In practice, magic and religion are often closely intermixed. However, two main varieties of magic may be distinguished. One kind of magic, such as that practiced by the Trobrianders in the cultivation of their gardens and in fishing, is used for group purposes and has much in common with religion. Such quasireligious techniques are sometimes known as _white magic_. The most secret antisocial varieties of magic, such as witchcraft and obeah, in contrast, have been termed _black magic_. One way of viewing the distinction between religion and magic is to regard each as occupying a polar extreme on a continuum. From this viewpoint the purest, most other-worldly manifestations of "higher" religions represent one extreme and black magic the other.

But there are many subtle blendings of magico-religious behavior along this hypothetical continuum. In addition, several types of behavior most commonly thought of as religious are seen on examination to fluctuate between the magical and religious poles. At the religious pole, for instance, prayer is exemplified by the belief of Brother Lawrence, for whom prayer is identical with the "practice of the presence of God"; whereas prayer at the magical pole is illustrated by the Tibetan's water-driven wheel, a mechanical contrivance that continues its "prayers" even while the worshiper sleeps. Or again, at the magical extreme, sacrifice may be an attempt to coerce, in a way, the supernatural with gifts; yet sacrifice may be conceived of in the meaning of the Hebrew psalmist who came to his God not with a burnt offering but with the sacrifice of a "broken and a contrite heart"—clearly a religious view.

Some of the social functions of white, or religious, magic have already been mentioned. Another question is what contributions black magic makes to the maintenance of human societies. Some scholars maintain that from a psychological point of view, witchcraft, the best-known instance of black magic, may operate to relieve group frustrations and distress by serving to project outside the group the hostile emotions so frequently associated with stress situations; or, alternatively, to focus these hostile feelings on a limited, special segment of the social group, as in the famous case of the Salem witches. In other words, black magic may help the group to maintain its internal cohesion and solidarity in the face of social stress.*

This function of magic is clarified in Clyde Kluckhohn's study *Navaho Witchcraft*. Kluckhohn shows how witchcraft in this case is associated with the almost unbearable psychological and social pressures occasioned in part by the extreme isolation of family life in a society of widely scattered sheep-raisers. Navaho culture prohibits all manifestations of overt hostility among family members; nevertheless, as psychiatric research conducted by Kluckhohn and others among the Navahos brings out, their living conditions stimulate considerable ambivalence of feeling and hostile (as well as cooperative) emotions. But most Navahos do not dare to give vent to these tabooed sentiments within the family circle itself, suffering guilt and anxiety if they admit even to themselves that they do in fact entertain such feelings. In this dilemma the assumed existence of malevolent witches provides the Navaho people with approved targets for their repressed hate, and by means of this black magic they can "get back at" their enemies, both real and imaginary.[21]

Since the Navaho economy might break down if individual families in their scattered hogans were not able to cooperate ef-

---

* Other students may feel that this line of reasoning constitutes a somewhat strained attempt to find a function for magic and may prefer more simply to regard such magic as dysfunctional.

fectively in their sheep-raising, and since witchcraft provides an agency for the relief of psychic guilt that might otherwise reach unmanageable proportions, in the absence of alternative techniques the latent function of witchcraft may be said to be positive. Whether among the Navahos or others, however, any relief from stress that witchcraft may afford is bought at a large social cost, evidenced not only in the possible victimization of the witches themselves, but also in the widespread fear and suspicion that witchcraft keeps alive in a social group. A still further cost of magical practices, as already indicated, is that once they have become accepted customs, they act to block the adoption of technically superior means to handle stress situations. In the case of the Navaho tribe, for example, in which witchcraft and black magic are closely linked with the maintenance of health, the acceptance of the aid of modern scientific medicine has been retarded.

Conflicting Social Values

Human stress, it has been noted, can be induced by psychological conflicts engendered by disparities and contradictions in different aspects of a society's institutional structure. These disparities and contradictions in turn give rise to conflicts in values. It is apparent, especially in times of rapid social change, that members of human societies are confronted from time to time with inconsistent or contradictory values.[22] Most persons in the course of their lives do indeed at certain stages of their careers need to abandon some values and accept others, to learn new priorities for behavior, to recognize the different conditions in which one value or another should be involved. Perhaps most people learn to make these adjustments rather smoothly.

But there are also in a society internal structural conditions that plunge many people into continual uncertainty over the choice of values or an ethic to govern their behavior. Such a dilemma may be experienced by some members of the society as a major stress situation. Anthropologist Claude Lèvi-Strauss has suggested that in such situations religious myth may play a reconciling role. Myths, in his view, are symbolic expressions and symbolic formulas for the resolution of value conflicts implicit in societies containing structural contradictions that place many people living "normal" lives in moral quandaries. Lèvi-Strauss regards religious myth as depicting the *course of resolution* of value conflicts intrinsic to the social structure of each society, even of stable societies. Hence the function of such myths is to act as a sort of bridge and thus to permit the society to maintain the partial advantages of each of its contradictory segments.[23] Furthermore, both myths and ritual also function as emotional vents, which provide relief for the tensions that such contradictions produce.

The Oedipus myth, in the interpretation of Erich Fromm, furnishes an excellent example of a myth that fulfilled, for archaic Greek society, the function described above.[24] In this myth the infant Prince Oedipus is abandoned by his mother to die but is rescued and raised by a shepherd. Not knowing his true identity, he grows up to kill his father, the King of Thebes, and to marry his mother, the widowed queen. In expiating for this unwitting patricide and incest to which he was destined by fate, he blinds himself. While Freud treated this myth as the classic symptomatic expression of a neurotic problem he felt to be universal in man, Fromm regards it as a symbolic expression of a structural contradiction in Greek society; he sees the struggle against paternal authority as the main theme of Sophocles' Oedipus Trilogy and also views this struggle as stemming from an ancient institutional fight between contradictory patriarchal and matriarchal systems. Oedipus, then, is seen as attacking an emergent patriarchal system while upholding earlier matriarchal forms. The functional utility that Fromm claims for the Oedipus myth is that it afforded the individual an emotional bridge with which to span contradictions of the social structure. Fromm views the myth as a recognition of the strong attachment to their ancient matriarchal system the Greeks at that time still felt, but he also sees it as a device indicating that when there was a clear confrontation between patriarchal and matriarchal values, the patriarchal values were to be given priority.

A similar function was performed by the Hindu myth of Prince Arjuna and Krishna his heavenly charioteer narrated in the *Bhagavad-Gita*. Arjuna was torn by the conflict between his religious values, which enjoined abstention from killing, and the values of his warrior caste, which demanded that he should fight. Krishna commands him to do his duty as a member of his caste but acknowledges the force of the religious prohibition in taking life by enjoining him not to be "attached" to his action. He also softens the emotional impact of the action on Arjuna by reminding him that while all must die sooner or later, nevertheless, all will be reborn.

Today many individuals are faced with a value conflict between duty to the state and religious conceptions of duty to humanity. The tragic war in Vietnam has revealed structural contradictions in our society in glaring fashion. But individuals today are less able to accept religious myths as furnishing adequate bridges of reconciliation to span the conflicting institutional structures of our society.

RELIGION AND SCIENCE AS ALTERNATIVE MODES OF ADJUSTMENT

Science supplies men with practical empirical means for adjusting to practical empirical situations. In religion both the ends sought and the means used are nonempirical. Moreover, science, in marked contrast with magic, employs practical, empirical means, although both science and magic seek practical, empirical ends.

Science, in contrast with magic or religion, may at first glance seem to be the very acme of modernity. This is because we are likely to think of science almost solely in terms of its familiar highly developed form. Very simple techniques, however, can be scientific in principle, as Malinowski has pointed out.[25] In fact, science viewed as empirical method rather than as a developed system is as old as society; human culture could not have evolved without some minimal scientific techniques. Long before the arrival of Europeans, for example, the American Indians of the Southwest had developed methods of cultivating corn that were and still are of demonstrable effectiveness in crop production. The fact that they did not achieve the results made possible by a more developed technology does not negate the scientific character of the simpler methods.

The conspicuous achievements of modern science and its consequent prestige convince many people today that science is the dominant method used by man to achieve his many purposes and to adjust to stresses of various kinds. Science's record of success in these respects is clearly impressive; there can be no doubt that from many points of view it performs positive social functions.[26] The question remains, however, whether or not the functions of science are unconditionally positive; for science does not apply itself but is applied by social beings to social purposes in terms of social values. Hence it may be asked if science, like religion and magic, does not also at times create additional stresses while alleviating others. A related question and one more intimately concerned with our central theme, namely, the social function of religion in stress situations, also arises: Does religion as a means of adjustment to stress situations become less important in human affairs as scientific means become more effective?

Social theorists have given quite different answers to the question of the future of religion's role in stress situations in societies characterized by a highly developed science. We shall digress somewhat at this point in order to consider two famous, and contrasting, interpretations. Any attempted answers to this intriguing question are, of course, intellectual projections into an unknown future. This fact explains in part their divergent nature. In addition, this divergence inheres in the contrasting views held about the character of religion by various distinguished scholars. The present discussion of religion's future role is limited to the theories of Durkheim and of Freud.

Durkheim, unlike Freud, considered the ultimate reference point of all religious symbolism to be the social group rather than any transcendental conceptions of the supernatural. He therefore concluded that religion, as he defined it, was necessarily a permanent characteristic of human societies. Precisely because it is grounded in society (and therefore not, in the final analysis, dependent on changing intellectual concepts of the supernatural), religion must endure as long as society endures. Techniques of adjustment to stress situations may indeed change as science develops. Nevertheless, since man's basic stress situation is inherent in his imperative needs to adjust to the compelling reality of the social group—"society divinized," in Durkheim's phrase—his need for *non*empirical (that is, religious) techniques for doing so is likely to remain. The remote possibility that the social and psychological sciences might develop to the point that human beings could relate themselves to society by purely rational and scientific means is not seriously considered by Durkheim.[27]

Freud not only takes a different stance concerning religion's future, but he also holds a radically different view of the nature of religion itself. Pivotal to Freud's theory is the conception of a transcendent supernatural deity of a strongly paternalistic character. In this belief Freud showed himself to be a true child of his nineteenth-century Jewish heritage. Furthermore, as pointed out earlier, Freud the psychoanalyst saw the Deity as a psychic projection of man's dependence on his parents, particularly on the father. In his stimulating essay *The Future of an Illusion* he claimed that one of the main functions of religion was that of supplying man with a shield of "illusion" against his fears of nature and his frustrations in human society. Freud, however, envisaged the possibility that with advances in psychological science the human race might eventually become more rational and learn to outgrow its "infantile" dependence upon religion. He regarded this eventuality as beneficial for the human race, since human beings would thus be freed to deal with their existential problems by the unfettered use of reason. But Freud was not optimistic that the triumph of scientific reason over religious illusion would take place in the foreseeable future. (As a psychoanalyst he was rather pessimistic about human

RELIGION: A SOCIOLOGICAL VIEW

nature, including his own.) Hence the emancipation of the human race from the domination of religion by the aid of science remained problematic for Freud.[28]

These illustrations, taken from the theories of two of the most influential scholars of modern times, suggest that the question of religion's future role in alleviating stress situations in societies characterized by a dynamic science opens up a number of divergent and far-reaching possibilities. The theories of Durkheim and of Freud are suggestive and have provoked a great deal of comment pro and con. With all due respect to these distinguished authorities, however, we would suggest, as we did earlier, that religion's role in alleviating stress can be most usefully discussed in terms of specific social contexts and particular models of society. Therefore we shall use once more our three societal models in pursuing this theme.

MAGIC, SCIENCE, AND RELIGION IN DIFFERENT TYPES OF SOCIETY

In Model One societies, of which Malinowski's Trobriand Islands furnish one example, magico-religious methods of adjustment are likely to be fairly dominant, and science and technology are relatively little developed and used. In nonliterate societies religion is frequently inextricably blended with magic, and magico-religious means are utilized to adjust to a number of stress situations that are often handled religiously in Model Two societies or scientifically in Model Three societies.

The magico-religious blend in these societies, however, is by no means of a uniform nature. In one society, for example, the main area of anxiety and stress may be concerned with the demonstration of prowess in warfare; in another, with the hazards of agriculture; and elsewhere, with threats to the maintenance of physical health.[29] In each case the magico-religious means are focused upon an area of special anxiety and stress that is important in the experience of the society in question. Frequently, although not invariably, situations of stress in Model One societies are closely related to uncertainties concerning the basic conditions for assuring physical survival.

In Model Two societies technology is more developed, and science therefore furnishes a somewhat more effective means of providing for physical needs. Scientific theory, however, is not highly developed, especially in comparison with Model Three societies.

Magic, both white and black, functions overtly and covertly in Model Two societies. Much popular religious magic survives from earlier days, witchcraft is endemic, and the hysteria of witchhunting recurs periodically in times of special stress, as the history of the European Middle Ages illustrates.

Religion in Model Two societies typically attempts to free itself from entanglement with magic and to become differentiated into a fairly self-consistent ethical system. The great founders of the ethical religions of the world aided this development, their teachings showing all of them to have emphatically repudiated magical methods. In spite of these teachings, however, magic persists in societies of this type as an important means of adjustment to stress situations for a great number of people. While the official religious organizations often disavow magic, they are forced to make compromises with it and in the name of religion rebaptize a great deal of earlier magic.

An interesting illustration of this process occurred in Burma in the eleventh century of the Christian era. The powerful Burmese king Anawratta introduced at that time a "pure" form of Theravada Buddhism into his country. At the same time he forbade his subjects to continue the magico-religious worship of local spirits, known in Burma as *nats*. Finding, however, that in this respect his royal commands were of no avail, he ordered his sculptors to make representations of the nats in postures of reverence before the Lord Buddha. The inference was that if the powerful nats revered the Buddha, people could continue to worship and make offerings to nats without prejudice to their veneration for the Buddha.[30] Even today in devout Burmese Buddhist homes, the visitor may see a central shrine sacred to the Buddha and usually containing a small image or picture of him. On either side of it, however, there are likely to be two smaller shrines containing offerings of bananas and coconuts to the nat spirits. For since the Buddha has entered Nirvana, it is not religiously appropriate to address petitionary prayers to him, but petitions for specific material benefits may instead be addressed to nats.*

The process just described is by no means confined to Burmese Buddhism. In medieval Europe, for instance, Catholic Christians transformed "pagan" festivals into Christian holy days and "pagan" spirits into Christian saints. To the latter the faithful could, and can, with perfect propriety direct their prayers for concrete benefits. For example, St. Christopher became the patron saint of travelers, who even today may wear his medal around their necks. St. Anthony stands ready to receive the petitions of those who wish to recover lost property. Some Catholic saints, such as St. Christopher, have been recently "de-sainted," but it is doubtful that this fact will inhibit those who wish to invoke their aid.

Although important areas of stress in these societies still remain in connection with securing the fundamentals for sheer physical survival, their increasing complexity gives rise to additional strains of a social and psychological nature. The mere acceptance of custom is no longer quite enough. Men are beginning to demand ethical explanations of the inequalities of institutional arrangements and often of the condition of man himself. These psychological and social strains are characteristically dealt with by distinctively religious means. The imprecations of the prophet Amos against the inhabitants of the bur-

---

* Actually there are many different kinds of nats, some friendly and a great many malevolent. It is the friendly household nats who have a place in domestic shrines. The threatening nats are propitiated from time to time by magical rites conducted by natwives (nat-kadaws). Manning Nash's *Golden Road to Modernity,* pages 166–174 (see footnote 9), has an excellent account of the part played by nats in Burmese village life. Another example of how nat worship has been absorbed by Buddhism is that nats, who are often thought to inhabit old trees, sometimes inhabit banyon trees, which are thought to be sacred to the Buddha. Hence veneration is sometimes offered at the same tree both to its nat resident and to the Lord Buddha.

geoning towns of Israel illustrate the point.[31]   Amos was a rural herdsman from Judah whose ethical sense was outraged by the oppression of the "new" urban populations by the more privileged classes.   In his attack against these injustices he invoked religious sanctions against established authority and custom. Hence Amos called upon the "higher" ethical law of the God of Israel and of Judah to oppose the inequities perpetrated by man.

Religion, too, often helps in the adjustment to the psychic tensions occasioned by the uncertainty men feel about their origin and destiny; it also furnishes in these societies the most commonly accepted official cosmologies.   The medieval church's conception of heaven, hell, and purgatory, dramatized so poetically by Dante, is a case in point.   So was the "religionizing" of the Ptolemaic system, which gave "scientific" sanction for the centrality of earth and of man in God's plan for the universe.

The fact that these official religious cosmologies, sometimes backed by punitive ecclesiastical authority, not only served to reassure the uneducated majority but might at the same time have stifled free intellectual inquiry by an educated elite emphasizes religion's capacity to perform opposite societal functions simultaneously.   For religion, in common with other sociocultural phenomena, can have multifunctions, including opposite ones.   We have just seen how Amos attempted to stir up the people of Israel by challenging the injustices of their society in the name of an ethical religion.   Nevertheless, history affords many examples of religion performing the opposite function, namely that of reassuring people about the rightness of the basic institutions of a given social order.   Thus religion has often given powerful support to many varieties of "establishment" and so has performed important conservative functions, as will be pointed out in Chapter 6.   Durkheim in particular has emphasized religion's conservative role.   Marx, on the other hand (in the context of a Model Three society), attacked religion, which he described as the "opiate of the people," precisely because of this reassuring function.   In his view religion "doped" working people into accepting social conditions favorable to the bourgeoisie—conditions that it was to their interest to unite against and strenuously oppose.

Model Three societies feature a highly dynamic science, both theoretical and applied, which is increasingly used as a practical means of adjusting to stress situations of many kinds. Science replaces in large measure magical and religious methods in meeting problems of physical and mental health and of maintaining a steady supply of food.

Magic is not entirely obsolete in these scientifically oriented societies, although it is usually applied to rather different types of stress situations than in Model One and Model Two societies. So-called old-fashioned magic as a means of adjustment to personal hazards still persists in the form of semiarchaic survivals; beliefs such as in the gardener's green thumb and practices like the avoidance of walking under ladders are retained by some individuals, partly in jest but partly in earnest. (Students will recognize various examples of semimagic practiced by themselves or by their fellows, for example, love magic and examination magic.) Organized religions, however, in greater or lesser degree tend to discard or reinterpret the older form of religious magic.

These "secular" societies, on the other hand, develop their own characteristic kinds of stress situations, less associated with the precariousness of natural forces than with the hazards of economic arrangements, status striving, and job security. A new streamlined secularized magic is used for the coercion of the secular deities: the gods of money, success, and power. The large sums of money some astrologers make today, the weekly sale of millions of astrology and numerology magazines, and the daily appearance of astrology columns in newspapers testify to the thriving character of this type of magic. Wherever money, success, and power are most assiduously cultivated, soothsayers of all kinds batten on rich and poor alike. Big-time gamblers in the financial districts, small-time gamblers in numbers and cards, many aspirants to stardom in sport, stage, screen, or even politics are among those who seek their aid. It has been said, perhaps mistakenly, that Adolf Hitler kept in attendance an astrologer whose advice he sometimes sought and that Winston Churchill also consulted an astrologer so that he might be informed as to what advice Hitler's astrologer had presumably been giving him.

A more important and certainly more pervasive example of the use of magic in Model Three societies may be seen in much of the advertising in the mass media. Brand name products, often described in scientific terms, are also, by implication, associated with enticing side effects that are purely magical. Toothpastes, deodorants, automobiles, and other products are linked with popularity and success, whether in status striving, in business, or in love, demonstrating vividly the commercial exploitation, with magical techniques, of common human anxieties.

The increasing use of science and its products helps to create new stress situations that magic is sometimes called upon to alleviate. Modern science as applied to warfare and transportation has exposed the members of modern societies to frightening new physical dangers. The use of quasimagic by many individuals who face extreme hazards, such as air pilots and combat troops, not only persists but also continues to exist side by side with the most modern technical equipment and gadgetry. The controller of the instrument panel of a supersonic jet may treasure in his pocket an ancient rabbit's foot.[32] It was reported in the press that an astronaut in a Gemini flight carried with him religious medals representative of three different faiths.

Again, the modern city, itself in large part a product of science, is marked by the social isolation, loneliness, and rootlessness of many individuals, some of whom are recruited by the new magico-religious cults that flourish in metropolitan areas (as well as in deprived and disorganized sections of the rural population).[33]

What, then, is the role of religion in the adjustment to both the older and newer types of stress situations in Model Three societies? The older types have not been eliminated, although they have been mitigated by the application of science. Nature's threats to human survival—floods, tornadoes, uncontrollable disease—are more likely to be viewed by religionists as occasional acts of God than as ever-present hazards to survival. The basic requirements of health and food supply are assured for most (but by no means all) people by modern technology. Nevertheless, and in spite of the fact that even rainfall is sometimes artificially produced by seeding the clouds,* adjustment to sporadic natural calamities is aided by religious as well as scientific techniques. Furthermore, individuals under the stress of grave physical handicaps, whether congenital or acquired in later life, frequently acknowledge their need of support from a superhuman power, as the writings of Helen Keller and other afflicted persons amply attest. And the lesser stresses that belabor most or all of us still often call forth prayers for superhuman aid.

The psychic tensions engendered by the great unanswerable questions "Whence does man come?" "Why is he here?" and "Whither is he going?" persist. The answers to these questions are partly intellectual and partly emotional in nature. The intellectual component commonly includes an explanation of the physical nature of man and his place in the universe as embodied, for example, in modern cosmologies. In Model Two societies religion supplies the officially accepted cosmologies, but in modern secular societies science provides the most commonly used explanations, and earlier religious cosmology is continually reevaluated in the light of the growing accumulation of scientific findings. It is in this area that much of the so-called conflict between religion and science has been and still is experienced. Modern science, however, leaves unanswered the basic moral and emotional questions about human destiny. Present-day psychology and psychiatry possibly help to allay some of the anxiety and stress created by these fundamental uncertainties. In addition, prolongation of the human life span and general increase in health and comfort enable many individuals to postpone facing these potentially disturbing issues. But sooner or

---

* During a drought in New York City, when the municipal government employed an expert to seed the clouds, the following cartoon appeared in *The New Yorker:* inside a church through whose Gothic windows the rain could be seen falling in torrents, two cassocked clerics looking dubiously at this scene asked of each other, "Is it *His* or ours?"

later in many or perhaps most lives these questions must be faced. At that point religious faith continues to supply an important means of human adjustment.

Finally, the new stress situations engendered by scientific technology pose new problems for religion. The use of the hydrogen bomb and jet planes in modern warfare has confronted all mankind, especially city dwellers, with the threat of mass destruction.* Furthermore, a highly complex mode of living featured by close functional interdependence, but characterized also by impersonality, has introduced unprecedented social and psychological pressures. These pressures emphasize a need experienced by some individuals in Model Three societies for the development of religious as well as scientific means for dealing with new types of stress. Current attempts to create a liaison between religion and psychiatry and the special training often given to ministers in techniques of psychiatric counseling are examples of new trends in meeting this need. But the growth of new religious interpretations and applications is markedly less dynamic than the development of science. This differential is partly the result of the great prestige that has been achieved by science and scientific activity in modern society.

The members of modern society, we believe, manifest a dual tendency regarding the use of religion as a means of adjustment to stress. Many individuals have almost entirely discarded the personal use of religion. Others, especially in times of personal or widespread distress, reaffirm religion. Apparently a large number of people alternate between these two patterns, a situation that deserves more careful sociological study than it has received.

The assimilation and the reinterpretation of evolving human knowledge have marked religious thought throughout human

---

* It is perhaps worth noting that in communities like Oak Ridge and Los Alamos, where many scientists working on problems of atomic energy either live or have lived, churches and religious organizations of many different types have rapidly sprung up. Again, the first astronauts to orbit the moon, on viewing the planet Earth from their lunar orbit, chose to celebrate that event by broadcasting to the world the biblical story of creation as recorded in the Book of Genesis.

RELIGION: A SOCIOLOGICAL VIEW

history. It is not surprising, therefore, that in Model Three societies religious leaders are attempting to bring new scientific knowledge, particularly psychiatry, into their purview and practice. They see this as an essential task if religion is to be a more effective means than it is at present for coping with the stress situations of the modern world.

REFERENCES

1. Kingsley Davis, *Human Society* (New York: Macmillan, 1949), p. 517.
2. Cf. Talcott Parsons, *Religious Perspectives of College Teaching in Sociology and Social Psychology* (New Haven: Edward W. Hazen Foundation, 1951), p. 10.
3. Bronislaw Malinowski, *Magic, Science, and Religion* (Glencoe, Ill.: Free Press, 1948; reprint ed., Garden City, N.Y.: Doubleday, Anchor Book, 1954), pp. 37–41. Also see Arnold Van Gennep, *Rites of Passage* (Chicago: University of Chicago Press, 1960), *passim*.
4. Parsons, *op. cit.,* p. 10.
5. *Ibid.,* pp. 11–12.
6. *Ibid.,* p. 13.
7. *Ibid.,* p. 11.
8. Reo Fortune, *Manus Religion* (Philadelphia: The American Philosophical Society, 1935), pp. 49–50.
9. Manning Nash, *The Golden Road to Modernity: Village Life in Contemporary Burma* (New York: John Wiley, 1965), p. 151.
10. Leroy Bowman, *The American Funeral: A Way of Death* (New York: Paperback Library, 1964), Chapter 10. In this chapter Bowman analyzes the effects of urban living on funeral practices.
11. Jessica Mitford, *The American Way of Death* (New York: Simon & Schuster, 1963), *passim*.
12. Evelyn Waugh, *The Loved One* (Boston: Little, Brown, 1948; reprint ed., New York: Dell, 1964), *passim*.
13. Émile Durkheim, *The Elementary Forms of the Religious Life,* trans. Joseph Ward Swain (New York: Collier, 1961), pp. 445–449.
14. Nash, *op. cit.,* p. 153.
15. Lucien Lévy-Bruhl, *How Natives Think,* trans. Lilian A. Clare (New York: Washington Square Press, 1966), pp. 88–117.
16. Malinowski, *op. cit.,* pp. 28–29.
17. Francis Hsu, *Science, Religion and Human Crisis* (New York: Humanities Press, 1952), pp. 85–96 and 119–134.

18. Malinowski, *op. cit.,* pp. 50–51.
19. *Ibid.,* p. 79.
20. *Ibid.,* pp. 88–89.
21. Clyde Kluckhohn, *Navaho Witchcraft* (Cambridge, Mass: Peabody Museum, 1944), pp. 67–70.
22. Anthony F. C. Wallace, *Religion: An Anthropological View* (New York: Random House, 1966), pp. 27–29.
23. Claude Lèvi-Strauss, "The Structural History of Myth," *Journal of American Folklore,* 68 (1955), 428–444.
24. Erich Fromm, *The Forgotten Language* (New York: Rinehart, 1951), pp. 204–205.
25. Malinowski, *op. cit.,* pp. 34–35.
26. Cf. Bernard Barber, *Science and the Social Order* (Glencoe, Ill.: Free Press, 1952), pp. 5–6 and Chapter 3.
27. Émile Durkheim, *op. cit.,* pp. 236–240.
28. Sigmund Freud, *The Future of an Illusion* (Garden City, N.Y.: Doubleday, Anchor Book, 1964), *passim.*
29. Ruth Benedict, "Religion," in Franz Boas, *General Anthropology* (Boston: Heath, 1938), Chapter 14, especially pp. 633–634. This entire chapter is a useful analysis of the social functions of religion and magic.
30. Maung Htin Aung, *Folk Elements in Burmese Buddhism* (London: Oxford University Press, 1962), pp. 74–75. In this book, Dr. Htin Aung, the distinguished former rector of the University of Rangoon, shows how these earlier folk elements were absorbed into and synthesized in Burmese Buddhism.
31. Amos 5:9–13.
32. Davis, *op. cit.,* p. 541.
33. For an earlier study see A. H. Fauset, *Black Gods of the Metropolis* (Philadelphia: University of Pennsylvania Press, 1944).

5

Religion, the Problem of Meaning and Society

THE PROBLEM OF MEANING IN INDIVIDUAL AND SOCIAL EXPERIENCE

In Chapter 4 we discussed some of the ways in which religion helps societies and their members adjust to the uncertainties and strains of life. In this chapter we will consider the *problem of meaning*, that is, the role of religion in providing an explanation with which human beings interpret in moral terms their personal distresses and successes as well as the past history and present circumstances of their societies. In other words, we are moving from the analysis of religion's contribution in answering some of the crucial hows of social life to a consideration of its related function in dealing with some of the equally crucial whys. In more formal language, we are passing from a consideration of the *conative* aspects of religion's social role to a discussion of its *cognitive* aspects.

Throughout the ages religion has not only given man rituals that provide emotional relief and techniques that fortify faith and thus enable him to carry on but also has provided generalized intellectual interpretations that have helped him to make moral sense out of his total life experience. These interpretations comprise much of the content of the great religious philosophies and cosmologies. The major religions of mankind—Judaism, Christianity, Buddhism, Islam, and the rest—have developed their own distinctive interpretations of the nature of God or gods, man, man's purpose on earth, the problem of evil, and man's destiny after death. Other explanations of man's nature and destiny, such as that supplied by totemism, are also attempts to answer man's quest for meaning. Furnishing such interpretations of meaning has been one of the main functions of religion throughout man's history. "Whence does man come?" "Whither is he bound?" and "Why is he here?" are perennial questions for which thinkers of all ages have striven to find answers. Few of them have been able to fashion answers that have not included at least some nonempirical—and *religious*—elements.

The notion that man is a kind of being *desirous* of finding morally satisfying answers to such questions is a large assumption. If such an assumption is made, it should be tempered by the recognition that there have always existed great variations among individuals regarding the urgency with which answers to these questions are sought. Some people, as Max Weber has expressed it, are "religiously unmusical." [1] Others may be content to experience life as "just one darn thing after another." But for still others, an important minority, the need to find a morally satisfying solution to the problem of man and his destiny, to plumb the meaning of the relationship between man and his fate and whatever God or gods may be, has amounted to a burning fever. Such individuals have been, over the ages, the developers of the great religious philosophies. Impelled on one hand by the strength of their own inner needs and on the other by the crises faced by society, or a particular segment of it, in their time, they have forged these "solutions" to the problem of meaning.[2] Perhaps a majority of people have been content, when confronted by personal crisis, to avail themselves of these "prefabricated" interpretations of meaning. But it must not be forgotten that however abstract and remote some of these interpretations may seem to us today, they were once hammered out in times of crisis by individuals and groups on the hard anvil of human history. Even though the exact historical circumstances may remain hidden from us, it is fairly safe to assume that man's need to make sense of his human experience and destiny stemmed initially from his existential plight and was not merely the outcome of philosophical speculation.*

For many people the problem of meaning is less a matter of finding systematic explanations of the meaning of human destiny than of answering the question of why untoward things happen, and especially, why such things should happen to *them*. Some answer to this question, which may be asked and answered on very different levels, is no doubt a necessity for human beings if they are to cope successfully with their frustrations. Here too religion has supplied a variety of "answers" to this universal human question.

The biblical character of Job epitomizes the eternal human *why*. By discharging both his social and religious obligations, Job had striven to revere the sacred values that were exemplified in the divine commandments as he knew them. "My face is red with weeping, and on my eyelids is deep darkness; although there is no violence in my hands, and my prayer is pure." How great, then, must be the injustice of God, and what kind of being must God be to let him suffer so much? "Behold, I cry out, 'Violence!' but I am not answered; I call aloud but there is no justice." [3]

Job, however, was not concerned only with the meaning of his own misfortunes. When he turned from the contemplation of his own miserable lot to think of the fate of his fellow men, he was forced to the conclusion that most human beings were sunk in misery and injustice. Thus he was led to ask God for an explanation not only of his own wretchedness but also of that of all mankind. Job confronted what is often referred to as the *problem of evil*.

Job was puzzled and distressed too by the apparent injustice with which a supposedly righteous God distributed His rewards and punishments in human society.[4] If God was righteous, why did He cause the righteous man Job to be stricken while on every side the "ungodly flourished like the green bay tree?" [5] Why does not God guarantee that people get their just deserts?

---

* This should not be taken as implying that subsequent to an initial formulation of an interpretation of meaning, scholars in succeeding ages have not elaborated upon it in calmer, and more academic, mood.

In the same vein the flyer's widow in Michener's story might well have asked why a just God should allow her husband to perish when many younger men with less combat service were holding down safe and profitable desk jobs at home. These disparities in men's fortunes and misfortunes are not readily explainable in accordance with ordinary human standards of what is fair and right. Therefore an important function of religion is to "justify the ways of God to man." In other words, one of the functions of religion is to assign moral meaning to human experiences, which might seem otherwise a "tale told by an idiot, full of sound and fury, signifying nothing" (*Macbeth,* Act 5, Sc. 5, ll. 26–29) .

A few years ago Archibald MacLeish in his play *J.B.* presented the theater audience with the problem of Job in a modern setting.[6] The J.B. of the play was a successful, generous, philanthropic businessman who revered God and loved both his family and his neighbors. His loss of wealth, position, reputation, family, and friends rather closely paralleled the misfortunes of Job. Both God and Satan appear in the play, which begins when the Devil dares God to find one righteous man who cannot be made to "curse" God if misfortunes were to overtake him. The God of the play takes up the Devil's dare, and they select J.B. for the crucial experiment.[7] Throughout the play God and Satan observe and comment on J.B.'s reaction to the "injustices" that are inflicted upon him.

As his trials accumulate, J.B. agonizes not only over his actual miseries but also over the character of the God he has tried to serve. He tries in vain to reconcile Almighty Power and Omniscience with Divine Love and Compassion. "If God is God [that is, the Almighty Creator] he is not Good; if God is Good, he is not God!" was his tormented utterance. The end of MacLeish's play left his audience still guessing, for the author never "justified" the ways of God to man. In fact, MacLeish's deity was a pasteboard figure and failed to inspire either respect or love. It will be remembered that the Job of the Old Testament did not find a watertight intellectual solution to his doubts. Yet in view of the majesty of God's creation he felt it behooved him to "doubt his doubts" concerning the justice of God. "Though He slay me yet will I trust in Him" was a moving confession of faith wrung from Job in the face of doubt.[8] Similarly J.B. does not work out a complete solution. And there have been several different guesses as to what "solution," if any, MacLeish himself had in mind. In the present writer's view, admittedly a guess, J.B.'s resolution of the meaning of his unhappy fate is an existential one. The moment when his estranged wife returns to him, when they are able to recover and express their love for each other and are thus able to share compassionately in the miseries of their fellow sufferers, is the high point of the play. Human love and human sharing thus appear as ultimate values, whatever other aspects of the human dilemma remain unexplained. Both God and Devil are made to appear largely irrelevant, but human existence is endowed with deep meaning on its own terms.

We have cited the modern instance of J.B. as well as the ancient biblical story of Job in order to show that man's attempts to find moral meaning in the human dilemma persist and also to point out that such attempts do not invariably find expression in conventionally religious terms. Indeed, some of these "irreligious" ways of approaching the problem of meaning are very old. Socrates, like MacLeish, found that whatever meaning he could ascribe to human existence resided in Man himself. His faith was not in God or gods but in the potential for continuing development of man's inquiring mind. Such an interpretation does imply the attribution to human existence of a meaning beyond everyday appearances; it ascribes to humanity a *moral* significance and not a purely naturalistic one. In this sense it is also an act of faith that invests humanity with a sacred meaning. Today many individuals and groups, including many college students, are seeking to find and to interpret the meaning of existence in the contemporary world by using forms of expression that may appear to some to be both strange and bizarre. The culture and life style of some segments of the "new youth," especially among those known as "hippies" (an outmoded term among youth itself), include elements, often distorted, of Far

Eastern beliefs and practices (for example, Zen, meditation, Yoga), North American Indian religions, primitive Christianity, and, increasingly, astrology, parapsychology, and even witchcraft.[9] Nevertheless, in ways that have often seemed unconventional to older contemporaries, the struggle to find significant meaning in man's predicament has been waged throughout human history. That struggle still goes on.

We have stated the problem of meaning in an individual context for the sake of both poignancy and clarity. This problem, however, is not essentially different when it is considered in the context of entire societies, each with its particular set of interacting institutions. Each society may be viewed from the *outside* and as differentiated from other human societies; but each society also may be studied as a social system from the *inside*. When we look at societies from the outside, that is, in historical perspective and in relation to other societies, we may ask why some tribes and nations attain power and success while others seem destined to poverty and impotence. When we view societies from the inside, we are confronted with inequalities in the distribution of wealth, power, and happiness among the members, inequities that inevitably stimulate moral interpretations of the social order.

THE PROBLEM OF THE MEANING OF SOCIETY

Every society that has persisted for any appreciable length of time through the wars and rivalries that have generally accompanied group life has developed some moral interpretation of its own way of life—some explanation of the problem of *societal* meaning. For if people are to fulfill their social obligations, there must be available a morally acceptable explanation of their society's particular system of institutional arrangements, including its social disparities.

Undoubtedly a larger measure of equality and human justice marks the social arrangements of some societies than of others; yet in none does the actual distribution of social rewards and punishments conform exactly to ideal requirements of justice, insofar as human beings in a particular society agree on what they mean by those requirements. Hence in all societies, contrasts between ideal and practice require explanation and interpretation.[10] Equally important is the fact that to date, no human group has been able to evolve an explanation of the meaning of its social system that is morally watertight, without drawing upon at least some elements outside the realm of empirical common sense. Apart from the acceptance of the viewpoint that regards human injustice as brute fact and social life as morally meaningless, no empirical or common-sense answer is readily available to the questions posed by the inequalities and inequities of social systems.

These considerations provide the general context for the role that religion (which by definition embraces the nonempirical in its purview) plays in making moral interpretations of human history and social arrangements. For all attempted moral solutions in purely empirical terms tend to break down in the face of glaring adverse balances on the moral side of the social ledger. Hence explanations of societal meaning that have gained wide acceptance invariably, in order to balance the moral books, introduce nonempirical, often including supernatural, elements.

Such explanations of meaning, attempts to explain the problem of evil, are often referred to as *theodicies*. Max Weber has noted three main types of theodicy,[11] all involving extensive nonempirical elements. The first is the Hindu conception of *karma*, an impersonal "automatic" system for the balancing of rewards and punishments for good and evil deeds. The working of karma is believed to be continuous throughout an almost endless series of lives. The concept of karma is thus coupled with a belief in reincarnation—a belief hardly susceptible to empirical proof. A second type of theodicy involves a belief in the absolute transcendence of God. All that happens to man is seen as predestined by the inscrutable will of a deity whose wisdom and power are infinite, mysterious, and beyond the reach of human understanding. Divine *predestination* allows no options;

men must accept on faith the full sovereignty of God. The third type of theodicy is less clear-cut, less logically watertight, than either of the first two. It stems from the teachings of Zoroaster, who viewed the universe as a battleground between the powers of good and evil—between God and the Devil. In this dualistic system the forces of good and evil are not entirely equally matched. It is believed that in spite of much hard struggle and some temporary triumphs of the Devil, God will win in the end, and man's good and evil deeds will be suitably rewarded on a final day of judgment.

Historically these three types of theodicy are rarely found in undiluted form. The first, involving reincarnation, is most characteristic of Hindu-Buddhist religion. But even the founder of Buddhism is on record as being tempted by Mara, a kind of Buddhist "devil." A good example of the second type is Calvin's teaching of predestination in seventeenth-century Europe. Islamic teaching also, in some of its aspects, stresses the absolute power and sovereignty of God. Both the second and third types, often in combination, are frequently found in the Judeo-Christian tradition. In the case of Job, as suggested earlier, both these types of theodicy are brought into play: the biblical story includes a contest between God and the Devil, but its conclusion is the acknowledgment by Job of his absolute submission to God's sovereignty even when he cannot understand His purposes.

In some societies the theodicy theme is present in muted form. Thus ancient China relied notably on "common sense" and rational interpretations of the social order, including the famous Five Relationships attributed to Confucius, which gave traditional sanction to great inequalities, particularly those based on age and sex. Although there was relatively little emphasis in China on supernatural explanations, the entire social system was assumed to be in accordance with the "will of Heaven," which perhaps may be viewed as a diffuse form of predestination. Confucius taught that man's efforts to establish harmony on earth were in accord with the "will of Heaven" and hence of his ancestors who were believed to reside there.

Some of the actual theodicies to be examined here are, as in the case of ancient China, mixtures of these three basic types. Furthermore, a number of different theodicies may coexist in the same society. They are likely to be associated with the various social classes or strata within that society and to be related to the different needs and aspirations of those classes or strata. A theodicy of escape may be "appropriate" for an underprivileged class; whereas, for a dominant class, justification of its power and standing, based on religious doctrine, is consistent with its position. A rising middle class may discover an affinity with a theodicy far different from either of the above. Different theodicies may exist together in a given society also because of the uneven incidence of social change and its differential effect on religious interpretations of societal meaning. Thus we see that the methods of "balancing the moral books" are likely to be, on occasion, extremely complex affairs.

Sometimes this moral balancing is thought of as occurring in the future of *this* world. The travail of an entire nation or tribe or social class may be tolerable to the group concerned because of a deeply held belief in a promised land of freedom, equity, and justice in the historical future.[12] On closer examination most beliefs of this kind may also be shown to be nonempirical in nature, particularly when the earthly utopia is not immediately attained. As the realization of the promised land fades into the indefinite future, the original concrete goal takes on nonempirical overtones; what was at first a goal to be worked for changes to a treasured dream for future generations. Finally this dream may become an article of faith whereby present sufferings may be more patiently endured. Thus the wheel has swung full circle, and the originally empirical goal has become a sacred value.

Our discussion of religious interpretations will first treat briefly societies in their entirety and consider variant ways in which their history has been given meaning by religion. We shall then view in more detail the problem of societal meaning as it affects the interrelations of various groups and institutions within societies. Special consideration will be given those groups and institutions of principal significance in defining differential social positions and in allocating rewards and punishments. For one of our main interests is the meaning ascribed by certain religions to the differences in position and prestige of various social classes. Differences in class standing are closely correlated with the distribution of economic wealth and political power. Therefore we shall also discuss religious interpretations of the meaning of economic and political institutions, especially those concerning the use and acquisition of material wealth and the exercise and abuse of political authority.

WHAT DETERMINES RELIGIOUS INTERPRETATIONS?

In the religious interpretations of the meaning of social arrangements presented below, the reader will observe a high degree of consistency between religious doctrine and actual institutional arrangements. To what degree a particular religion has impressed its own ethical meaning on a given society's thoughtways or, conversely, to what extent religious doctrine merely reflects or rationalizes the political and economic status quo, has been and remains to some degree a central question for scholars in this field. We will not concern ourselves with this problem at this point.

However, a word of sociological caution is in order. Some readers may perhaps hold the opinion congenial to Marxist thought that all religious interpretations are merely rationalizations, possibly even deliberate and hypocritical ones, which meet the interests of dominant classes. In reply to this point of view it must be stressed that all idea systems that have been accepted by an entire society or by large segments of it are the products of many years of interacting influences. These include groups concerned with the promulgation and maintenance of religious and ethical values, as well as economic and political groups, including, of course, dominant power groups. Although particular moral interpretations of the social order often are consistent with their interests, the extent to which they are deliberate inventions of dominant groups can easily be exaggerated. There would appear to be, as Weber has pointed out, an "elective affinity" between the economic and political arrangements of a given society and the interpretations of societal meaning that it develops over a period of time.[13] But it should be borne in mind that no religious ethic, even in its purest and most "original" form, ever emerged in complete isolation from the currents of opinion about social, economic, and political conditions. This statement holds for all the great religious systems, whether formulated first by Moses, Buddha, Mohammed, Christ, or Calvin.[14]

Consequently, the following discussion makes no attempt to establish the independence or priority of material factors on the one hand and religious factors on the other. Rather, we present some of the situations, both historical and contemporary, in which explanations of the meaning of the social world have been couched in religious terms and reinforced with religious values. We shall also indicate how these solutions are generally consistent with political, economic, and other social institutions of the societies in question.

RELIGIOUS INTERPRETATIONS OF THE SOCIAL ORDER

Adversity and Religious Beliefs

The classic example of a religious explanation of the meaning of the suffering of an entire society is the doctrine evolved by the Jewish people. At the height of their religious creativity the Jews worked out, although gradually, a moral interpretation of the meaning of their society that was of a more universal, comprehensive, and revolutionary nature than had previously been developed by any other group. In their earlier history their existence as a people was given meaning by the idea of their having been chosen as the faithful servants of a single sacred being, Jehovah, who had revealed His Will to them in the Commandments through Moses. In the light of this faith they took possession, under Joshua, of the promised land of Canaan. The great Jewish moral interpreters, the prophets, explained many of their later calamities as the result of their failure to fulfill Jehovah's Commandments. During their captivity by the Babylonians and Persians it must have seemed to these people that their service to Jehovah, imperfect as it was, was at least more worthy than that of the heathen around them; hence their long-continued sufferings must have appeared as both cruel and undeserved.

In these times of bitter adversity the earlier, more limited religious interpretation of their history and experience gradually broke down. Why should they endure prolonged travail when the kingdoms of the heathen, who neither knew Jehovah nor worshiped Him, flourished? By asking this question, however, they were driven to think of Jehovah as the God of the surrounding nations as well as of their own people.

The mental anguish entailed in the attempt to wrest a moral meaning from such apparent injustice has been recorded by Hebrew psalmists and prophets. A later prophet, a nameless genius known as the second Isaiah, likened the destiny of his people to that of Jehovah's "Suffering Servant"; and their tragic burdens then became a central part of the plan of the Creator and Ruler of the Universe for the salvation of all mankind. This was a high and terrible destiny indeed, but this doctrine enabled the prophet to present a moral and meaningful interpretation of the history of his people.

The keystone of this interpretation consists, of course, in a nonempirical belief in the existence of a single supreme supernatural being who is deeply involved in the entire course of human history, including that of the Jewish people. There can be no purely scientific grounds for either accepting or rejecting this interpretation. On the other hand, it is a matter of record that this nonscientific doctrine has had tremendous practical consequences for the survival of the Jews. Neither the persecution by pagans and Christians nor dispersal to the ends of the earth nor, more recently, Russian pogroms and Nazi gas ovens

RELIGION: A SOCIOLOGICAL VIEW

have extinguished the religious and cultural vitality of this people.

Although Jewish interpretations of the meaning of their history involved primarily and centrally the role of the Jewish people themselves, at the peak of their religious creativity their prophets reached out for *universal* interpretations with a meaning for all mankind.* This universalism, it may be argued, was largely an outcome of the loss of their own national territorial base and of the repeated migrations and dispersions of the Jewish people, which meant that interpretations of the meaning of their history and destiny were very likely to transcend territorial boundaries and so become delocalized.[15] In contrast, many other peoples, particularly those who have retained possession of their ancestral lands for many centuries, have tended to develop interpretations of the meaning of their history that have been culturally and territorially limited. Shinto, the indigenous religion of Japan, is a prime example of a religion tied to territory; [16] and Hinduism until very recently afforded another illustration of such culture-bound religious interpretations of meaning.

A secondary solution of the problem of societal meaning, a solution utilized by the Jews in situations of desperate crisis, is the messianic one.[17] Jewish doctrine in this instance is the prototype of the kind of interpretation that has evolved in a number of small, weak societies faced by the possibility of cultural extinction or otherwise without hope. The belief in the imminent coming of a messiah, or supernatural deliverer, who by means of other-worldly power will right the wrongs of a particular society and usher in a new era of justice and righteousness, clearly accents supernatural explanation. Messianic doctrine is largely a product of desperation, resorted to when a social group can visualize little possibility of continuance. Various societies, if

---

* In spite of such universalistic interpretations, however, Judaism was— and has remained—primarily an ethnic religion. It was Christian leaders, notably Paul of Tarsus, who made some of the principles of Judaism "exportable" and detachable from Jewish ethnicity. However, as the leaders of Reform Judaism pointed out in the nineteenth century in Germany, Judaism was *in principle* universal.

faced with impending cultural extinction by the advance of a dominant group, will resort to messianism as did the Jewish people at various periods of their history and particularly when threatened by the destruction of the Jerusalem Temple by Imperial Rome.

Messianic or quasimessianic cults, such as cults of the return of ancestors or culture heroes, may be either actively militant or passively expectant. Jewish messianic cults, in New Testament times, provide examples of both types. Some, like the Zealots, looked for a messiah who would place himself at the head of a militant movement to overthrow Roman rule. Other cultists were prepared to wait peacefully for a scripturally promised messiah—or for the return of one of the great prophets—who would miraculously restore their kingdom.

Both types of cult have also appeared in the history of North American Indian societies during the period that their cultures were threatened with extinction by the white man. The Ghost Dance spread in the last quarter of the nineteenth century among Plains Indian tribes at a time when the destruction of native culture was well advanced.[18] The meaning of life for the Plains Indians had been bound up with the hunting of the great herds of buffalo that roamed the Plains and also with the almost constant wars between the various tribes. The religious ceremonials of one of the Plains tribes, the Pawnee Indians, were largely concerned with the handing down, from generation to generation, of their hunting and fighting lore. A cardinal tenet of Pawnee religious ideology was the sacred character of buffalo meat, which was used in connection with all of their important ceremonies. With the appropriation of tribal lands by the white man, the American government's prohibition on intertribal warfare, and, even more important, the annihilation of the great herds of buffalo, the Pawnee way of life became largely meaningless and its traditional religious ceremonials pointless and impotent. The feeling of desolation that spread among these tribes made them ripe for any message of hope.

The Ghost Dance doctrine, so anthropologist Alexander Lesser has maintained, did indeed bring hope. It promised the destruction of the white man, a return of the buffalo and of old Indian ways. It also promised—perhaps some Christian influence may be detected here—a reunion of Indians with their deceased forebears. The sanction for this hope, claims Lesser, was native to the Indian mind. It was based on the *vision*, on the direct supernatural experience. It was a visionary experience of the return of the ancestors; messages were received from the deceased, telling the living what to do and what would happen. In the hypnotic trance of the Ghost Dance the Pawnees saw their ancestors in the "beyond," gathering for war dances and the hunt. By means of this visionary experience it was possible to revive Pawnee tribal lore, which formerly could only be passed down by the living to the living. Thus the Pawnees revived the Horn Dance, the Young Dog Dance, the Doctor Dance, the handgame, and many other ceremonies in danger of becoming extinct. In short, the activity of the Ghost Dance, with its nonempirical religious emphases, restored meaning to Pawnee culture, fostered its renaissance, and so contributed to its survival, at least for a time. It is instructive to note that Navaho Indians, who unlike the Plains Indians did not face the possible extinction of their historic culture, developed no equivalent of the Ghost Dance.

The cult of the Ghost Dance was, for the most part, antiwhite, and part of its meaning was a defiance of the whites. It had political and activist overtones and was indirectly connected with the Sioux rebellion. As the situation of the Indians became more and more hopeless, however, later Indian cults, such as the Peyote cult [19] and the Dream Dance cult, became more passive in character, more purely religious and less political, more compensatory and resigning and less actively rebellious.

British colonial governments have also been confronted by militant messianic revolts. One of the most famous was that of the Mahdi, which sparked a revolt of tribesmen in the Sudan, a revolt that was quelled by armed forces under the leadership of General Kitchener. Today we read of new outcroppings of messianic movements in Africa and elsewhere.[20] The fact that such unrealistic beliefs sometimes arouse sufficient vitality in a deprived people to resist effectively a much stronger power bears striking witness to the vital importance to the society concerned of some acceptable solution in moral terms for the meaning of its existence.

A somewhat different problem confronts oppressed peoples who are handicapped in their struggles with their oppressors because they have been cut off, through slavery, from their own cultural past. In such cases attempts are often made to "invent" a cultural identity that emphasizes their superiority to and their difference from those who, for the time being, are exercising domination over them.[21] J. Milton Yinger has suggested that the nonempirical elements involved in the fabrication of this pseudoidentity increase in direct proportion to the hopelessness of the group members' actual situation and their inability to ameliorate their position by empirical, that is, by political, means. Yinger has posited a hypothetical continuum, at one pole of which may be found the weakest and most helpless groups who must accept their condition and at the other pole those groups who are more powerful in a worldly sense and are able to utilize some practical aggressive means to resist their oppressors.[22] At the former pole might be placed American Negroes in the South during the height of the slavery period. Most of them "accepted" their situation, refraining (in their helplessness) even from verbal aggression.* Their "real" identity was a heavenly one, and they were prolific in their invention of symbolic nonempirical utopias, such as the one that the play *Green Pastures* affectionately caricatures. The words of many Negro spirituals illustrate the type of other-worldly compensatory identity that gave meaning to the Negro slave's generally miserable this-worldly lot. Near the opposite pole of Yinger's continuum might be placed the Black Muslims of recent years. Negroes today have more actual power—Black Power—than did their forefathers. They have some economic and political leverage and hence can "afford" organized, overt aggression. Nevertheless, many of them have adopted a nonwhite, non-Christian, "Is-

---

* Nevertheless, even under slavery an important minority of militant activists, such as Nat Turner, existed. Modern scholarship has revealed increasingly the extent of the slave revolts.

lamic" identity. The Black Muslim movement has been described by sociologist Eric Lincoln as a "dynamic social protest that moves on a religious vehicle." [23] This "religious" stress, however, should not obscure the fact that the Black Muslims rely less and less on nonempirical factors, and, in keeping with the Black Power movement in general, are becoming more aggressive and more realistic.

Somewhere between these two extremes might be placed a movement such as the Ras Tafari in Jamaica, West Indies. The Ras Tafari have invented a "meaningful" history for themselves in connection with the kingdom of Ethiopia, looking to the Emperor Haile Selassie as their religious and political leader and Ethiopia as their true home. The main themes of the Ras Tafari movement, as seen by sociologist George E. Simpson, are the wickedness of the white man, the superiority of the black man, the hopelessness of the Jamaican situation for blacks, the desire for revenge, and—here the movement looks to nonempirical solutions—the insistence that Ethiopia is their homeland, their heaven, and the only hope for blacks.[24] There is some reason to believe that, as the economic situation of most Jamaicans is improving, the Ras Tafari is becoming somewhat more actively militant and practical. In 1955, when Simpson studied them, none of the members had been to Ethiopia and no attempt had been made to communicate with the Emperor Haile Selassie. But the situation had changed by 1967, when Haile Selassie visited Jamaica and received a welcome that rivaled the one given to Queen Elizabeth. For the most part, however, Ras Tafari members no longer attend political rallies or vote, thus withdrawing from the political means by which they might improve their lot. They have kept up a violent verbal attack on the white man, as well as on "establishment-minded" fellow Jamaicans. But while they have talked about returning to Ethiopia as if to their real homeland, they have remained in Jamaica, and whether or not the Ras Tafari movement will shift further to the more aggressive (and, in some ways, empirical) pole of Yinger's hypothetical continuum is problematic.

Yinger's continuum is useful, as these illustrations suggest, in drawing attention to the fact that the mixture of religious and empirical elements in interpretations of the meaning of the history and current situation of given societies or groups varies both in amount and in intensity and also changes over a period of time.

Success and Religious Interpretations: The Case of Imperialism

Both types of religious belief discussed above are moral interpretations of societal adversity. Almost equally important for a society is a morally acceptable explanation of its successes. Since a successful society often enjoys its worldly accomplishments at the expense of less fortunate peoples, its members are frequently driven to find a moral formula that will not only provide positive meaning for their own good fortune but also will help diminish any guilt they feel about the less happy situation of other groups.[25]   Such explanations may stress the superior worth of the members of the successful group and emphasize as well the benefits conferred by their social dominance.   Most great imperialistic societies, including Rome, Britain, and Soviet Russia, have developed moral formulas of this sort, marked by at least some nonfactual elements.   And when the United States, at the turn of the present century, was about to take over the government of the Philippines from Spain—a patent departure from her earlier anticolonial policy—an uneasy President McKinley was impelled to justify this move in quasireligious terms by his famous phrase "manifest destiny."   The introduction of these nonempirical factors is all but inevitable, since the exercise of rulership over subject peoples always involves some degree of exploitation, and neither the benefit conferred by the rule nor what may be the superiority of the rulers is necessarily self-evident to mere common sense.   Hence justifications of imperialism solely in factual terms have never entirely stood the test of moral adequacy.

A familiar illustration of a moral formula of this kind is the one current among the British at the height of their imperial success.   To many a Victorian Christian the thought that his country had been chosen by God to shoulder the "white man's burden" and to bring the benefits of British civilization and Christianity to "lesser breeds without the law" helped to make the undoubted fact that his country had subjugated and exploited many people socially legitimate and morally acceptable. Although a few hard-boiled rationalists among nineteenth-century British were capable of accepting matter-of-fact explanations of their country's success as implied in the caustic couplet

> Whatever happens we have got
> The maxim gun which they have not

most members of Victorian society would not have slept comfortably had they been required to believe that Britain's imperial rule was justified by sheer force alone. Moreover, such a nonmoral interpretation probably would not have induced a sufficient number of British to persevere with the practical and sometimes uncomfortable and lonely tasks necessary to maintain the empire. Some interpretation of the meaning of imperial success acceptable in terms of current morality, such as we have described and which Kipling's famous poem *Recessional* epitomizes, was needed both for the psychic comfort of British society and the mobilization of the vitality of the empire builders.*

An inseparable part of this interpretation was a belief in the superiority of the white man,[26] another nonempirical element in the moral formula. For the most part this belief was an unthinking assumption, common, of course, to many peoples. When this assumption was challenged, many British (and Americans) were inclined to justify it on biblical, and therefore highly moral, grounds. The Book of Genesis was cited as authority for the belief that God created different races of men and that in

---

* It may not be out of place to mention here that many of the most ardent empire builders were the sons of English clergymen. Although these young men (like Admiral Nelson) had the spur of economic interest, they may have needed a religious justification as well.

the wisdom of the Creator, these races were created of unequal worth. Various scholars have pointed out that prevalent ideas of racial superiority came into prominence when, after the seventeenth century, European whites began to expand their rule over many colored peoples. Nonscientific theories of qualitative differences between races, whose assumed superiority and inferiority could be attributed to the all-wise purposes of a supreme creator, served to augment the self-confidence of the whites and to allay any gnawings of guilt that they might feel. It should be noted in this connection that such highly selective interpretations of biblical authority enabled many Christians to make moral sense of the institution of slavery.

Furthermore, fundamentalist Christians, especially members of rural societies in comparative isolation, have been particularly prone to justify racial dominance and policies of racial segregation in biblical terms. The hard core resisters to the civil rights movement in the South are often found in the churches, and they frequently cite scriptural authority for their segregationist position, even in the face of an opposing stand taken by other Christians on grounds that appear to *them* to be religious. The case of the rigid segregationist stance of the up-country Afrikaans farmers in South Africa is an even clearer example of a society of rural fundamentalists who, after their courageous trek deep into the veldt, were virtually cut off for some three hundred years from the liberalizing influences of European religious culture, including that of their own former homeland, Holland. For these puritanical, hardworking farmers of the South African veldt the Bible was almost their sole literature and the patriarchal days depicted in the Old Testament their most congenial inspirational source. Dangerously outnumbered, condemned by world opinion as expressed in the United Nations, it is perhaps not surprising that they should continue to moralize *apartheid* in biblical terms.

RELIGIOUS INTERPRETATIONS OF SOCIAL INSTITUTIONS

We turn now from the consideration of the different meanings that societies, whether faced by adversity or success, have imputed to their own history, to religious interpretations of social stratification and of economic and political institutions. Class systems assign different and unequal statuses to a society's members; sometimes the resulting social inequalities are not only extreme but also rigidly fixed. This situation once more poses the problem of interpreting the social system in moral and meaningful terms.

The Hindu Caste System

The Hindu caste system of ancient India, currently undergoing considerable change, is an outstanding example of the moralization of radical social inequality. The salient fact about this sytem is that, in principle and largely in fact, the individual's life station, usually including his occupation, was fixed at birth, and no individual effort on his part could change it. Furthermore, in assigning highest caste ranking to the Brahmins, Hindu society was granting priority within its social system to the very group whose hereditary occupation connected it most closely with the society's dominant cultural value, namely the assurance of a favorable destiny for each individual in future lives by means of an extremely complicated religious ritual.[27] The right to perform the most important and sacred portions of this ritual was reserved for members of the Brahmin caste. The status of other castes * was determined by their social and religious distance from the Brahmins.

---

* There were (and are) literally hundreds of castes and subcastes, not to mention unfortunate multitudes who were outside the system of caste ranking. However, only the principle of caste concerns us here. The four "classical" castes are Brahmins (priests), Kshatriyas (warriors and administrators), Vaisyas (merchants), and Sudras (servants).

The Hindu caste system clearly poses a large moral problem. Why, for instance, should some lazy and possibly worthless Brahmin enjoy the greatest social prestige, whereas an upright and diligent Sudra (a member of the servant caste) or an outcaste is not only segregated occupationally but also spurned socially and deprived religiously? The Hindu answer to this question, an answer giving the caste system moral justification, was found in the supernatural world. Interpretation of this answer requires some understanding of the Hindu religious outlook.

The Hindu doctrine of reincarnation, which carries the main burden of justifying the inequities of the caste system, is bound up with Hinduism's conception of the ultimate spiritual destiny of the individual.[28] This spiritual goal is the reabsorption of his individual soul, or *atman,* with the Universal World Soul, or *Brahman.* In the course of his journeying to this goal, the individual is thought to persist through thousands of years and thousands of lives. Throughout the journey he is bound by his personal *dharma,* the relentless chain of causation set in motion by all his past actions in all his previous lives. His *karma,* or destiny in any subsequent life or lives, is considered to be the direct result of his dharma. An individual is believed to be subject to the possibility of reincarnation as human being or animal, male or female, high-caste or low-caste member. According to this religious doctrine, whatever the caste position of an individual, he receives no more and no less than his just deserts earned in previous lives.

There are two striking points about this interpretation. First, it fitted extremely well the concrete conditions of Hindu society: as a justification for a rigid system of caste, the religious doctrine of reincarnation seems custom-made. Secondly, there is the preeminently other-worldly, nonempirical character of the doctrine.[29] The Hindu emphasis on the attainment, through myriad lives, of an other-worldly spiritual state gave religious sanction for placing the main focus of all human striving in the superempirical world. This had the further effect of devaluing concrete activities and engendering attitudes of indifference and

130

apathy toward the social and economic sufferings and injustices
endured by human beings in this mortal life.

The Class System of Medieval Europe

The medieval European system of social classes, or estates,
differs in important respects from the Hindu caste system.
The method by which religious thought endowed the medieval
class system with moral significance also differs. Although
medieval Europe, in common with ancient India, institutionalized its status differences, the latter were not as rigid or as
irreversible as those of ancient Hindu society. Furthermore, the
two systems embodied very different cultural values. Whereas
the key cultural value of the Hindus, to which their status system
was geared, was the furtherance of the individual's long-term
spiritual destiny by means of religious ritual, that of medieval
Europeans was the possession of land. In the medieval system
the relation in which the individual stood to the feudal system of
land tenure determined his class standing more than any other
single factor. The members of the different classes, landowners
great and small, clergy, burghers, and tenants-in-villeinage were
bound to one another, and thus to the society as a whole, by
reason of the particular character of their relationships to the
land. Each individual's relationship to the land also defined the
whole gamut of his rights and obligations to his fellows.
The medieval system, then, perpetuated substantial inequalities
that required moral interpretation. It may seem strange that
Christianity, with its doctrinal stress on the value of every Christian soul and the equality of all sinners in the sight of God,
could have succeeded in morally justifying a system of class
inequality. Its explanatory task, to be sure, was not easy. One
possibility was to have interpreted the equality of Christian
souls in a purely spiritual sense and to have ignored earthly
differences in status as religiously irrelevant. But Christian
philosophy did not venture far along such an interpretative
path. True, Christian creeds were explicit in the declaration of
belief in a supernatural future world. In heaven, purgatory, or

hell appropriate rewards and punishments for the conduct of this-worldly affairs were promised to all. If we are to believe Dante, those who occupied the positions of greatest prestige in this world stood less chance of gaining positions of privilege hereafter than those of low estate.

Christian philosophers, however, were aware that according to orthodox Christian belief the fate of the individual soul throughout all eternity hung on the conduct of a single this-worldly life. The grace of God was freely offered to all, but grace had to be received by the Christian in this life. Thus worldly life, related to salvation itself, was invested with a crucial value. The Christian, then, unlike the Hindu who contemplated eternity through vistas of successive incarnate lives, could not afford to regard known social arrangements as spiritually unimportant.

Accordingly, in the eyes of Christian philosophers, Christian civil society, including its class system and its economic and political arrangements, was imbued with a moral purpose. St. Augustine, whose *City of God* most clearly expresses this conception of purpose, explained that the moral justification of civil society is to maintain such conditions that Christians are able to conduct their earthly lives so as to save their immortal souls.[30] The chief agency within civil society, as St. Augustine saw it, that enables individuals to attain salvation is the organized Christian Church, the divinely ordained means for the dispensation of grace. Since this Church existed within the framework of a feudal society, which after the collapse of the Roman Empire was the only organization capable of defending Christianity against the threats of heathens and barbarians, the whole feudal order was endowed with moral meaning. In some such terms as these medieval Christian thought gave moral meaning to the medieval class system. This religious endorsement of the class system and of civil society itself, however, was a conditional one. The arrangements of civil society were not religiously underwritten for their intrinsic merit but as the means to a supernatural objective.

RELIGIOUS INTERPRETATIONS OF ECONOMIC AND POLITICAL SYSTEMS

Economic institutions, as well as the class systems with which they are intermeshed, call for moral interpretation. The distribution of wealth and the means by which it is amassed may give rise to feelings of injustice and inequity. In the social system of ancient India we pointed out how the concrete world was strongly rejected by religion: it was regarded as *māyā*, or illusion. This radical rejection of the world not only devalued economic activity but also relegated it to an unregulated moral limbo. Since material wealth and economic activity were illusory, religious thought could, so to say, wash its hands of them. The propertyless ascetic was both supported and revered, but economic exploitation of the masses and the extortion of usurers went unchecked.*

The situation in medieval Europe was strikingly different. Christian religious thought, as we have seen, assigned a moral meaning to civil society on conditional terms. It was only in the light of the other-worldly, nonempirical goals that life in this world was sanctified. The gaining of heaven was the Christian's major objective. Therefore, his moral problem concerning economic activity was how to engage in it without falling into sin and so jeopardizing his chance of heaven.

In this dilemma the social objectives of wealth and economic activity were emphasized. Wealth was to be regarded as essentially for use and was neither to be hoarded nor avidly amassed. Hence usury and the taking of unfair profit were religiously condemned, and attempts were made to maintain fair prices by the regulations of merchant and craft guilds. This conception

---

* Here again, we must beware of exaggeration—brief general statements can be misleading. In India much economic activity, apart from agriculture and village handicrafts, fell into the hands of non-Hindu groups, such as the Jains, Parsees, and Muslims.

of economic activity, the student of sociology should note, was not only morally but also economically appropriate in a society of poor communications, undeveloped urban life, and scarcity of monetary metals.

Moreover, medieval Christendom, in contrast to ancient India, also gave a moral interpretation to political authority.[31] In India the village *panchayats* embodied the belief in corporate responsibility for the control of local community affairs, but the authority exercised over larger areas by rajahs and princelings was generally despotic, capricious, and relatively meaningless morally.* Christian thought, in contrast, which regarded political institutions as means for the Christian to pursue both his sanctified earthly purposes and his heavenly goal, interpreted political authority in moral terms. All earthly authority was assumed to be ordained by God, the Supreme Ruler of the World, and was believed to be delegated to its earthly wielders as a sacred trust. Political authority, thus religiously sanctioned, was expected to be exercised by earthly rulers for the benefit of the ruled, while dutiful obedience was required from all those lawfully subjected to it. St. Thomas Aquinas, whose writings depicted in moral terms the social and political order of medieval times more systematically than those of any other contemporary, maintained that only in the most extreme cases, in which rulers through flagrant abuse of their delegated authority might be assumed to have forfeited their sacred trust, could rebellion against such authority be justified religiously.

In the cases of ancient India and medieval Europe, religious interpretations of political and economic systems are clear-cut and relatively easy to discern. In contrast, religious interpretations of the political and economic arrangements of modern

---

* This statement is emphatically not true of the great rulers of India, such as the Emperor Asoka (269–232 B.C.). He assumed responsibility for the welfare of ordinary people and also regarded himself as the protector—and discipliner—of all the religious groups in his vast empire. It is true, by and large, of great numbers of rajahs and princelings throughout much of Indian history.

industrial societies are much less clear-cut and more difficult to trace. It is usual in modern societies to "moralize" various types of social arrangements in "secular" and humanistic, rather than religious, terms. In the United States, for instance, political and economic rights are guaranteed in political documents, notably in the Declaration of Independence and the Constitution. These documents, to be sure, are avowedly man-made, but the Declaration of Independence nevertheless legitimates the break with the English Crown by an appeal to the "Laws of Nature and of Nature's God." Moreover, such "secular" documents may themselves in course of time take on a quasisacred significance and come to be revered rather than read. Consequently, they may be invoked to legitimate diverse types of institutionalized behavior. Since such political documents usually embody the views of more than one man, they are commonly couched in "compromise" language that glosses over inherent contradictions. It is well known that the Constitution of the United States (unlike the Declaration of Independence) stresses property rights rather than human rights; and the Declaration of Independence claims for Americans "inalienable rights" to *both* "liberty" and the "pursuit of happiness," ignoring the fact that one man's unbridled pursuit of his individual "happiness" may on occasion infringe upon the "liberty" of his fellows. It is apparent that quasisacred political documents have been used by contending groups particularly in times of rapid social change to legitimate conflicting interpretations of societal meaning.

THE PROBLEM OF MEANING IN DIFFERENT TYPES OF SOCIETY

Thus through the ages men have sought solutions for the ultimate whys of social experience, and in these solutions they have attempted to reconcile the concrete facts of social systems with men's highest standards of morality and justice. Since there is an ever-present disparity between the justice meted out to people by social institutions and ideal conceptions of justice and right, there is a need for legitimation in religious terms, that is, in terms transcending common sense or science.

In simpler societies, of the kind described earlier as Model One, religious interpretations of the meaning of society may be implicit rather than explicit. In such societies the human group itself may constitute a basic sacred value for its members; hence distinctions between ideal morality and actual customs may not always be clearly drawn. In this case the very existence of the group is its own moral justification: whatever is, simply is, is just and right. No further legitimation is necessary. But even in these simpler societies the degree of correspondence between the ideal and the actual is relative rather than absolute.

The greater complexity of Model Two societies is accompanied by larger differences between the fortunes of rich and poor, of rulers and ruled. With an increase in the division of labor, moreover, the opportunities for the exploitation of man by man are augmented, and so too, perhaps, is the total reservoir of human guilt. In the early stages of these societies emergent ethical religions enunciate codes that are in important respects challenges to encrusted custom. As these societies mature, religion also serves to furnish an explanation of the meaning of society that enables the mighty to feel assured of the justice of their station while the poor and humble are kept content with their lowly estate. When in the later stages of their development these societies undergo social convulsions of various sorts and new interests challenge a former distribution of power, new outcroppings of religion provide new interpretations, which help to justify in moral terms both the challenge itself and the new social order.

In Model Two societies, in which religion typically underwrites and legitimates the values of the basic social institutions, the part played by religion in investing traditional institutions with moral significance stands out in clear relief. Can the same be said of the part played by religion in societies of the third type, our modern industrial societies? What interpretation does religion give to the relationships of modern urban man to the state and to the economic order? What meaning does it assign to the vast network of conflicting power relationships in our shrinking world?

In these societies the injustices and inequities in the diverse fates of individuals and of nations are plain. However, secular interpretations of the meaning of the social order exist alongside religious ones. In modern industrial societies, as we pointed out earlier, secular entities, such as the nation or the state or a particular form of government, may be suffused with religious overtones. Hence nationalism, communism, and even democracy itself may become quasireligions, rivals to the traditional spiritual religions of the world.

Can the interpretations of these secular religions, as they are sometimes called, suffice to invest the huge inequities of the modern world with moral meaning? History has not yet given the answer to this question. There are some who think that the moral doctrines of these secular faiths are becoming threadbare and that in this time of crisis modern societies are on the brink of evolving vast new spiritual and religious interpretations of the meaning of our world society.[32] Meanwhile other pundits exhort us to "embrace secularity" and to "learn to speak of God in secular fashion." [33]

CONCLUSION

In this chapter we have cited only a few of many possible illustrations of ways in which religion has helped, in varying degrees of emphasis, to assign moral meaning to human social arrangements. It is far from our purpose to maintain that the "religionizing" of the history and destiny of a nation or group is necessarily "a good thing," or, in sociological parlance, that it serves a *positive function*. There are times when the plight of a society is seemingly so hopeless that the injection of some supernatural elements seem almost inevitable requirements if its members are to make any adjustment, even one of resignation, to an unkind fate. But since long persistence is a characteristic of most religious interpretations of meaning, it might be argued that, in the long run, such religious interpretations may be "a bad thing"—that is, they may perform *negative functions*. The latter evaluation is especially likely to be made when the circumstances of a society or group have improved to a point where active, this-worldly measures to better their lot might appear to some to be feasible, whereas long-accepted religious interpretations of a compensatory nature might foster a possibly needless continuance of passive, resigning attitudes. Such a viewpoint is frequently expressed regarding "old-time" Negro religion by contemporary black activists. In the final analysis, however, whether a particular religious interpretation of societal meaning is adjudged, by sociologists or others, as performing a positive or negative function depends in large part on who does the evaluating. Persons for whom harmony, order, and stability are paramount may assess a given religious interpretation as being positive and useful, while those who are concerned with change and betterment, even at the price of conflict, may view the same interpretation as negative and harmful.

In this chapter we have been mainly concerned with ways in which religion has helped to provide meaningful interpretations of a variety of societal situations viewed, for the most part, in static terms. In the following chapter we shall consider the functions of religion with respect to social change.

REFERENCES

1. See Talcott Parsons, "Introduction," in Max Weber, *The Sociology of Religion,* trans. Ephraim Fischoff (Boston: Beacon Press, 1963), p. xlvii. According to Parsons, Weber postulates a basic "drive" toward meaning. At the same time, Weber is aware of the individual differences in religious interest and potential. See also Max Weber, *From Max Weber: Essays in Sociology,* trans. and ed. Hans H. Gerth and C. Wright Mills (New York: Oxford University Press, Galaxy Book, 1958), p. 287.
2. See Weber, *Sociology of Religion, op. cit.,* p. xxxiii (Parsons' "Introduction") and Chapter 4, pp. 58–59, in which the author gives

his conception of the role of the prophet and the part played by prophets in assigning meaning to the historical events of their time.

3. Job 16:16–17; *Ibid.,* 19:7–11.
4. See Weber, *From Max Weber, op. cit.,* pp. 275–276.
5. Job 21:7, 8.
6. Archibald MacLeish, *J.B.: A Play in Verse* (Boston: Houghton Mifflin, 1958).
7. See Job 1:6–12 for the agreement between God and Satan in the biblical story.
8. *Ibid.,* 13:15.
9. See Andrew M. Greeley, "There's a New-Time Religion on Campus," *The New York Times Magazine,* June 1, 1969.
10. See Talcott Parsons, *Religious Perspectives of College Teaching in Sociology and Social Psychology* (New Haven: Edward W. Hazen Foundation, 1951), pp. 13–14, and also Weber, *Sociology of Religion, op. cit.,* p. xlvii and p. 59.
11. Weber, *Sociology of Religion, op. cit.,* pp. 112–117.
12. Parsons, *Religious Perspectives, op. cit.,* p. 14.
13. See J. Milton Yinger, *Religion, Society, and the Individual* (New York: Macmillan, 1957), pp. 214–218, for an excellent discussion of this complex problem. See also pp. 295–302, especially p. 299, for a discussion of "elective affinity," and see Gerth and Mills in their introduction to Weber, *From Max Weber, op. cit.,* pp. 62–63.
14. See Yinger, *op. cit.,* p. 304.
15. See Talcott Parsons, "Christianity in Modern Industrial Society," in Edward Tiryakian (ed.), *Sociological Theory, Values, and Sociocultural Change* (Glencoe, Ill.: Free Press, 1963), pp. 33–70; reprinted in Louis Schneider (ed.), *Religion, Culture, and Society: A Reader in the Sociology of Religion* (New York: John Wiley, 1964), p. 277: "First, Jehovah became a completely universal transcendental God who governed the activities not only of the people of Israel but of all mankind. Second, the people of Israel became, through the exile, depoliticized."
16. See Sokyo Ono and W. P. Woodard, *The Kami Way: An Introduction to Shrine Shinto* (Tokyo: International Institute for the Study of Religions, 1959), pp. 1–4.
17. See Weber, *From Max Weber, op. cit.,* p. 273:

Among people under political pressure, like the Israelites, the title of 'Savior' (Moshuach name) was originally attached to the saviors from political distress, as transmitted by hero sagas (Gideon, Jephthah). The 'Messianic' promises were determined by these sagas, with this people, and in this clear-cut fashion and under other very particular conditions, the suffering of a people's com-

munity, rather than the suffering of an individual, became the object of hope for religious salvation.

18. See Alexander Lesser, "Cultural Significance of the Ghost Dance," *American Anthropologist,* January–March 1933, pp. 108–115; reprinted in Yinger, *op. cit.,* pp. 490–496.

19. See Bernard Barber, "A Socio-Cultural Interpretation of the Peyote Cult," *American Anthropologist,* October–December 1941, pp. 673–675.

20. See Vittorio Lanternari, *The Religions of the Oppressed: A Study of Modern Messianic Cults,* trans. Lisa Sergio (New York: New American Library, Mentor Book, 1965), pp. 19–62, in which appear accounts of a number of modern African nativistic movements.

21. See C. Eric Lincoln, *The Black Muslims* (Boston: Beacon Press, 1963), especially pp. 10–17.

22. J. Milton Yinger, *op. cit.* pp. 174–179.

23. Lincoln, *op. cit.,* pp. 250–251.

24. See George E. Simpson, "The Ras Tafari Movement in Jamaica," *Social Forces,* December 1955, pp. 167–170, and also Sheila Kitzinger, "The Rastafari Cult of Jamaica," *Journal for the Scientific Study of Religion,* 7, no. 2 (Fall 1969), pp. 240–262, especially p. 262. On the basis of Kitzinger's more recent (1966) data, it would appear that the Rastafaris are still geared to seek psychological compensation rather than organized political action.

25. Weber, *From Max Weber, op. cit.,* p. 271: "Religion provides the theodicy of good fortune for those who are fortunate. This theodicy is anchored in highly robust needs of man and is therefore easily understood, even if sufficient attention is often not paid to its effects."

26. *Ibid.,* p. 276. "[Social] strata in possession of social honor and power usually tend to fashion their status-legend in such a way as to claim a special and intrinsic quality of their own, *usually a quality of blood"* (italics added).

27. *Ibid.,* pp. 396–397.

28. See Huston Smith, *The Religions of Man* (New York: New American Library, Mentor Book, 1962), pp. 77–78. See also Max Weber, *The Religion of India: The Sociology of Hinduism and Buddhism,* trans. and ed. Hans H. Gerth and Don Martindale (Glencoe, Ill.: Free Press, 1960), Chapter 3, especially p. 121. See also D. S. Sarma, "The Nature and History of Hinduism," in Kenneth Morgan (ed.), *The Religion of the Hindus* (New York: Ronald Press, 1953), esp. pp. 4 and 5; R. N. Dandekar, "The Role of Man in Hinduism," in *op. cit.,* esp. pp. 125–130; and Sivaprasad

Bhattacharyya, "Religious Practices of the Hindus," in *op. cit.*, esp. pp. 202–203.

29. See Weber, *Religion of India, op. cit.*, pp. 132–133 and 178. There are some modern scholars, such as Milton Singer, who are of the opinion that Weber—and many other westerners, not necessarily scholars—have exaggerated the other-worldly implications of Hinduism.

30. See Talcott Parsons, "Christianity and Modern Industrial Society," *op. cit.*, pp. 47–48.

31. *Ibid.*, p. 260.

32. See, for example, Pitirim Sorokin, *The Crisis of Our Age* (New York: Dutton, 1941), Chapter 9, especially pp. 322–326; and Arnold J. Toynbee, *The Study of History*, Abridgement of Vols. I–VI by D. C. Somervell (New York: Oxford University Press, 1947), pp. 544–554.

33. See Harvey Cox, *The Secular City* (New York: Macmillan, 1965), p. 241.

6
Religion and Social Change

INTRODUCTION

Changes in religion, whether theological, liturgical, or organizational, are highly publicized today. Popular magazines carry articles about theologians who claim that "God is dead," about masses celebrated "family style" in the homes of Roman Catholics of the "underground" church, about priests and nuns who discard their distinctive clerical habit, about priests who defy their bishops and protest the rules enjoining celibacy, and about Protestant ministers who are jailed for inciting resistance to the draft.*

Such happenings, notwithstanding the publicity given to them, are from the standpoint of sociology only illustrations of the well-known fact that religion, in common with all other social institutions, is inextricably involved in social and cultural change. Moreover, this involvement is no new departure; it has always existed, although admittedly the rapidity of change in the modern world has dramatized religious—and other—changes.

There is a long-standing and much-debated question about whether "society" changes "religion" or vice versa. Such a question, in the form just stated, is misleading. In taking account of institutional changes we are not concerned with either-

---

* All deviant ministers, however, are not involved with civil rights and other "radical" causes. A forthcoming book, by Rodney Stark *et al.*, *Wayward Shepherds* (New York: Harper and Row, 1971), documents prejudices of various kinds—right wing as well as left wing—among the Protestant clergy.

or propositions but (as implied all along) with *interaction,* the key to understanding change not only in religious institutions but in all major institutions.

In this chapter, we will deal with the mutual interaction between religious change and social change.* Religion will be viewed as a force that is one of a complex of causes that mutually condition one another. This interactional and multicausational position carries with it complexities and analytical difficulties. For example, this approach precludes easy generalizations about the influence of religion on social change, or the influence of secular changes on religion. Moreover, an additional complication is that those who use this approach must be continually aware that the actual influence of one institution upon another is often unintentional rather than intentional, and that the consequences of institutional interaction are often latent rather than manifest. These interactive influences, in fact, vary considerably from situation to situation. It becomes the task of sociological analysis, then, to discover those conditions that maximize and those that minimize religion's influence.[1] Clearly we shall not expect to find situations in which religion is *the* cause of social change, nor situations in which religion is *nothing but* a reaction to other changes. We shall indicate, however, some combinations of historical and institutional conditions under which religion and its institutions may be expected to exert more or less influence.

The analysis of any particular situation of religious and social change usually reveals an intricately woven "chain of causation." Sometimes, for analytic purposes, it is useful to hold the religious strand of the skein motionless—to treat it as a "given" while investigating its influence on politics and economics. Or, in reverse, economic institutions may be defined as the "given"

---

* We shall not be concerned here with two other possible points of view. The first of these is that religion is the "prime mover" in history—a contention that is not common today. Indeed, if religion were the prime mover, how should we explain changes in religion itself? The second view is that religion is a mere reflection of other changes in history and society, not an integral part of causal interaction. Religion and its institutions would thus be no more than mere "epiphenomena," as Marx maintained.

while we attempt to assay the changes that have occurred in religion. Such procedures are useful and legitimate as long as it is realized that they can give only a partial picture and that there exist other strands of the causal chain which play a greater or lesser part in the emergent reality.

Furthermore, it is important in estimating the extent of the influence of religion on social change to distinguish between its influence as a system of ideas, that is, as a belief system influencing individuals, and the influence of religious organizations. As we shall see, the historical role of the Protestant Ethic is one factor, while that of the Protestant churches is quite another.

In the opinion of most sociologists there are certain conditions usually conducive to societal change. Situations of crisis within a society and contact with alien cultures (the first sometimes stimulated by the second) both provide a favorable milieu for change. The weakening of existing social institutions, which often accompanies societal crises, may create a disposition among a society's members to experiment with new or borrowed solutions to unfamiliar problems that their established customs are proving inadequate to handle. Whether religion or some other sociocultural factor plays a significant role in bringing about subsequent changes may depend on the strength and adequacy of the secular institutions as opposed to the degree of autonomy, rationality, and dynamism in the religious sphere. In times of great danger and confusion men react in diverse ways. Some may turn from religion and reject God, seek the fleshpots or follow secular saviors, while others may be more open to accept other-worldly explanations for their calamities and supernatural direction for their conduct.

In the following pages we shall consider factors that rather typically accompany and interact with religion's role in three types of situations: those in which religion plays an active part in furthering changes in society; those in which it acts as a barrier to change; and those in which religion reacts, rather than acts independently, in *response* to social change.

We begin our discussion of the first type of situation (that in

which religion plays an active, instigating role) by a consideration of Weber's conception of the "prophet," especially of the
"ethical" prophet, as a precipitator of change even in custom-
bound Model One societies. We then present two historical
examples in which religion appears as an active agent of change:
the case of the Prophet Mohammed, and the Islamic religion he
founded, as a vital force in the integration of Arabian society
and the emergence of a vast theocratic empire; and Weber's
well-known case of what he conceived as the "independent" role
of the Protestant Ethic in the rise of modern "rational" capitalism.

Situations in which religion has played an appreciable role in
blocking change, whether intentionally or unintentionally, are
discussed in more general terms, with, however, some special
attention to factors reinforcing religion's role in Spain and
Latin America.

Finally, as examples of the third type of situation, in which
religion's role is mainly a reactive one, we will consider two
situations, far apart in time: first, the modifications undergone
by Buddhism (which originated in India) after its contact with
Japanese culture; and, secondly, the changes that took place in
many Christian churches and sects after they were "imported"
from Europe to America and were subsequently exposed to the
influences of American frontier life.

RELIGION AS AN ACTIVE AGENT IN FURTHERING CHANGES IN SOCIETY: THE ROLE OF THE PROPHET

Religion's potential to stimulate change, as noted above,
is likely to be greatest in crisis situations. The transition from
one type of society to that of another—for instance, the passage
from a Model One to a Model Two type of society, or from
Model Two to Model Three—sometimes (although not always)

coincides with an acute societal crisis. In the following discussion of such types of crisis situations our indebtedness to Max Weber will be apparent.

In the Model One type of society (discussed at some length in Chapter 2), generally very little change takes place as long as the society remains small, isolated, and self-enclosed. Such a society, as noted earlier, offers a relatively meager range of culture models to its members, who are, moreover, largely debarred through lack of communications from borrowing new cultural items from outside. In addition, as long as religion is deeply embedded in tradition and magic and remains an aspect of most of the institutional activities of the society rather than a distinct institution in its own right, it can possess scant leverage with which to exercise a dynamic influence for social change. On the other hand, in Model Two societies religion is typically differentiated from the other institutions and possesses a systematic, rationalized ethic of its own. This ethic, insofar as it is a *social* ethic, is often in considerable tension with the custom-derived behavior of the society's members and, insofar as it gains acceptance, may be a potent influence for social change.

In view of the relatively static nature of Model One societies, the question arises: How does the initial change to the Model Two society come about? What are the circumstances under which the "cake of custom," so tough and seemingly impermeable in Model One societies, can be effectively broken? Although Model One societies must not be considered completely static, it would seem nevertheless that some special circumstances would be needed to precipitate significant change. Max Weber was concerned with precisely this type of problem. His special interest was in the emergence of what he called "rational" (that is, ethical, nontraditional) religion from the stranglehold of magic. Hence he focused his analysis on the conditions that he believed made possible such a crucial breakthrough.[2] But how, under the conditions of Model One societies, could such a rationalized ethic come into existence?

The prime essential for this breakthrough, in Weber's view, was the presence of outstandingly gifted religious specialists whom he termed "prophets." The power of the prophets to move men and events resided in their "charisma"—an awe-inspiring quality of attraction whereby they exercised an almost mesmeric effect upon their hearers. These prophets, moreover, were proclaimers of a "religious truth of salvation through personal revelation." They were vital emotional preachers, orators with a touch of the demagogue about them, and they held a belief in their transcendent mission that distinguished them from ordinary men. Prophets, as Weber conceived of them, were very different from the priests and magicians of Model One societies, for the latter were usually tradition-bound, whereas prophets were likely to be laymen outside the priestly ranks who believed themselves to have had a direct revelation from a transcendent deity. The belief in his supernatural mission enabled the prophet to "break the cake of custom" and to supersede tradition.[3]

Furthermore, according to Weber, an individual merited the title of prophet only if his message was a call *to break with an established order*.[4] Weber distinguished between two kinds of prophets: *ethical* (or emissary) and *exemplary*. Ethical prophets exercised the more dynamic influence, since they were "instruments for the proclamation of a god and his will." Because of his divine mission the ethical prophet could demand obedience from his listeners as an ethical duty. The exemplary prophet, on the other hand, provided a model for others to follow if, as individuals, they were moved to do so; he gave individuals the *opportunity* to walk the path of salvation that he himself had trod, but he did not promulgate a divinely revealed ethic binding on his fellows as a *duty*. Thus, while the exemplary prophets demonstrate the "way" of salvation mainly to individuals, the ethical prophets offer what is potentially a *social* salvation. Weber noted that exemplary prophets were more likely to be found in China and India, whereas the ethical type was confined to the Near East. Zoroaster and Mohammed are examples of ethical prophets, and the Buddha is an outstanding example of an exemplary prophet.[5]

Weber considered the power of charismatic prophecy particularly strong in the early stages of a prophetic movement, at the time when the prophet's charismatic appeal is fresh and keen. Once the prophet has succeeded in attracting a group of followers and has founded a religious movement, his followers are then likely to *routinize* his charisma.[6] Eventually such routinization may result in the creation of a *priestly,* hence more conservative, religious organization. Thus, as routinization progresses, the dynamic cutting edge of a prophet's radical message of salvation and therefore its potential to change society become blunted.

This stress on the prophet as an agent of change has been regarded by some as only another version of an exploded "Great Man" theory of history. In this view Weber elaborated only one strand of the causal chain mentioned earlier and treated religion as a "prime mover" and the religious leader as an "uncaused cause." [7] We believe, however (especially in view of his general propositions concerning social change), that Weber, for analytic purposes, was holding the other strands of the chain constant and that he was by no means unaware of the broader social, political, and economic factors that played a part in the emergence and conditioning of dynamic individuals. To be sure, he does at times appear to have regarded the appearance of the religious genius as in some respects sporadic and unpredictable. Nevertheless, the important point is that his *focus* was on the crucial breakthrough, on the historical moment that the logjam of tradition began to give way. In a complex concatenation of circumstances he saw the prophet as a precipitant.

Weber did, in fact, look at another strand of the causal chain when he considered what kind of social "soil" was likely to be most receptive to the prophet's message.[8] He argued that, on the whole, members of a newly emergent urban middle class were likely to offer the most fertile soil for the prophetic seed. In a society in process of transition from an agricultural to an urban economy Weber saw the new urban classes as those most "hungry and thirsty for salvation" and therefore open to receive a new ethical and religious interpretation of the meaning of their lives and of their place in a shifting social order. In a period of transition these were the people who were most likely to be uncertain of their place in the social scheme of things, who felt that relative to others they were being given less than their due, that they were being left out of the status system of their society. In modern sociological terms Weber was indicating classes of people with a *propensity for alienation.* Furthermore, the urban classes who were occupied with trading and merchandising could be expected to have experience in planning and calculation and hence to have a tendency toward rational rather than traditional ways of thought.[9] The existence of such susceptible individuals depends on at least some development of an urban way of life that in turn depends on the development of communications and the breakdown of the isolation characteristic of Model One societies.

Case One: Mohammed and the Rise of Islam

The role played by Mohammed and the Islamic religion in the rapid transformation of Arabia in the seventh century is a dramatic example of the potency of religious factors in stimulating societal change. Before Mohammed's time Arabia, with the exception of the commercial center at Mecca, was mainly a society of rivalrous nomadic tribes hemmed in by the two great empires of Byzantium and Persia. In part as a result of Mohammed's leadership, the warring tribes were united; and ten years after his death in 632 Islam gave rise to a powerful and expansive military and commercial empire, able to defeat in battle both the Byzantines and the Persians. A hundred years later the empire of Mohammed's successors extended from India to France and challenged Christendom as it expanded. Furthermore, the territories under Islamic rule were transformed internally by a new system of religiously sanctioned law and government and new forms of architecture and scholarship.

What can be said about the part played by religious factors in bringing about these large-scale changes? It is readily apparent that Mohammed corresponds closely to Weber's conception of the ethical prophet.[10] In the first place, he was a man with a message revealed to him by a supreme, supernatural being, Allah. This message is recorded as having been imparted to him in a series of trancelike encounters. It is also recorded that even against his personal wishes he felt compelled to deliver the message that had been revealed to him, for the Angel Gabriel had appeared to him and commanded him to "recite." In the second place, partly by virtue of his claim to be Allah's spokesman and partly because of his own personal qualities, he became a powerful charismatic figure in the eyes of the inhabitants of Mecca and Medina. A man who had received a direct revelation from God could surely be no ordinary man! Finally, Mohammed was commissioned to deliver an ethical message that did indeed entail an obligation to break with an established social order, namely, the corrupt order established in Mecca by the monopolistic power of the dominant group of rapacious caravaneers. This group of wealthy merchants controlled the lucrative trade of Mecca, taking toll of all rivals, and, in common with many other Meccans, they also grew rich at the expense of the numerous pilgrims who flocked to the city to worship the Black Stone and share in its magical properties.

Mohammed's stress on the ethical obligation of his hearers to act in accordance with his message was exceedingly strong. He claimed that he had been commissioned by Allah to be a warner of impending doom and called upon the Meccans to submit to the Will of Allah in order to avert it. In submitting to His Will they were required to adopt a new and upright way of life and to forego the urge to amass large personal fortunes. They were no longer to be preoccupied solely with themselves and their wealth but were to practice generosity and give alms to the needy. In effect he was challenging the lucrative monopoly of an inner group of wealthy traders, while attempting to allay the financial anxieties of those less fortunate.

The content of Mohammed's message was indicative of the new social order that was to emerge. The famous "Four Pillars of Islam" had consequences for society as well as for religion.[11] The obligation to engage in public prayer five times daily, for instance, meant that Islamic believers had to "stand up and be counted," and thus to identify themselves as apart from non-Muslims. Moreover, the duty to make a pilgrimage to Mecca not only gave Islam a central focus but also entailed the mingling of Muslims from many lands under conditions that minimized cultural distinctions and maximized their Islamic brotherhood. Such injunctions, when faithfully carried out, furthered the emergence of a new kind of community, based on "universalistic" theocratic sanctions rather than the earlier narrow community based on tribe and kinship. In addition, the injunction to give alms made this new religious community responsible for the mutual aid that formerly kinsmen had supplied.

Mohammed and his preaching, powerful precipitants of change as they were, must not be regarded as the only factors operative in this dynamic situation. Aspects of his message may, in fact, be viewed as a response to a Meccan crisis created by social and economic changes already under way. Thus the "soil" was already prepared to receive the "seed" of the Prophet's preaching. Significantly, this "seed" was sown at a strategic crossroads of the middle eastern world. Mecca was a commercial and religious center where merchants from east and west converged, and where desert tribesmen, for the most part magic-ridden polytheists, also flocked to worship the Black Stone.[12] Furthermore, novel religious ideas of a monotheistic sort were being introduced into Mecca. A Jewish community had been established there, and the Meccans appear to have had some knowledge, not always accurate, of both Jewish and Christian beliefs and practices. It is an interesting fact that Mohammed's revelations, as recorded in the Koran, contain many passages borrowed from the Judeo-Christian Bible. These borrowings, to be sure, were interpreted from an Islamic viewpoint, but the fact of such borrowing was by no means inconsistent with Islamic teaching, nor did it deny the basic doctrine of Islam, namely that Allah, the One God, was the God of the Whole World. Thus the central teaching of Islam directly challenged the magical and polytheistic beliefs of Arabian tribal society.

Sociologically, it is also important that a relatively disprivileged class, likely to be receptive to Mohammed's message, had been emerging as a result of the crisis in Meccan society that accompanied the early stages of the transition from nomad tribalism to a more settled urban way of life. This class of relative disprivilege was comprised of the moderately wealthy traders. For the nomadic trader, in contrast to the town-based caravaneer, had been forced by the nature of his nomadic business to share some of his profits with his helpers and associates. In Mecca, however, the urban-based traders were able to increase their wealth almost without limit and to create a near-monopoly, so that the economic gap between the very rich townsmen and those of moderate means was continually growing wider.[13] The resentment of the less wealthy traders was increased by the fact that the change had been so rapid that older individuals could remember the profit-sharing customs of earlier times, as well as the obligations formerly discharged by wealthy kinsmen to the weaker members of the tribe. Mohammed himself, in all probability, was born into this "weaker" group of Meccan traders. (He was, to be sure, aided by his more powerful kinsmen, for older customs of mutual aid had by no means completely disappeared.)

This moderately wealthy group, with its propensity to alienation, did in fact contain the individuals who responded most readily to Mohammed's early preaching. They were the ones who, in Weber's terms, were most "hungry and thirsty for salvation" and who may well have felt that they were unfairly left out in the newly emergent social and economic order. From the point of view of Weber's theory, an important fact about the members of this group of relatively disprivileged traders was that their training and experience in business organization and profit calculation would predispose them to rational rather than traditional ways of thinking and acting. These men, therefore, would be likely to possess the necessary skills for organizing the new religious movement.

As we have pointed out, not all of these dramatic changes were due to Mohammed's preaching alone. When the Prophet entered the Arabian scene, the desert tribes were on the eve of a period of expansion. However, the convergence in time and in place of the Prophet's personal attributes and the content of his message with the crisis situation in Mecca and in Arabia generally resulted in conditions highly favorable to societal changes, conditions in which religion was able to play a dominant role. Thus Mohammed and his preaching provided a vital precipitant, and without him subsequent changes in the Arabian peninsula would not have been so rapid nor have taken the form that in fact they did. After the Prophet's death, to be sure, Islam was all but destroyed by a bitter struggle over the succession. Yet under the Caliph Omar, its second founder, the movement was consolidated and Islam's characteristic combination of secular and religious authority was assured. In the second half of the seventh century Islam was able to enter an era of rapid expansion before a complete routinization of the prophetic charisma had set in.[14] This absence of routinization, it will be recalled, was one of the conditions specified by Weber as being especially favorable to religion's influence on societal change. An important additional ingredient favoring the powerful impact of Islam was the absence in Arabian society of central political and economic institutions sufficiently developed to compete with the emergent Islamic theocracy.

Earlier in this chapter it was noted that great societal changes often coincide with crises occasioned by the passage from one type of society to another. Pre-Islamic Arabia was not, however, a Model One society in all respects. Even before the advent of Mohammed, Arabian society had begun in some areas to develop complexities approximating societies of the Model Two type. But Model One societies themselves, as we have seen, are not totally immune to change; indeed, in preliterate societies many happenings go unrecorded and forgotten. Therefore, it is reasonable to suppose that the great "historic" prophets, such as Mohammed, had been preceded by "minor" prophets, early protagonists of change, whose exploits are lost to history. Nevertheless, the Arabia into which Mohammed was born came much closer to our Model One type of society than does the society in which religious influences on societal change will next be discussed, namely, Western Europe in the seventeenth century.

Case Two: Protestantism and the Rise of Capitalism

The economic and political revolutions * that ushered in the modern world coincided in their early stages with the religious revolution known as the Protestant Revolt. The latter part of the sixteenth and early part of the seventeenth centuries were, for Europeans, years of crisis. The prolonged crisis accompanied the transition, which first took place in the West, from a Model Two to a Model Three society. What was the part played by religion in this epoch-making societal change?

As in the case of Islam, in this case also religion played an active formative role. Nevertheless, religion made less apparent impact on this more highly developed, Model Two type of society than it had on a society more nearly approximating the Model One type. It is much more difficult, for example, for an ethical prophet to challenge effectively an established order characterized by highly organized political and religious institutions, which are controlled by individuals strongly protective of their own vested interests. In such societies prophecy has typically become routinized, and religious institutions are more rigid, priest-controlled, and conservative. The priestly hierarchy is typically able to mobilize considerable power to resist changes that threaten it and to receive the backing of secular governments that rely on existing religious sanctions for their own legitimation. In such societies, then, a powerful alliance of religious and political interests confronts the religious innovator.

In Model Two societies, however, the provocation to challenge an established order is often extreme. The teachings of ethical prophets tend to be forgotten or glossed over in the course of time, and the separation of religion from magic is rarely permanent or complete. Thus a formerly "rationalized" religion may

---

* An interesting sociohistorical study that relates the theological outcome of the Protestant Reformation in some forty European societies to the nature of the *political* and *governmental* organization of the societies in question in the period immediately preceding the Protestant Revolt is by Guy E. Swanson, *Religion and Regime* (Ann Arbor: University of Michigan Press, 1967).

become reimmersed in magical tradition, and the hold of a priestly hierarchy over an unlearned population may be powerfully reinforced. Therefore the ethical challenge to the religion of Model Two societies is typically a challenge to the religious establishment and not to the secular order alone. Only if a rising social class of aggressiveness and growing power becomes the carrier of a competing, highly rationalized religious ethic congenial to its own interests and convictions is such an ethical challenge likely to be effective. New religious ideas, often associated with the opening of new avenues of communication and the bringing together of formerly isolated cultures, are as essential to success as are material considerations of political, economic, and military strength. New religious ideas and convictions not only strengthen the *will* of the contending classes but also enable them to fight existing religious justifications of an established order with counter religious justifications. Otherwise, their opposition to the establishment is likely to appear to their contemporaries as not only political revolution but also as religious sacrilege.

All of this bears upon the situation in Western Europe in the first half of the seventeenth century. By then the exploration that had begun in medieval times had enormously widened the boundaries of the known world. England and Holland in particular had become leaders in commerce and navigation, and northwestern Europe had become the center of a new system of maritime communication. New products and ideas as well as new types of commercial organization were continually being introduced. The urban middle classes, rather than the landed gentry, were eager to exploit the new opportunities.

It is not surprising, therefore, that the carriers of novel religious ideas should be members of these same upwardly mobile urban commercial classes. Like the less wealthy Meccan traders in the seventh century, they too felt themselves to be alienated from the establishment. They were debarred for the most part from positions of political influence and social prestige. In many cases they were forbidden by law to hold certain offices and follow certain professions unless they subscribed to the religious establishment. Nevertheless, they were well aware that it was their commercial enterprise and their monetary contributions that chiefly sustained the ruling monarchs and financed governments. When these rising commercial classes became strong enough to play an aggressive role, they were in need of a powerful moral justification for their challenge to the established order. They found it, according to Max Weber, in the doctrines of that form of Protestantism known as Calvinism.

Weber would not have us suppose, however, that the Calvinistic Puritans deliberately chose radical religious doctrines for the express purpose of combating existing political and religious forms of government. But he believed that there was an "elective affinity" between certain religious ideas and certain economic and social classes.[15] Thus the convergence of the radical religious ideas and the newly powerful classes was a semiconscious one.

Calvinism, unlike Lutheranism, was both ethically and socially radical. In common with some other Puritan groups, Calvinists strongly condemned the existing economic, political, and religious institutions. Moreover, John Calvin's headquarters were in Geneva, which was becoming an important commercial center. It was no mere accident, then, that the people attracted to Calvin's teachings were drawn from the urban and commercial classes whose aggressive character and rising aspirations have just been discussed.

One of the major distinctions between medieval and modern societies is the existence in the latter of a "free" capitalistic form of economy. The medieval restrictions on certain forms of economic activity were, to be sure, more often ignored than observed. Furthermore, greed and the desire to amass wealth are found in many societies, past and present. But capitalism as a rational system, dedicated to the pursuit of profit in a calculated and systematic way, in Weber's opinion was something peculiar to the modern world and intimately related to other major changes that accompanied the emergence there of a Model Three type of society. It was capitalism in this sense that Weber viewed as significantly related to new religious ideas.[16]

RELIGION: A SOCIOLOGICAL VIEW

The Protestant Ethic and the Spirit of Capitalism, which is Weber's best-known work, brings out specifically how the Calvinistic variety of Protestantism and emerging capitalism reinforced one another. It is a study of the *interrelations* between developments in religious thought and concurrent changes in economic and political institutions.

Calvinistic belief not only strictly enjoined hard work and prohibited all manner of extravagance and frivolity, but it also denied the validity of the ecclesiastical system for the attainment of the good life on earth, and of heaven through the dispensation of sacramental grace. The duly authorized administration of this sacramental system was, and is, central to Catholic Christianity. Calvinist doctrine held, however, that only God knew who was saved and who was damned eternally; neither individual effort nor sacramental grace could alter His predestined purposes. The Calvinist concept of God emphasized almost exclusively His transcendent aspects, viewing Him as the Omniscient and Terrible Ruler of the Universe, the Inscrutable Dispenser of justice and doom. Whereas the medieval Christian, in thinking of the world to come, was mainly concerned with the gaining of heaven (and in this objective could rely on the help of Christ, the Virgin Mary, and the Saints as well as the entire sacramental system of the Church), the Calvinist was obsessed by an overpowering fear of hell and the dread necessity of facing alone his fate with a transcendent and terrible God.

The political correlate of Calvinism may seem obscure. An overwhelming impulse to avoid hell for themselves and to warn others of the awful danger in which they stood, instead of paralyzing Calvinists as one might suppose, gave them a powerfully dynamic driving force.[17] Since in their view God alone possessed the knowledge of who was saved and who was damned, they found it easy for practical purposes to think of powerful people, especially those among their religious and political rivals, as in imminent peril of doom. They regarded themselves as God's elect, charged with the destiny of waging moral and physical war on the wicked rulers of the world and threatening them with both deposition and impending hell.

At the outset of this revolutionary movement, Calvinist John Knox, in Scotland, trumpeted against the monstrous rule of royal women,* and largely due to his fulminations the autocratic and ineffective regime of the luckless Mary Queen of Scots was overthrown. A little later Holland, a tiny country whose booming commercial and financial activities typified the spirit of the new age, under the leadership of its Calvinist rulers and with the aid of a Puritan England successfully defied the ancient despotisms of France and Spain. Meanwhile in England, Calvinistic members of Parliament, spurred on by those of other independent Protestant groups, not only resisted the tyrannical government of the Stuart kings but also advanced religious justifications for radical political doctrines in which they anticipated the more extreme democratic theories of a later day. These religious enthusiasts, moreover, were ready to back up theory with force. The Puritan Cromwell, with the support of radical Protestant sectaries in the army of Ironsides, defeated Charles I in battle, beheaded him, and finally undertook to enforce the "rule of the saints with the sword."

Of crucial significance, particularly for the development of economic institutions in the West, was the interpretation Calvinists gave to their central doctrine of predestination. Far from inferring that since nothing a man may do will suffice to save him from hell and that therefore he may with impunity spend his life in this world in idleness and self-indulgence, they drew the rather astonishing conclusion that because no man can possibly know his other-worldly destiny he should, for the greater glory of God, live as if, in fact, he *were* saved. The Calvinists were taking no chances. Whatever their fate, they were duty bound to practice the virtues of industry, self-denial, and thrift. They held, too, that the exercise of these virtues should take place in the individual's occupation, or *calling*.[18]

There were, of course, several other possible interpretations of

---

* The full title of Knox's famous pamphlet was *The First Blast of the Trumpet Against the Monstrous Regiment of Women,* the women being Mary Queen of England; Mary of Guise, Regent of France; and Mary Queen of Scots—all Roman Catholics.

Calvinist doctrine. A do-nothing fatalism, for instance, might with equal plausibility have been selected. The interpretation actually chosen, however, was chosen in part by "elective affinity" because of its congeniality to the way of life of those commercial classes already increasing in power.

Weber called the Calvinists "inner-worldly ascetics" because they brought to the conduct of their worldly business affairs the virtues practiced by the monks in the cloister. We can see how this harnessing of business activity with self-denying industry and thrift was productive of savings and surplus, vital essentials for capitalist investment. Moreover, just as the enterprise of a Calvinist's salvation was a lonely, individual risk, so also did the development of capitalist enterprise depend on risks taken by venturesome individuals.

As the Calvinists became influential, however, they faced a grave problem that many successful religious groups have had to face. As more and more people joined the Calvinist ranks, the movement could no longer regard the world as something external to itself. Furthermore, since the social and economic standing of their members was continually advancing, Calvinists could not perpetually justify their existence by contrasting their own humble virtues with the proud pretensions of evil men in power. The time came when they themselves were the men in power. Their challenge to the old order having succeeded, they were forced by this very success to evolve a moral interpretation of the meaning not merely of their social challenge but also of the newly established economic and political order that they had helped to create.[19]

Max Weber regarded the Calvinist sects as the religious precipitants of the revolutionary movements in economic and political life that ushered in the modern world. In this section we have largely followed Weber's analysis. However, several eminent scholars disagree with Weber's interpretation. Some writers have emphasized the contribution to the rise of modern capitalism of various *non*-Calvinistic independent congregational sects. Others, notably Lujo Brentano, have drawn attention to capitalistic developments among Catholics, especially in the

Italian merchant cities, *before* the time of Calvin. Still others, like Werner Sombart, have stressed the part played by the Jews (in pre-Reformation times) as "pioneers" of capitalism. R. H. Tawney, whose *Religion and the Rise of Capitalism* is in some respects sympathetic to Weber's interpretation, sees nascent capitalism as the "prime" factor that "conditioned" Calvin's attitude to economic enterprise and the accumulation of wealth. The most radical criticism of Weber comes from Kurt Samuelsson. In his *Religion and Economic Action* he contends that *no* connection in fact existed between Calvinistic ideas and capitalistic development. He also claims that Weber had overly selected his data and had therefore exaggerated the distinction between Catholic and Protestant (including Calvinistic) economic ethics.[20]

Pro-Weberian scholars have, of course, argued at length against these critics, sometimes claiming that they have not understood the special sense in which Weber used the term "capitalism." Such has been the fascination of Weber's ideas, however, that the controversy about them is by no means dead.

Whether or not "capitalism"—or its "spirit"—antedated Calvin, the fact remains that the resurgent religious sects succeeded in impressing upon their contemporaries much of their belief in the moral significance of self-denying activity in one's calling. Even today, echoes of their moralizing, often in secularized form, still reinforce the sense of almost sacred obligation experienced by some individuals, who strive without ceasing in their professional and business life. Whatever may be the fate of Weber's thesis at the hands of scholars, it has, somewhat ironically, become popularized—and often distorted—both in the mass media and in the hands of certain overenthusiastic researchers who sometimes misapply Weber's historically rooted thesis, out of context, to situations in present-day life.* Weber would doubtless

---

* John Maynard Keynes is reported to have said that "practical men, who believe themselves to be exempt from any intellectual influences, are usually the slaves of some defunct economist." Although the economist Keynes had in mind was probably Adam Smith, his dictum might also be applied to

be horrified by such neglect of historical context as seen in some (although not all) current attempts to explain contemporary differences between Catholics and Protestants by invoking his thesis.

In comparing the role of religion as an agent of change in the two examples just discussed, Islam and Calvinism, it seems apparent that many of the factors that facilitated religion's role are similar. In both cases a revealed, ethical type of religion was preached by a charismatic leader at a cultural crossroads. In both cases the leader claimed to be directly commissioned by a transcendent deity. In both cases there was a clear challenge to an established order, and in both cases this challenge was made at a time of societal crisis when new communications were facilitating the introduction of new artifacts and new ideas and when old solutions to social problems were felt to be increasingly inadequate. Furthermore, in both cases the challenge was taken up by new urban classes who felt themselves to have been denied their rightful power and status by the contemporary establishment.

In the early development of capitalistic society, however, the impact of religion would appear to have been less potent. Calvin was not an ethical prophet of the same dimension as Mohammed. The secular institutions that Calvin challenged were more firmly rooted, more fully united, and more efficient than those on which Mohammed successfully placed a religious stamp. Finally, the existing religious institutions in the seventeenth century were more fully unified and better organized and were thus able to revitalize themselves to a considerable extent and thus to set limits to the changes that the new religious-political groups were able to effect. The stand taken by the Catholic Church at the Council of Trent, the so-called Counter Reformation movement, and the bloody religious wars served to limit the extent of the changes that radical Protestantism had helped to set in motion.

some contemporary "practical" individuals who sanctify their devotion to work by reference to their notion of Weber's Protestant Ethic.

RELIGION AS A BARRIER TO
SOCIAL CHANGE

In the preceding pages we considered the role of religion in helping to change established social orders. We will now discuss briefly some of the circumstances that favor the function of religion as a barrier to social change.

Sociologists have been more interested in the dynamics of prophetic movements than in the mechanics of the stabilizing process. No sociologist of the stature of Weber has concentrated on the analysis of the conditions under which religion functions to block change. Durkheim, who viewed society as imbued with a sacred quality, drew attention to religion's conservatism. For men do not lightly change that which they hold in awe. Anthropologists such as Malinowski, who have studied religion's role in societies of the Model One type, have emphasized the prevalence of magic in such societies.[21] Since magic is likely to be highly traditional in its emphasis, as Weber also noted, magical religions are presumably inimical to societal change. But even in Model One societies, where religion is most likely to be interwoven with magic, changes do in fact occur.

Of more interest to sociologists, it appears, is the fact that religion can be a strong barrier to change in Model Two societies. What, then, are the characteristics of religion that, in combination with certain societal conditions to be considered shortly, are most likely to maximize religion's power to obstruct change?

First of all, a given religion would appear to be especially powerful in discouraging change after the prophetic charisma has been routinized for a considerable time. Apart from sporadic outbreaks of "prophecy," the capacity of the various modes of religious expression, whether of symbolic ritual or sacred scripture, to evoke a sense of the sacred depends largely on the worshipers' respect for the continuity and antiquity of the beliefs and practices in question. Since the alleged antiquity of a religious tradition commonly increases man's sense of its sacredness, the length of time that a religion has been "established" generally (although not always) increases its change-obstructing potential.

[In the second place, a religion that has developed a strong and largely autonomous organization, with a centralized priestly hierarchy, frequently acts as a barrier to societal change.] [If, in the third place, this priestly hierarchy can tighten its hold on a largely illiterate populace because its members alone can mediate to the faithful the sacramental means of grace (which most persons are likely to view in magical terms), the difficulty of effecting social changes is magnified still further, for most members of the priesthood will be unwilling to acquiesce in any changes that threaten their power over the mass of the people.] [Fourth, if the priestly establishment has come into the possession of large accumulations of wealth and landed property, an already powerful establishment has yet another potent incentive to protect its vested interests by opposition to any changes in the status quo.]

The general characteristics of religion just described are commonly tied in with certain definable aspects of the social structure in those cases in which an established religion has formed a strong barrier to social change. When the membership of a particular religious body comes to include all, or nearly all, the members of its environing society, it is almost inevitable that the religious interpretation of the social order will also include a legitimation of the entire power structure of that society. This situation, however, is likely to occur only after many years of reciprocal interaction between the religious institutions and the other institutions of the society in question; that is, as noted earlier, only after an initial prophetic charisma has been thoroughly routinized. [Therefore an important factor enhancing religion's potential to block change is likely to be an alliance between an established religion and an established government in circumstances when both stand to gain by maintaining the status quo.[22] [This situation is particularly likely to obtain in the case of autocratic governments that possess a monopoly, or near-monopoly, of military power, as in some Latin American countries. It may also exist, however, in the case of a rigidly traditional bureaucracy, such as that of ancient China. [Religion's power to block change is still further augmented when the presence of an ignorant peasantry makes it relatively easy for both secular and ecclesiastical landowners to cooperate to keep a reactionary government in power for their mutual benefit.] Not only do ignorant and pauperized peasants furnish cheap labor, but, partly because of their inclination to believe in magic and to fear it, they are also likely to acquiesce readily to a dominant priesthood and its demands for fees for the performance of sacramental rites.

Usually absent in situations favorable to the power of religion to obstruct change, be it noted, are those conditions previously mentioned that favor religion's influence over the course of change—namely, a crisis situation triggered by accelerated urbanization, developing commerce, and proliferating communications leading to the emergence of an organized and rationally oriented middle class.

No attempt will be made here to discuss in detail any particular cases in which religion has obstructed social change. Numerous examples of the alliance between religion and reaction will doubtless occur to the reader. It is often observed that as secular governments have gained power, they have not only used religion to legitimate that power but have also used religious institutions and religious personnel to carry out their secular purposes. This is one reason why Voltaire so bitterly attacked the part played by the Catholic Church in prerevolutionary France. And in prerevolutionary Russia as well as in contemporary Spain and parts of Latin America, examples may be cited of a similar alliance between religion and reaction.

While religion can be a potent force for delaying change, it does not, in the long run, prevent change, even though it has often been used in attempts to do so. Sometimes, indeed, the delaying force of religion may help to make periods of transition less sudden, violent, and radical, as pointed out in Chapter 3. On the other hand, however, stubborn attempts by rigid and uncompromising religious establishments to block changes promoted by powerful elements within the society may eventually precipitate drastic and revolutionary changes accompanied by violence.[23]

An example of this situation is the intransigence of Czarist Russia and the extreme violence of the revolution of 1917, in which both the Czar's regime and the Russian Orthodox Church were overthrown and atheism was officially promoted. If the pressures toward change are not sufficiently powerful, however, the religious sanctions for the existing order (along with the other sanctions available) may be sufficient to prevent change for long periods.

Max Weber has analyzed some of the ways in which traditional religious values prevented the emergence of a "modern" economic order in the ancient civilizations of India and China.[24] In China, indeed, the Confucian tradition exerted for centuries such a stabilizing influence that few people were prepared for the violence of the contemporary revolution in that society.

The Moslem rulers of the modern world's Islamic countries have been able to control change and to bolster their own authority in part by appeals to religious symbols, but it is doubtful that they will be able to do so much longer. Rumblings of discontent in the Islamic world are increasing, and the attempts to block change may only contribute eventually to an even greater explosion of extremism and violence.

In large part because of the modern revolution in communications, situations in which all of these change-inhibiting factors may be found interacting together are rapidly decreasing. Even in Latin America, where ecclesiastically supported military dictatorships persist, and where the great majority of the inhabitants are illiterate peasants, the winds of change are blowing. Particularly in the new urban centers the status quo is being challenged, and noninstitutionalized religious enthusiasm is sometimes allied with the forces of political revolution.[25]

SOCIETAL CHANGE AS A MAJOR
FORCE IN RELIGIOUS CHANGE

We know that religions *do* change. No clearer indication of the interdependence of religion with society can be found than the changes that religions undergo when their social settings change.[26] Religions are not totally malleable, particularly if they possess written records, even when they receive the strong impress of a culture alien to that in which they originated. In this section, however, we shall point up situational factors that favor the maximal influence of society and culture on imported religious belief, ritual, and organization.

Classic examples of the influence on religions of different social settings may be seen in the changes that have occurred in the world's great founded religions—Buddhism, Christianity, and Islam—as they have spread from one cultural milieu to another. An almost equally impressive but more limited and nearly contemporary example may be found in the changes undergone by the beliefs and practices of Christian and Jewish religious bodies as a consequence of their transplantation from European to American soil. The following discussion considers the cases of Buddhism in Asia and Protestantism in the United States.

Case One: Transplanted Buddhism

James Bissett Pratt's *Pilgrimage of Buddhism* provides a fascinating account of ways in which ancient, "original" Buddhism became modified as it traveled in three directions from its point of origin in northern India in the sixth century before Christ. From there it journeyed southward to Ceylon and on to Southeast Asia, northward to the Tibetan Plateau, and eastward across the vast plains of Central Asia to China and Japan.[27] In the course of these journeyings of many centuries the religion preached by Gautama the Buddha underwent some rather surprising changes.

We have selected for analysis an example of a dramatic contrast in Buddhist beliefs and practices taken from the contemporary scene, namely, the contrast between the Amida Buddhism of Japan and the Theravada Buddhism of Ceylon.* Theravada Buddhism is derived from the Pali Scriptures, recorded in writing by monks in Ceylon at the beginning of the Christian era and believed by the Sinhalese (and also by many Buddhist scholars) to contain the earliest version of the Buddha's teachings.[28] Amida Buddhism, on the other hand, is one of the many sects of "Pure Land" Buddhism that were the result of a series of developments stemming from Mahayana Buddhism after it had migrated from India to China and later to Japan.[29] The contrast between the Theravada Buddhism of Ceylon and the Amida Buddhism of Japan is so sharp that Americans who visit Japan after staying in Ceylon or any one of the other Theravada Buddhist countries, such as Thailand or Burma, might find it hard to believe that some of the many forms of Buddhism practiced in Japan are, in fact, really manifestations of a common Buddhist faith. Yet eminent Buddhist scholars have claimed that underlying the easily observable differences there is in fact a basic unity, a kinship of religious spirit that is perhaps easier to feel than to describe.[30] If, then, we accept the thesis that Buddhism is one faith, we are faced with the problem of explaining how certain of these observable differences came about.

These differences are indeed outstanding and include modifications in belief and ritual systems as well as in organizational patterns. As to belief systems, Theravada Buddhism of Ceylon, following the Pali Scriptures, regards the Buddha as neither God nor Savior, but rather as a *Wayshower*, pointing to a Path that He himself had taken but encouraging others to follow it by their own efforts. Japanese Amida Buddhism, and Pure Land Buddhism in general, is less concerned with the historical Buddha than with transcendental Buddhas such as Amida, who is looked

---

* Theravada Buddhism is the most acceptable name for the Buddhism of Ceylon and Southeast Asia. The term means *The Way of the Elders* and is preferred by Theravadins to the term "Hinayana," meaning *Little Vehicle*, a name given by the Mahayana Buddhists. "Mahayana" means *Great Vehicle*.

upon as preeminently a Savior, by means of Whom devout individuals can attain salvation by grace, faith, and the repetition of Amida's sacred Name. The way in which these two branches of Buddhism conceptualize "salvation" also differs markedly. In Ceylon Buddhism, Nirvana, the equivalent of salvation for the Theravada school, is thought of as a psychological and spiritual state of consciousness, indescribable to be sure, but not as a heavenly place. Amida Buddhists, in contrast, are prone to picture salvation as the gaining of entrance into the "Pure Land" of the Western Paradise, a heaven of pure delights and the abode of thousands of benevolent transcendental beings.*

The ritual observances of Theravada Buddhism of Ceylon and Amida Buddhism similarly are far apart. Strictly speaking, Theravada Buddhism has little in the way of ritual. Even though the Buddhism of the Ceylonese includes many colorful ceremonies,[31] such ceremonies are traditional rather than scriptural.** The rituals derived from Early Buddhism, the only ones that are considered essential, mainly concern practices of the Buddhist Order, such as ceremonies for admission to the novitiate and for the higher ordination. These ceremonies are simple. The worship of Amida Buddhism, on the other hand, is much richer in ritual, and its ceremonies are accompanied by bell-ringing, gong-sounding, and chanting in front of lavishly decorated altars.[32]

----

* Members of modern Pure Land sects, however, do not invariably interpret the meaning of the "Pure Land" in a literal-minded way. The "Pure Land" can be understood as something in the heart of man, and the Western Paradise as a spiritual condition and not merely as a place. By such interpretations the distinction between Early Buddhism and the modern Pure Land sects becomes much less sharp.

** In Theravada Buddhist countries today, that is, in Ceylon, Burma, Thailand, Cambodia, and Laos, the visitor will see numerous colorful religious ceremonies, public processions, and the like. According to official explanation, such ceremonies are not mandatory for a practicing Buddhist but are found helpful and enjoyable by the mass of the people. For the uninitiated foreign observer the distinction is sometimes hard to grasp, and Buddhist observance might well be the poorer without these "popular" ceremonies. Among Theravada countries Thailand has the most highly developed ritual.

In the transformation of Buddhism during its long pilgrimage, changes in environment have played a major role. Nevertheless, the influence of changed environments does not, by itself, furnish the sole explanation of the changes in Buddhism described above. Certain characteristics of Buddhism itself have facilitated the influence of new environments upon it, including internal developments of a philosophical nature. Buddhism began to be transformed even in India, where it had originated. Less than three centuries after the death of the Buddha, the subtle minds of Indian philosophers and metaphysicians began to modify the austere ethical and philosophical doctrine He had bequeathed to his followers, thus laying the foundations of Mahayana Buddhism.[33] This Buddhism of the Great Vehicle, the form in which Buddhism traveled across Central Asia to China and Japan, had already in India begun to look to the Buddha as a Savior and to emphasize His grace and compassion, made freely available not only to monks but also to ordinary folk.

From its beginnings in India, Mahayana Buddhism was a religious tradition with a tendency to innovative speculation. Furthermore, inasmuch as Buddhism was founded by an exemplary prophet, a Wayshower rather than by an ethical (or emissary) prophet such as Moses or Mohammed, Buddhism has tended to be nonauthoritarian, nonexclusive, and markedly tolerant. For these reasons Buddhism may well have been more susceptible to influences from the outside and more willing than a less tolerant religion to coexist, and even to blend with, the religions already existing in the areas to which it spread. This last explanation must not be pressed too far, however, for Christianity and Islam, religions founded by ethical prophets, have also changed (although probably less so than Buddhism) as they spread from one sociocultural setting to another.

What, then, were the main environmental factors that facilitated the transformation of Buddhism in Japan? Anthropologists have identified some of the general considerations that must be reckoned with in all cases of cultural borrowing, including the assimilation of borrowed cultural elements. The assimilation of an imported religion by a host culture presents a complex instance of cultural borrowing of this kind. [In the first place, the prior existence of a strong indigenous religious culture is rather generally believed to increase resistance to the influence of the imported religion and to increase the possibility of a partial absorption of a new religion by an old faith—especially if an ancient faith has been strongly identified with national history and patriotism.] Shinto, the indigenous faith of Japan was (and still is) a hardy religious tradition with a strong patriotic emphasis. It was not, however, strong enough to exclude Buddhism, at least partly because the belief of the Japanese people in the *kami,* godlike beings capable of bestowing benefits and misfortunes on human beings, can be rather readily accommodated to the Mahayana form of Buddhism, which stresses the beneficent activity of numerous heavenly beings, such as the Bodhisattvas, and preaches salvation through faith in heavenly grace.[34]

[A second factor to consider is the strength and prestige of the carriers of a new religion relative to the strength of the forces supporting an indigenous religious establishment.] In Japan the monarchy was intimately bound up with the indigenous religion, Shinto. Japanese monarchs were thought to be sacred, since they were mythically descended from the Sun-God, from whose godlike progeny the Japanese islands were believed to have magically sprung. It was the obligation of the monarch to uphold the worship of the *kami,* the local spirit-deities; to give hospitality to a new imported religion at the risk of offending them would be judged highly dangerous.[35] Consequently, even though some of the early Buddhist missionaries were emissaries of neighboring monarchs who addressed themselves directly to the Japanese royal house, they at first received a very uncertain reception from both kings and courtiers. For a considerable time Buddhism in Japan experienced fluctuating fortunes depending largely on its rise and fall in royal favor.[36] The situation was one in which the emissaries of the new faith were both foreign and few, and the indigenous religion firmly entrenched and royally sanctioned. Hence the acceptance of Buddhism was a gradual affair in which

RELIGION: A SOCIOLOGICAL VIEW

the imported religion had to come to terms with both Shinto *
and Confucianism.[37]

[In the third place, the particular religious needs of the different social classes in the receiving culture, and the extent to which they are able to modify an imported religion by molding it to meet these needs, must also be taken into consideration.] In Japan's dark ages, from about the seventh century to the turn of the millennium, Buddhism as well as Shinto fulfilled purposes that were mainly magical. The twelfth and thirteenth centuries, however, witnessed a turning point in Japanese religion. By then feudalism was thoroughly established, and almost all of the various sects of Buddhism that had developed in China and Korea had found a home in Japan. Some of these sects, such as Zen, the disciplined religion of an elite, made its chief appeal to members of the Japanese nobility. The practices of Zen and the code of chivalry of the feudal nobility therefore became closely interwoven, as D. T. Suzuki has shown in illuminating fashion in his *Zen and Japanese Culture*.[38] The Jodo, or Pure Land sects, on the other hand, made their chief appeal to people of lower status. The Japanese peasants were the main sufferers in the almost constant warfare waged by the feudal nobility. In the thirteenth century the great Japanese teacher Shinran, the founder of Shin Buddhism and the originator of the cult of the Amida Buddha by the Pure Land sects (which include Shin Buddhism), addressed his preaching to the religious needs of the masses. Shinran knew that it was hard to strive for spiritual perfection on an empty stomach or to contemplate the infinite when one's mind was preoccupied with the unremitting worries and labors of a poor man's life. But faith in Amida Buddha and the repetition of His Name was within the power of the poorest and most ignorant.[39] In succeeding centuries the Pure Land sects were to become the most popular form of Buddhism in Japan, in very large part because they spoke to the condition of the great majority of Japanese people.

---

* Buddhism was at first a court-sponsored religion with its focus in Nara. It only gradually came to terms with Shinto, the popular religion of the masses.

The impact of Japanese culture on Buddhism might have been much weaker had the imported faith swept into the islands on a wave of conquest followed by a colonial occupation, or had Buddhism itself been a less malleable religion. As things were, the very gradualness of the Buddhist infiltration and the variety of forms in which it came, coupled with the strength and nationalistic character of the Shinto establishment, made for a very strong impress of the indigenous culture on the imported faith.

At the risk of much oversimplification we chose to describe changes that have occurred in Buddhism as it traveled from one social setting to another. We could equally well have discussed the factors underlying changes that have occurred in other great traveling religions—in Islam or in Christianity. For Westerners, however, it is probably easier to be objective in recognizing major changes that have taken place in a religious tradition far removed from our own. The spread of Christianity throughout the world, like the spread of Buddhism, has been far-reaching, and the changes that it has undergone considerable. Many Christian biblical scholars would, in fact, agree that their religion *has* been influenced by social changes and changes in milieu, although most of them would probably deny that such changes have affected the essentials of the faith.[40]

The long history of the Roman Catholic Church provides remarkable instances of adaptation to changing circumstances. Its motto, *semper idem* (that is, always the same), holds only in a stable society. For it has been "always the same"—with numerous important exceptions. For example, the Church dropped its defense of medieval cosmology after decades of opposition to astronomers; it reversed its opposition to trade unions in environments where Catholic workers were finding unions useful. More recently Pope John XXIII, in his encyclical advocating *aggiornamento,* gave recognition to the fact that the updating of some former practices and attitudes is essential if the Church is to retain large sections of its membership.

It is far from our intention to deplore all changes in religion in response to changes in social milieus, in Buddhism, in Christianity, or in any other religion. The changes in the Roman Catholic Church cited above (which do not, to be sure, affect the centrality of the Christian faith), it may be argued, illustrate how wisely, if sometimes tardily, it has adapted itself in some respects in order to be more effective in a changing world.

Case Two: Modifications of Protestantism on the American Scene

We now turn much nearer home for an example of the modification of religion by reason of environmental change. The New World, as is well known, was a haven for many Protestant groups who were persecuted in Europe. Their encounter with the American environment, and particularly with the frontier, was accompanied by changes in their doctrines, liturgies, and modes of organization. The story of these changes has often been told,[41] and we shall touch on them but briefly here.

One of the most interesting doctrinal changes was the abandonment, or at least the substantial modification, by Calvinist churches and sects, particularly by the frontier Baptists, of hard-shell doctrines of predestination. The frontier experience brought home to most men and women the importance of individual effort, and the notion of an inevitable divine decree determining in advance those destined either for eternal bliss or infernal torment seemed clearly "undemocratic." Preachers like Methodist ministers, who emphasized God's *free grace,* had an advantage on the frontier over Presbyterians and other sects who believed in predestination. Hence occurred the softening of hard-shell predestination doctrines by many of these frontier sects.[42]

In ritual and liturgy there was a tendency for European formality to give place to American informality. The American Methodists, for instance, resolutely forbore to use the Methodist Prayer Book that Wesley's missionaries, Asbury and Coke, urged the American Methodists to adopt. The loneliness, the emotional and aesthetic deprivations of pioneer life, favored the spontaneous expression of heartfelt religious feeling and engendered a distaste for formal liturgies. Hence American Protestant groups, more than most European Protestant bodies, were cool to formal ritual and welcomed the rowdy informality of revivalism and camp meetings with their stress on the emotional experience of conversion.

Changes in organization tended toward a greater degree of lay participation and control. To be sure, Protestant groups who in Europe had resisted the autocratic control of the political state were often themselves equally autocratic in their ecclesiastical control of their own lay members. Such ecclesiastical control, even approaching tyranny, was a well-known characteristic of the New England Protestant churches of early colonial times. After 1789, however, in the religious free-for-all that developed in the United States, the clerical monopoly of power was largely broken and American Protestant groups, especially those outside New England and on the advancing frontier, became increasingly subject to lay control. By degrees the various Protestant organizations began to take on some of the characteristics of the American political government. Even the Episcopalian and the Lutheran churches, which in Europe had been "established" (that is, state-supported and -controlled), began to develop more democratic forms of church government. In the absence of the endowments they had enjoyed in Europe, the churches were forced to rely on their own members for financial support. Not surprisingly, there was an increasing demand on the part of those who paid the piper to call the tune.

European churches brought later to America by successive groups of immigrants had to come to terms with the American religious establishment as it had been set up by the earlier Protestant settlers. In every case some accommodations were made to this dominant Protestantism.

The adaptations that took place within the Roman Catholic Church, particularly in organization, are especially impressive. At an early date in the Church's American history, a disposition to seek increased lay control in "secular" and financial affairs was evident. Before the middle of the nineteenth century an American "nativist" Catholic movement, known as the Trusteeship movement, became so strong that, had it succeeded, it might have resulted in the creation of an autonomous American Catholic Church, independent of Rome.[43]   Largely through the Irish, who rallied to the support of the Roman hierarchy, the Trusteeship movement failed, and the Catholic Church in America became a bulwark of Papal power.   Meanwhile, the Americanized Irish obtained control of its hierarchy and proceeded to put their own unmistakable stamp on the church's organization and also on its cultural and intellectual atmosphere.[44]

Groups of Catholics who arrived later, whether Italian, Polish, French Canadian, or Puerto Rican, were forced to accommodate themselves, in some measure, to this Irish-American pattern.   In this way, although the Trusteeship movement was unsuccessful, over the years American environmental influences transformed and subtly "de-Romanized" the customs, attitudes, opinions, and behavior of Catholics both inside and outside the walls of their churches.   Thus in 1966 it was possible for a Roman Catholic priest and a lay journalist, both trained in sociology, to collaborate on a book published under the provocative title *The De-Romanization of the American Catholic Church.*[45]

A similar process of acculturation also resulted in some changes in Judaism in America.   The development of Conservative Judaism in particular was a response of Americanized Jews to conditions they encountered in the American environment as well as to their own economic advancement.[46]

In spite of vast differences in time and place, the changes undergone by European religions transplanted to American soil involved factors similar to those involved in the transformation of Buddhism in Japan after its arrival from India. In the American case, to be sure, the changes in the imported religions were less dramatic, and the contrast between the exporting and importing cultures less marked.   But once the Protestant churches, and the Protestant culture that went along with them, were firmly established in the United States, most of the members of these churches came to consider that they represented the national religious culture.   The adherents of the religious groups that came over in the nineteenth and twentieth centuries were therefore regarded as members of religious and cultural minorities by the "original" Protestants. Furthermore, for many persons, to be Protestant was to be "American," while to be Catholic was to be "foreign"—and possibly disloyal as well.[47] The minority status of the members of these later immigrant churches and the imputation of "foreignness" by the dominant Protestants constituted powerful pressures toward a degree of conformity in organizational forms and practices, although not always in belief, with the American Protestant establishment.

CONCLUSION

Our main concern in this chapter has been to consider types of situation in which religion has shown a potential to be an active agent of social change, or to block it. We have also considered situations in which religion is more likely to be in the position of reacting to changes in other social institutions rather than that of itself stimulating or blocking changes. We have, however, had little to say about religion and social change in modern industrial societies, that is, those of the Model Three type. Nor do we propose to discuss the topic in detail at this point. The examples of change discussed above have been deliberately drawn from past history, for it is much easier to "observe" the interplay of religious and societal factors in the context of past situations, especially with the inestimable benefit of hindsight.

But are not our Model Three industrial societies undergoing a prolonged crisis, and, in the light of our earlier analysis, should not they too be potentially susceptible to the influence of active religious forces? This is a hard question to answer, for it is an extremely difficult matter to disentangle the respective roles played by religious and other cultural factors in a complex, kaleidoscopic, contemporary situation in which we are personally involved. However, we believe that it is unlikely, even in times of crisis, that religious forces will influence the course of social change in the modern world to the extent they did in earlier times. Members of modern societies are more likely to look to secular solutions, especially to science, for answers to their problems.

We are helped in our understanding of how religious and societal factors influence one another in Model Three societies if we are clearly aware that a given set of factors may act in different ways at the same time in different sectors of the same national society. For instance, religion may act as an agent of change in one situation and as a barrier to change in another; or as an active force in one set of circumstances but as a mainly reactive one in another. The segment of the society being analyzed, then, is a crucial consideration.

The diminished potential of religion as an active force for change in Model Three societies (as compared to Model One or even Model Two societies) has coincided with the enormously increased power of the secular institutions in these Model Three societies. The strength of the latter's governmental, economic, and scientific institutions contrasts strongly with the relative weakness of institutions concerned with the religious life. In Model Three societies, religion has, on the whole, tended to reflect societal changes to a greater degree than it has impressed its own image upon them.[48]

Nevertheless, this does not appear to be the entire story. Religion has retained a considerable potential to block societal change. Particular religious institutions, such as the Roman Catholic Church, have retained this power to a considerable degree, although by no means to an unlimited extent. For example, Pope Paul VI's encyclical forbidding the use of all "artificial" methods of birth control constitutes an important attempt to erect a barrier to changes in family mores. It will undoubtedly influence a certain number of devout Catholics. The Papal encyclical may indeed retard social change, but it is very unlikely that the Pope's prohibition will slow it significantly. In the long run, even for most Catholics, considerations of education and economics, and of sexual love uninhibited by fear of pregnancy, rather than conviction of religious duty, are likely to be the decisive factors determining the use or nonuse of contraceptive devices.[49]

Furthermore, strict adherence to orthodox Christian doctrine may also serve as a barrier to social change. Not only does orthodoxy, by its very nature, serve to maintain religious beliefs unchanged, but there is some evidence that seems to indicate that the more "doctrinally orthodox" members of Christian churches are more likely than others to be politically and economically conservative.[50] Hence the holding of certain orthodox beliefs may indirectly act as a barrier to societal change.

Insofar as they reflect societal change, and on occasion block it, religious forces in Model Three societies appear to be playing a rather passive, negative role. However, it is at least doubtful whether, even in such societies, the innovating potential of religion has been eliminated completely. In our opinion religion still can play an active part in bringing about change within a limited social context. Especially among deprived and alienated groups, strongly held religious beliefs still retain the potential to spark new movements. And, as a matter of record, new religiously inspired movements continue to arise. To be sure, the initial religious impulse that was important in the instigation of such movements often becomes later overlaid with secular objectives and incentives. The latter may be economic or political or concerned with racial and social status. Yet, without the initial religious incentive these movements might never have gotten off the ground. Such movements as the Black Muslims in the United States and the Sōka Gakkai in postwar Japan afford examples of movements, religiously propelled in the first instance, that have had a strong impact on the social and economic behavior of their members and also considerable indirect influence on the larger societies of which they form a part.

REFERENCES

1. J. Milton Yinger, *Religion, Society, and the Individual* (New York: Macmillan, 1957), pp. 265–312. Yinger's insights into the problems of religion and social change are well worth reading.
2. Max Weber, *The Sociology of Religion,* trans. Ephraim Fischoff (Boston: Beacon Press, 1963), especially pp. 35–36.

3. *Ibid.*, p. 51.
4. Talcott Parsons, "Introduction," in *ibid.*, pp. xxxiii–xxxv.
5. Weber, *op. cit.*, pp. 55–56.
6. *Ibid.*, pp. 60–61.
7. Yinger, *op. cit.*, p. 304.
8. Weber, *op. cit.*, Chapter 6. See also Parsons, *op. cit.*, pp. xxxviii–xlii.
9. Weber, *op. cit.*, pp. 96–97.
10. *Ibid.*, p. 55.
11. Wilfred Cantwell Smith, *Islam in Modern History* (New York: New American Library, Mentor Book, 1957), pp. 26–27. Smith points out the paramount position of the community in Islam but insists that this community is based on, and is integral to, *individual* faith.
12. John Noss, *Man's Religions*, 2nd ed. (New York: Macmillan, 1956). See pp. 687–690 for a consideration of Mecca as a religious and commercial crossroads. Chapter 16, in its entirety, gives a brief but useful account of the rule of Mohammed and the spread of Islam.
13. William Montgomery Watt, *Islam and the Integration of Society* (Evanston, Illl.: Northwestern University Press, 1961). This work is a useful analysis of the impact of Islam on Arab society.
14. Weber, *op. cit.*, pp. 60–61. In Weber's view the relatively brief preroutinization period is the time most favorable for effecting changes; hence the importance of the rapidity of the spread of Islam.
15. Max Weber, *From Max Weber: Essays in Sociology*, trans. and ed. Hans H. Gerth and C. Wright Mills (New York: Oxford University Press, Galaxy Book, 1958), pp. 62–63.
16. Max Weber, *The Protestant Ethic and the Spirit of Capitalism*, trans. Talcott Parsons (New York: Scribner, The Scribner Library, 1958), p. 17.

> The impulse to acquisition, pursuit of gain, of money, of the greatest possible amount of money, has in itself nothing to do with capitalism. . . . It should be taught in the kindergarten of cultural history that this naive idea of capitalism must be given up once and for all. . . . But capitalism is identical with the pursuit of profit, by means of continuous, rational, capitalistic enterprise. . . .

17. *Ibid.*, Chapter 5, pp. 156–164.
18. *Ibid.*, pp. 121–122.
19. *Ibid.*, pp. 175–180.
20. Lujo Brentano, *Die Anfänge des Modernes Kapitalismus* (Munich: Academie der Wissenschaften, 1916); Werner Sombart, *The Jews*

and Modern Capitalism, trans. M. Epstein (London: Unwin, 1913) ; and Kurt Samuelsson, *Religion and Economic Action: A Critique of Max Weber* (New York: Harper & Row, Harper Torchbook, 1964). See also R. H. Tawney, *Religion and the Rise of Capitalism* (New York: Harcourt, Brace, and Co., 1936). See also Tawney, "Foreword," in Weber, *Protestant Ethic, op. cit.,* pp. 1–11.

21. Bronislaw Malinowski, *Magic, Science and Religion* (Garden City, N.Y.: Doubleday, Anchor Book, 1948), p. 90. "Magic fixes on . . . beliefs and rudimentary rules and standardizes them into permanent traditional forms."

22. Weber, *Sociology of Religion, op. cit.,* pp. 60, 67–169. Chapter 6, in its entirety, contains many examples and insights relevant to the process whereby a religious tradition is reinforced by alliances with secular castes, classes, and institutions.

23. Yinger, *op. cit.,* pp. 30–31.

24. Weber, *The Religion of China: Confucianism and Taoism,* trans. and ed. Hans H. Gerth (Glencoe, Ill.: Free Press, 1951). See especially Chapter 5, "The Literati"; pp. 416–444.

25. Gonzalo Castillo-Cardenas, "Christians and the Struggle for a New Social Order in Latin America," Donald R. Cutler (ed.), in *The Religious Situation: 1968* (Boston: Beacon Press, 1968), pp. 498–518.

26. Yinger, *op. cit.,* pp. 266–272.

27. James Bissett Pratt, *The Pilgrimage of Buddhism and a Buddhist Pilgrimage* (New York: Macmillan, 1928). Also, Bhikkhu J. Kashyap, "Origin and Expansion of Buddhism," in Kenneth W. Morgan (ed.), *The Path of the Buddha* (New York: Ronald Press, 1956), pp. 3–66.

28. Walpola Rahula, *History of Buddhism in Ceylon* (Colombo, Ceylon: M. D. Gunasena, 1956), pp. 48–61, and also Ananda Maitreya, "Buddhism in Theravada Countries," in Morgan, *op. cit.,* pp. 113–124.

29. Mitsuyuki Ishida, "Shin and Jodo Buddhism," in Morgan, *op. cit.,* pp. 331–339.

30. Hajime Nakamura, "Unity and Diversity in Buddhism," in Morgan, *op. cit.,* pp. 364–400.

31. Rahula, *op. cit.,* "Ceremonies and Festivals," pp. 266–286. See especially pp. 266–267.

Although rituals, ceremonies and festivals were not in keeping with the spirit of Buddhism, they were natural and inevitable developments, bound to come when the teaching of the Buddha became a popular state religion. . . . Almost all public activities were connected with religion. . . . Religious festivals provided both entertainment and satisfaction of religious sentiment.

32. Ishida, *op. cit.*, pp. 338–339.
33. Susumi Yamaguchi, "Development of Mahayama Buddhist Beliefs," in Morgan, *op. cit.*, pp. 153–181.
34. Shinso Hanayama, "Buddhism in Japan," in Morgan, *op. cit.*, pp. 307–331. Bishop Hanayama makes the point that Buddhism in its Mahayama form was accepted in Japan in 594, at a time when the indigenous Shinto religion was "still in a primitive stage and was undoubtedly far below the cultural level of Buddhism as it had developed in all the countries of Asia" (p. 308). Buddhism, however, "fitted in" the Japanese family system and the pattern of relationship between the people and the Imperial household. For example, in Japan, Buddhist temples have "as a matter of course served the primary function of having memorial services for their followers and keeping custody of their family graves" (p. 310).
35. *Ibid.*, p. 308.
36. *Ibid.*, p. 309. The much-respected Prince Shotoku is credited with the establishment, by royal ordinance, of Buddhism in Japan in 594.
37. *Ibid.*, pp. 323–342. The Heian Era (794–1184) saw the beginning of a conciliation between Buddhism and Shinto. For instance, the ancient Japanese gods (Kami) were identified as Bodhisattvas.
38. D. T. Suzuki, *Zen and Japanese Culture* (New York: Pantheon, 1959).
39. Ishida, *op. cit.*, p. 339. "All Pure Realm [Land] sects arose among the masses."
40. Yinger, *op. cit.*, p. 266.
41. For example, see Willard L. Sperry, *Religion in America* (Boston: Beacon Press, Beacon Paperback, 1963; first published in 1945).
42. Elizabeth K. Nottingham, *Methodism and the Frontier* (New York: Columbia University Press, 1941).
43. John Tracy Ellis, S.J., *American Catholicism*, ed. Daniel J. Boorstin (Chicago: University of Chicago Press, 1956), pp. 44–46.
44. Sperry, *op. cit.* p. 207. Sperry calls the Trusteeship conflict "the most serious crisis in the whole history of American Catholicism" for it was in effect "an attempt to set up an independent Catholic Church in America, free of all reference to Rome."
45. Edward Wakin and Father Joseph F. Scheuer, *The De-Romanization of the American Catholic Church* (New York: Macmillan, 1966).
46. Marshall Sklare, *Conservative Judaism: An American Religious Movement* (Glencoe, Ill.: Free Press, 1955).

47. Will Herberg, *Protestant, Catholic, Jew* (Garden City, N.Y.: Doubleday, Anchor Book, 1960), pp. 140–142.

48. J. Milton Yinger, *Sociology Looks at Religion* (New York: Macmillan, Macmillan Paperback, 1966), pp. 65–74. Yinger questions the validity of opposing the concept of "secularization" to that of "religion." He argues that much of what has been termed by some sociologists as "secularization" is in reality *religious change*. (See page 71.)

> What Berger, Herberg, and others are saying is that the church has too little relevance for the "prophetic task" of reforming the world. . . . Such a view ought not to be used, however, to obscure our analysis of the fact that the churches of those who are comfortable in a society are almost always well accommodated to that society. This is not secularization. It is instead one of the most persistent functions of religion—whether we applaud or lament the fact.

49. Charles F. Westoff, Robert G. Potter Jr., and Philip C. Sagi, *The Third Child* (Princeton, N.J.: Princeton University Press, 1963). Although the contraceptive practices of Catholics are being modified by various factors, Westoff *et al.* found that nevertheless "religion is the dominant factor determining contraceptive behavior . . . [and] number of pregnancies" (p. 195).

50. See Jeffrey K. Hadden, *The Gathering Storm in the Churches* (Garden City, N.Y.: Doubleday, Anchor Book, 1970). Hadden finds (p. 110) that "for clergy, rejection of orthodoxy is strongly associated with more liberal social and political ideologies. While the data for laity are not as adequate as for clergy, the evidence would seem to indicate that this relationship does not hold for laity." See also Rodney Stark and Charles Y. Glock, *American Piety: The Nature of a Religious Commitment* (Berkeley; University of California Press, 1968), chap. 11, p. 214, table 69.

7 Religion and Revolution in the Non-Western World

INTRODUCTION

Religion and revolution are strangely and intricately interwoven in the non-Western world. In those Model One societies where tribalism still persists, prophetic religions of liberation have flamed across the world from the peyote cult of the American Indian to the Mau Mau of the Kikiyu. In more sophisticated Model Two societies, in India and throughout Southeast Asia, where ancient religions are preserved in written scriptures, these traditional religions are being reasserted and reinterpreted. Thus reasserted, they have frequently become the vehicles of a resurgent national spirit. In other segments of such Model Two societies (particularly among Western-educated persons in the universities and in the cities), however, the drive toward "modernization" has weakened the hold of traditional religions and introduced powerful secularizing influences. In some cases, notably in Mainland China, but also elsewhere, communism, which was earlier characterized as a secular religion, has moved in to fill the vacuum.

To discuss this worldwide socioreligious revolution within the limits of a single chapter necessitates an exceedingly brief and schematic approach. However, a modern sociology of religion that makes no effort to encompass religion's role in these massive socioreligious changes is shirking one of its major obligations.[1] The societal models used throughout this study offer one useful way of approaching the problem. Accordingly, this chapter will deal with some of these complex issues in terms of the enforced and massive confrontation of the Model One and Model Two societies of the non-Western world with the technologically developed Model Three societies of the West.

THE MODERN PHENOMENON OF MASSIVE SOCIETAL CONFRONTATION

We must understand that the large-scale enforced confrontation of societies of Model One and Model Two types by Model Three societies is something new in the history of the world.[2] Imperialism and colonialism are by no means new, but modern * colonialism differs from earlier colonialism both in intensity and pervasiveness. Ancient imperialists and colonialists did not possess the technical skills to transform military conquest into long-term, nearly total political, economic, and cultural domination. Nor, in the absence of the media of mass communication, were they able to exercise so potent a sway over the minds of men. Hence the *shock* that modern Western colonialism has caused to the peoples of the non-Western world today is greater by far than that which was the result of Greek or Roman colonialism in the ancient world. So great has been the impact of this kind of confrontation that the revolutionary character of the social and religious changes that have arisen as a consequence should occasion no surprise.

When Western peoples reflect on the advantages they enjoy in comparison with those living in less "developed" parts of the world, they are likely to stress their "higher" standard of living, greater wealth, and technological superiority. They may also congratulate themselves on their free and democratic forms of government. For good measure, they may include their participation in a "Christian" civilization and their greater freedom from religious superstition and terrorizing magic. In counting

---

* We use the term "modern" in a broad sense to denote all European colonialism from the sixteenth century on. However, most of our discussion deals with nineteenth- and twentieth-century colonialism.

their blessings, however, they are usually unaware of one stupendous piece of sheer luck; namely, that the European West had the chance to develop into a Model Three society with very little interference from the rest of the world. Precisely because it was the first society to develop modern technology (including, of course, modern weapons of war and modern methods of communication), it had the great benefit of some three hundred years free from massive interference from other societies. Europeans and Americans in those years had the opportunity to assimilate, more or less at their own rate, the changes—technological, political, and religious—that were taking place. Even so, as is well known, the emergence of a Model Three society in the West was accompanied by bitter revolutionary struggles throughout most of that three-hundred-year period.

In striking contrast, it has been the fate of the Model One and Model Two societies of the non-Western world to endure the confrontation (whether they liked it or not) with the militarily and technologically dominant nations of the West. And even today, when political colonialism is largely a thing of the past (although economic colonialism is still alive), the non-Western world is embarked, necessarily, on policies of modernization in order to survive. Hence non-Western societies are compelled to attempt to accomplish in decades a series of political, economic, and intellectual-religious adjustments that required centuries in the West. What wonder, then, that this stepped-up modernization has been revolutionary in its impact and that much of the non-Western world has been undergoing a process of "shock and renewal."

CHRISTIAN MISSIONS AND REVOLUTION

Christian missionaries from the West have played a role, although not of course an exclusive one, in furthering revolutionary tendencies in the non-Western world. These missionaries have come from various European countries and are representative of the different phases of the period of European colonial expansion. The policies of the first Catholic missionaries from Spain were by no means identical with those from the Baptist denominations of the American Middle West. Nevertheless there are a few generalizations that can be risked about the impact of all Christian missions on the non-Western world.

In the first place, the consequences of missionary activity have been both *intended* and *unintended* by the missionaries themselves. Indeed, it seems probable that the unintended effects of missionary work outweigh those that were intended.

It was the manifest aim of the missionaries that their preaching of the Christian Gospel should bring benefits to their hearers by pointing out to them the "true" road to salvation and replacing the "erroneous" teachings of the indigenous faiths.[3] They wished to bring the knowledge of the redeeming love and compassion of Christ to all and to demonstrate by their lives and teaching their belief in the equal value in the sight of God of every human soul. One measure of the success of these conscious intentions, although by no means the only one, was the number of "conversions" made.[4] By this measure the success of the Spanish missionaries to the New World was greater than those of almost any other country or period.

In the second place, it should be borne in mind that the Christian Gospel itself carries a "built-in" revolutionary dynamic, and if that Gospel were fully accepted, the Western world as well as the non-Western would undoubtedly have to undergo a radical revolution.* However, the conscious intentions of most Christian missionaries did not usually envisage in such radical terms the impact of their Christian teachings on native populations.

In the third place, most missionaries until quite recently have been little aware of the distinction between the essentially religious values of Christianity and the various social structures that had grown up in the West to embody those values. We

---

* Readers may recall the film *The Gospel According to St. Matthew,* a dramatic and beautiful portrayal of Christ as a compassionate leader of radical social reform. The director of the film, Pasolini—himself a Marxist—has emphasized the revolutionary aspects of the Gospel message.

RELIGION: A SOCIOLOGICAL VIEW

pointed out earlier that these various types of religious organization have been created by man and are subject to human error. Nevertheless, most missionaries have attempted to transplant Western forms of religious organization along with their preaching of the Gospel. Some missionaries assigned an almost sacred significance to the particular form of churchly, sectarian, or denominational organization of the religious body "back home" that sponsored and financed their own missionary activities, and downgraded all other forms. Such a stance not only made Christians appear quarrelsome and divided, but it denied to their non-Western converts the power and self-determination to create their own religious organizations more in accord with their own customs and needs. This deprivation was a potential source of discontent and even rebellion, which was not at all what the missionaries had intended. Nevertheless, it was their own organizational policies that had helped to give to Christianity the stamp of a religion that was narrowly Western and colonial, rather than universal.[5]

Furthermore, the evangelical missionaries of the nineteenth century, especially the Protestants, were firmly convinced of the superiority of Western culture in general. Most of them were sincere and dedicated individuals, but they often came from provincial backgrounds and had little or no experience of any culture except their own. Innocent of anthropological training or cosmopolitan sophistication, they were all too likely to equate essential Christian teachings with the social customs of their own home town. The culture of the American Middle West, British suburbia, or French and German provinces was all that many of them knew—and such provincial customs they would impart devoutly along with their Bible teaching.[6] These well-meaning missionaries were thus the uncritical and often unconscious carriers of the Western racial attitudes, class prejudices, family customs, and sexual restrictions.[7] In short, many of them attempted to change the behavior of their converts far more than was strictly necessary for the achievement of their intended aims. What many of these missionaries did not reckon with, however, was the impact of their "incidental" teachings on in-

digenous cultures. A rather frequent, if unintended consequence, of these social teachings was the weakening of the social
control systems of indigenous cultures rather than the firm establishment of Western "Christian" social standards. For instance, in societies where polygamy is sanctioned by local custom, the missionary teaching of monogamy has sometimes helped
to weaken a husband's responsibility for his secondary wives and
their offspring while failing to impart an understanding of the
values of monogamy.* In some cases, as we shall see, this
weakening of social controls facilitated later revolutionary activities.

Finally, another unintended, and still more potent, precipitant
of revolution stemmed from the disparity between the Christian
principles professed by Western missionaries and the kind of social relationships they themselves maintained with colonial peoples. Insofar as the missionaries became assimilated to the value
system of the colonial society, their way of life was likely to negate, in the eyes of the subject population, the Christian values
they preached. And if, as was sometimes the case, the missionaries' teaching of the equal value of every individual soul in
the sight of God was canceled by the racial and social arrangements within the missionary compound itself, the disillusionment
of those who had been exposed to their teachings could be bitter
indeed.

The chief dilemma of the missionaries, who were mostly Westerners, lay in the fact that they were caught in the middle between "colonial" society and "native" society. Since the "colonial" society was dominant politically, it was often difficult for
them to avoid at least partial assimilation to its way of life or to
refrain from encouraging "colonial" attitudes in their converts.
For other reasons also, such as lack of habituation to diverse
climatic conditions, missionaries found it difficult to adopt a
"native" way of life. Furthermore, even when missionaries made
efforts to dissociate themselves from the more arrogant practices

---

* In some other cases a tribe's hitherto viable system of land cultivation
has been disrupted by the loss to the constituent families of the agricultural
labor of a man's secondary wives.

of Western colonialists, by reason of their nationality and race they might still, in the eyes of the subject people, appear as members of the ruling class and come under the same condemnation.[8]

One of the most important activities of missionaries throughout the world has been the maintaining of hospitals and schools. The schools in particular have been agencies for the dissemination of Western attitudes and skills. In many cases mission schools were the only schools in which ambitious individuals among the subject peoples could find the necessary preparation to qualify them for employment in the lower or middle echelons of colonial governments.* In these schools the propagation of the Christian religion and Western culture went hand in hand. Many individuals, to be sure, were ready to submit to exposure to the religious indoctrination (to which they could turn a deaf ear) in order to acquire skills that would facilitate their economic and social advancement. From the point of view of some colonial governments, the mission schools provided a useful means of training house servants and lower administrative personnel.

Nevertheless, one of the unintended results of many of these missionary schools was also the fostering of revolutionary attitudes. The exposure to certain aspects of Christian teachings and, in some colonies, the further exposure to a classic literature of revolution and democratic freedom, inevitably drew the attention of the subject peoples with education to the contrast between the liberties the colonizers claimed for themselves and their fellow nationals and those that they saw fit to grant to their colonial subjects. It is not surprising that this situation produced in a good many individuals feelings of bitterness and alienation that sometimes led to outright rebellion.**

---

* This situation is especially characteristic of colonial areas such as the Belgian Congo, where mission schools were the only source of education beyond the primary level.

** Many rebel leaders, such as Kenyatta, Kasavubu, and Lumumba, were mission-educated. So, also, were many "conservative" leaders. In many cases missionary education was the only readily available prerequisite for higher education of any kind.

Furthermore, insofar as mission schools equipped some individuals for positions in the colonial hierarchy, they provided them with a vantage point from which to gain familiarity with the more intimate workings of the colonial "system" and with the living habits of the ruling class. Such knowledge, especially if it included training in the use of firearms, acquainted disaffected "natives" with some of the means for combatting colonial rulers. As a writer in the English journal *The New Statesman* has remarked, "A native who has had close association with the boss-class is often one who has learned their tricks, and admired their gadgets, and come to hate their guts." [9]

Much of what has been said above about Christian missions is applicable only to the missions of an earlier day, especially those prior to World War II. Many missionaries today have considerable anthropological sophistication and aim at understanding and appreciating—as well as transforming—"native" religions. Many of the younger missionaries are less occupied with evangelism and with mission schools than they are with medical work, public health, technological aid and community development.* Some, indeed, have come to feel that it is part of their Christian duty *not* to support colonial or neocolonial governments but rather to identify themselves openly with those who are rebelling against them. In South Africa, for instance, Anglican leaders, such as Father Huddleston, have publicized their opposition to *apartheid* policies. In some Latin American countries, such as Brazil, Roman Catholic bishops have declared their support for some of the political rebels, and in Colombia Father Camilo Torres felt impelled by his Christian conscience to join the guerrillas and to resist, by force of arms and the risk of his life, what he felt to be the oppression of a neocolonial government.[10]

It should be stressed that it is not our purpose to debunk all Christian missions—or to defend them. Some missionaries, indeed, have pioneered in supplying subject peoples with humani-

---

* It is an interesting fact that the children of missionaries often take overseas assignments in such fields as medicine, technological aid, and community development.

tarian services that no other persons or agencies were, at a given time, prepared to undertake. Many of these services have subsequently been taken over by secular agencies of education and welfare. But rather than evaluate missions, the intention here is to draw attention to some of their disruptive consequences, largely unintended, for indigenous people and their cultures and more particularly to the role of missionary education in the stimulation of revolt against colonial rule. In sociological parlance we have been dealing with some of the *latent* consequences of missionary endeavor. Whether these consequences are to be viewed as eufunctional or dysfunctional is likely to depend on who does the viewing.

Needless to say, missionary education has produced conservative as well as revolutionary leaders, particularly in those countries where the only form of education above the primary level has been that supplied by missionaries. Furthermore, missions have produced sincere and creative Christians, such as Kagawa in Japan, whose Christian observance goes far beyond that which is customary in the West.

It must also be clearly understood, as was pointed out earlier in this chapter, that Christianity and Christian missions are but one among many factors that have helped to produce in the Third World both the revolution against colonialism and a revolutionary urge towards modernization.

RELIGION AND THE CONFRONTATION OF SOCIETIES OF DIFFERENT TYPES

In considering the confrontation of westernized Model Three societies with other societies, we shall deal separately with the confrontation of Model Three with Model One societies and with that of Model Three with Model Two societies. The tribal societies of the African continent, New Guinea, and Oceania furnish examples of the first type of confrontation, whereas the great Asian civilizations of India, Southeast Asia, and the

Far East afford examples of the second type. It should be understood, of course, that no individual society represents a "pure" type of either Model One or Model Two societies: we are concerned with *relative* predominance. The predominantly Model Two societies of Asia include tribal minorities more nearly approaching the Model One type, and similarly the predominantly tribal societies of Africa and other parts of the world contain elements of complexity more nearly akin to Model Two societies. The considerable variation among the individual societies means that all generalizations must be made with great caution.

Any consideration of the relationship between religion and revolutionary change must take account of a number of variables. The religion in question may be either imported or indigenous. The imported religion may be Roman Catholic or Protestant or Islamic. It may have been introduced hundreds of years ago or within the last century. The indigenous religions also present a great variety, although an important distinction can be made between those that possess a written tradition and those that depend entirely on oral transmission. A distinction can also be made between those having a clearly differentiated religious organization with a hierarchy of religious professionals and less "bureaucratic" religions.

In spite of the existence of these and other variables, two tentative generalizations may be offered about the encounter between Western and non-Western religions in both Model One and Model Two types of society. First, Christian missions appear to have been more successful among preliterate people near the tribal level (Model One) than they have been among more sophisticated peoples who adhere to one of the world's "higher" religions and possess written scriptures (Model Two).[11] In Burma, for instance, Christian missions made more converts among the hill tribesmen, most of whom were animists, than they did among the Buddhists in Burma proper.* Similarly, in

---

* The activities of the British colonial power and of the missionaries included a major effort to convert some of the "minority" groups, especially the Karens. Some of these groups were open to the preaching of missionaries

India more Christian converts have been made among outcastes and low-caste members than among Brahmins.[12]   In other words, Christian missions scored their greatest successes in a given society among people whose status was *marginal* or *disprivileged* with respect to the dominant systems of religious, ethnic, and social ranking.

The second generalization is that the introduction of an imported religion generates some degree of religious blending, or syncretism, in Model One and also in Model Two societies. However, the elements borrowed and incorporated from the imported religion into the indigenous religion and the way in which they are interpreted and used are likely to vary between Model One and Model Two societies.   In both types of society, converts and those who are merely "hearers" are alike prone to adopt and incorporate those aspects of an imported religious tradition that meet their felt needs.   They are likely to seize most readily on those new teachings that supplement an indigenous religion in useful and acceptable ways or that fit in with existing social customs, or both.

In a Model One society, preliterate peoples, even though they may borrow elements of the beliefs and practices of an imported religion relatively freely, are more likely than the relatively more sophisticated inhabitants of Model Two societies to "misunderstand" some of these borrowed elements.   Furthermore, in the course of the syncretic process, they may reinterpret and even distort them to suit their own needs.   Some African and West Indian peoples, for example, have "borrowed" those parts of the Old Testament that describe the family customs of the Hebrew patriarchs, customs that have more affinity to their own traditional behavior than the New Testament sexual morality taught by Christian missionaries.   Furthermore, they sometimes interpret Old Testament stories of the bloody wars between the Hebrews and their neighbors in the land of Canaan as prototypes of conflicts between themselves and colonial rulers.[13]   Such in-

---

partly because they had been victims of discriminatory treatment by the Burmese Buddhist majority. By 1921 some 180,000 Burmese were Christians, but among that number 70 percent were Karens.

terpretations have been known to give rise to nativistic messianic cults that have stirred up revolt against the white man's rule.

Inhabitants of the Model Two type of society—especially the more literate and sophisticated among their number, who are familiar with their own written scriptures—are likely to be more resistant to imported beliefs and practices than are preliterate peoples. In addition, the vested interests of a professional religious class still further increases the probability of such resistance. Nevertheless, even the religions of Model Two societies have not been altogether immune to syncretism. For example, Hinduism, an admittedly tolerant and hospitable religion, has not infrequently accepted Jesus Christ as one of the avatars of Vishnu, that is, as an incarnation of divinity. Furthermore, the thinking of such outstanding Indians as Gandhi and Rabindranath Tagore has been influenced by the New Testament even though neither of them ceased to be Hindus. Intellectuals in Model Two societies have sometimes been interested in Western Christianity partly because it was the religion of a "successful" people and was therefore presumed to have a certain prestige.* Sometimes, however, this interest has had the rather paradoxical result of stimulating renewed interest in indigenous religious traditions, whether Hindu, Buddhist, or Islamic. Moreover, such revivals of a traditional religion have at times taken on nationalistic overtones and thus have helped to kindle resistance to Western colonial rule.

So far we have noted some of the processes and principles involved in the confrontation of Model Three societies and their religions with societies of the Model One and Model Two type, respectively. When we examine more closely some of the "confrontations" themselves, as we shall do shortly, the situation becomes more complicated and more concrete. More than principles and processes are involved, and we must take into account particular cultural configurations, idiosyncrasies in the personalities of leaders, and the sequence of historical events.

---

* It was brought to my attention that a Japanese girl, on being asked why she had converted to Christianity, replied, "Because I want to own an automobile."

Innumerable examples of the confrontation of religions (and their related cultures and civilizations) could be cited. It is clearly impossible to take account of them all. In North Africa, for instance, Islam is engaged in confrontation with indigenous tribal religions; and in Latin America, European religious culture confronts that of American Indians. Two examples only will be discussed in some detail below. The scene of the first is Africa, and that of the second, Burma. In the first case the confrontation is between a Model Three and a Model One society, whereas in the second a Model Three society confronts one that more nearly corresponds to a Model Two type.

RELIGION AND THE CONFRONTATION OF MODEL ONE BY MODEL THREE SOCIETIES

The confrontation of Model One by Model Three societies involves the contact of societies of extremely disparate types, who are ill-prepared and usually ill-equipped, to understand one another. The shocks engendered by such confrontations are frequently severe, especially to the members of the Model One societies. Furthermore, since World War I and especially since World War II, the contact of industrial with preindustrial societies has become closer and more penetrating than it had been in earlier times. In the twentieth century such contacts have been characterized by the introduction of a highly developed and complex technology that has the capacity radically to transform indigenous ways of life.

A dramatic instance of such a transformation that took place in the islands of the Manus Archipelago, which were used by the Americans as an amphibious base during World War II, has been described by Margaret Mead. In her book, *New Lives for Old,* Mead describes how the islanders, whose lives and customs she had studied and described in *Growing Up in New Guinea* twenty-five years earlier, had been greatly transformed by a massive infiltration of American servicemen, military supplies, and equipment. An outcropping of new religious cults, known as Cargo Cults, was one of the ways in which the Manus inhabitants responded to this, for them cataclysmic, state of affairs.[14]

Vittorio Lanternari has drawn attention to the worldwide nature of the religious transformations in primitive (Model One) societies. He has especially emphasized the role of these transformations as precursors of rebellions against Western colonial rule. In Lanternari's view the religious transformations of the primitive world and the new religious movements that accompany them are the natives' way of "talking back" to the Western world. Therefore, he stresses, it is important that the leaders of the West understand the meaning of these religious movements and learn to "listen" to this kind of religious "talk." [15]

The case of the Kimbangu cults in the Belgian Congo is drawn from the heart of the African continent. Lanternari's statements about the role of religion in that part of the world, his conclusions being based upon the findings of a number of missionaries and anthropologists, are highly instructive. He claims that "when the first tremors of rebellion ran through the Belgian Congo, Nyasaland, French Equatorial Africa, Kenya and West Africa, neither the seasoned observer nor the discerning ethnologist was taken by surprise. These were the inevitable if perturbing manifestations of a religious ferment that had been ripening in Africa for well over fifty years." He is also of the opinion that "premonitory religious movements of revival and transformation usually lie at the origin of every political or military uprising among the native people, and take the form of messianic cults promising liberation." [16]

Lanternari points to numerous occasions in which members of colonial societies of the Model One type, both in Africa and elsewhere, have sought relief from their frustrations and miseries through religion before turning to political means. He sees religious protest as their most readily available weapon of revolt against the white man's religion, his appropriation of their land, and his racial policies. Such religious cults are not only seen to express the popular yearning for liberty but also to fulfill the role of the "secular" leadership sometimes exercised by religion in primitive societies.

In the light of our general knowledge of Model One societies, this conclusion of Lanternari's is understandable. Since in such societies the political, military, and legal institutions are likely to be weak, their members respond to the threat of cultural extinction through the medium of the strongest, most inclusive, and most pervasive institution—apart from the family or tribe—that they possess: their religion. By making a display of their religious independence, such peoples strive to fight racial discrimination and segregation, forced acculturation, or the destruction of their tribal life at the hands of either missionaries or colonial administrators.

The Case of the Congo Cults

The region lying between the Middle and Lower Congo River has been a focal center for cults that have expanded into French Equatorial Africa and the Belgian Congo. An eighteenth-century chronicle records strange ways in which the impact of Christianity had affected traditional religious beliefs. A Belgian monk, working among the Bakongo tribes, came upon a prophetess known as Beatrice, who, by virtue of dreams and visions and her memory of deaths and births, claimed to be the reincarnation of Saint Anthony. Announcing that the day of judgment was at hand, Beatrice surrounded herself with "angels," and to one of them, named Saint John, she bore a son. Shortly thereafter, she founded a movement called Antonian, after the saint she embodied. It attracted a huge following dedicated to the restoration of the native kingdom of San Salvador and to the revival of all customs banished by the missionaries. For her heresies the monk saw to it that she was burned at the stake, but her large following remained united in pursuing the goals set by the martyred prophetess.[17]

This story provides an early recorded example of the religious syncretism discussed above. Here we find that a Christian saint, usually portrayed holding the Child Jesus in his arms, has been given a connotation of a protector of fecundity and fertility. It is also recorded that Bakongo Christians used the crucifix as a fetish for their protection, again illustrating a rather distorted result of the impact of two cultures unprepared to understand each other.[18]

Fetishism, the worship of inanimate objects having specific uses endowed with magical powers, is a typical religious form in the Congo and has played a major role in messianic movements. In general the intention of fetishism has been to fulfill two major functions: [to express hostility to the white man and to protect the natives from the effects of sorcery and black magic.] The first messianic movements in the Congo occurred in the early years of the twentieth century and were both fetishist and anti-white. Secret religious societies grew up whose members were pledged to passive resistance to European rule. They boycotted European textiles and other products and refused to pay taxes or serve the white man in any capacity whatsoever. Thus, as emphasized earlier in this chapter, these first revolts against imperialism started under cover of religious worship. When, as in 1905 and thereafter, the white man's bullets killed the rebels, it was easy for the natives to believe that their defeat was due to their own transgressions of the rules of their secret societies. Hence they lost neither their faith nor their determination to persevere.

New cults grew up, like that of the Bashilele, which began to expand in 1933, according to which the advent of a Messiah was to be preceded by such extraordinary events as the collective rising of the dead, the eclipse of the sun, the appearance in every village of a black talking dog, and the coming of a man, part white and part black. The natives were to acquire invincible powers by drinking a special magic potion from special magic cups. Not long after the sect had gained a footing, secret rituals were performed around ancestral tombs, and the people stopped working in order to wait for the return of the dead, who would bring them untold riches with which to inaugurate an era of happiness and well-being.

Highly important in this case is the combination of *old* beliefs, such as that in the end of the world and in regeneration, with a *new* belief in the expulsion of the white man. The secret societies, which operated simultaneously against sorcery and against the white man's rule, flourished chiefly among those of the Congolese who had been removed from their tribe after World War II and made to work for foreign masters. On the other hand, another aspect of syncretism was involved in the religious movements of messianic character that had Christian overtones. These latter movements gained a following largely among the natives who had remained in their own villages, as in the following cases.

In 1921 Simon Kimbangu, a powerful personality, founded a movement known both as the *Kimbangu* and as the *Ngunzi* * movement.[19] This movement found fertile soil wherever Christianity had been preached. Eventually the Ngunzi movement gave rise to several autonomous churches and to a number of political groups working for independence. In the Congo this early religious phase produced some remarkable prophets, such as Simon Kimbangu himself, André Matswa, Simon Mpadi, and Mavonda Ntangu. In view of our earlier discussion, it is interesting that all these Congolese leaders, influenced mainly by the Protestant missions, had committed themselves to Christianity. It is of further interest, however, that their teachings harked back almost entirely to the Old Testament, from which they carefully culled only the passages best suited to furthering their nationalistic and anti-Western goals.

Kimbangu had been educated by Baptist missionaries and had also learned about Western ways as a house servant to Europeans. He embarked on his evangelistic career as the result of a vision of the Supreme Being of ancient Bakongo tradition, who then became identified in his mind with the Judeo-Christian God—yet one more example of religious syncretism. Kimbango then identified himself with the prophet Moses and urged his people to forsake polygamy and idolatry and worship a single

---

* The word "Ngunzi" means prophet.

God. He interpreted the story of David and Goliath as the struggle of the blacks against the whites and later regarded himself as performing a reenactment of Jesus Christ's sacrifice for the redemption of mankind. Kimbangu was subsequently sent to prison, where he languished for many years, and died in 1950, thus becoming a martyr.

After 1930 Kimbangu's work was carried on by André Matswa, who even more than Kimbangu came to be regarded as the savior of his people. Matswa had been raised as a Roman Catholic and had fought in France during World War I. Thus his personal contact with colonial rulers and their ways had been as close as, although rather different from, that of Kimbangu. While in Paris, moreover, Matswa had been in contact with Negro freedom groups. He too was imprisoned, and he died in 1942. When alive, he had been the Negro Messiah, and when dead, he became the Negro Christ. His followers called him Jesus Matswa. Lanternari points out that Christianity itself offered the example of a "Messiah sacrificed to the blind intransigence of public powers no less than to the infamy of his enemies, yet rising triumphant for the redemption of the faithful." [20] This is a striking illustration of the revolutionary potential of Christianity, as discussed earlier in this chapter. The martyrdom of Matswa and his identification with the role of Christ set the seal of religious approval on the demand for religious and cultural independence and self-determination.

After 1939 a third prophet, Simon Mpadi, carried on the work of Kimbangu and Matswa. He also was imprisoned, but by this time the martyrdom of their messiahs had awakened a revolutionary spirit in the Congolese. The Christian promise of a kingdom and a millennium was interpreted as a call to rebellion against the repressive rule of the colonial powers. It was indeed a gospel of salvation, and for the natives salvation meant freedom.

Churches of the Ngunzi cult sprang up in the Congo, and these churches were militantly autonomous. After the imprisonment of Simon Mpadi, Mavonda Ntangu continued his teaching. Once again, a combination of the old and the new was characteristic of the liturgy of these native churches. The sign of the cross was used, but its meaning was radically altered, for the ritual gesture was accompanied by the words "In the name of the Father, of Simon Kimbangu, and of André Matswa." Thus a nativistic and heretical trinity superseded that of orthodox Christianity. Furthermore, the altars in native chapels were draped in red, with a huge wooden *V* encasing the Cross of Loraine, the symbol of the Free French. In the minds of the Congolese, however, the red was identified with the blood of the Congolese martyrs, and the gigantic *V* gave tangible expression to the natives' faith in rebellion and ultimate victory. They believed that their freedom would be established when Simon Kimbangu and André Matswa came back with power to rule the "Kingdom" —and that the Kingdom would be African. And when they prayed, they prayed thus: "God of Abraham, God of Isaac, God of Simon Kimbangu and God of André Matswa, when shall we receive the blessing and be free? Thou shalt no more hear the prayers of the whites, for Thou hast heard them for a long time and they have received blessings enough. Hear us now! Amen." [21]

The Kimbangu movement gave rise to numerous submovements, but by 1956 it was gathering its local groups into a single force called *Église de Jésus Christ sur la Terre par le Prophète Simon Kimbangu* (Church of Jesus Christ on Earth through the Prophet Simon Kimbangu), which closely follows the original ritual and doctrine established by Simon Kimbangu. At present the official leader of the Église is a son of Kimbangu. Although the Église was officially a strictly religious organization, political drives were nevertheless inevitably developed within its religious context. For instance, the Église supported the belief that the spirit of Simon Kimbangu was reincarnated in the leaders of the Congo uprisings of 1959. The religious texts used by the Église denounce the oppressive practices of the white man. Many of the leaders of the political movement for Congo independence were also members of the Église.

For the sociologist of religion the revolutionary religious cults in the Congo provide a challenge. Certainly there exists in the world today a wealth of material in terms of which Weber's hypotheses regarding the functions of prophecy and the conditions favoring its emergence (discussed in Chapter 6) could be put to an empirical test.[22] Furthermore, those of us inclined to view the prophetic tradition in Judeo-Christianity in highly abstract terms as something remote in ancient history may be stimulated to take a more concrete, realistic view of prophetic situations in general and of the conditions that produced those Old Testament prophets, such as Amos and Elijah, whose names are so familiar.

RELIGION AND THE CONFRONTATION OF MODEL TWO BY MODEL THREE SOCIETIES

The confrontation of Model Two by Model Three societies is less recent and possibly less dramatic than is the confrontation of the primitive world by modern industrial societies. The expansion of Western Europe into India, China, and Southeast Asia, which dates back to the fifteenth and sixteenth centuries, was a more gradual affair. In some respects, especially in the earlier days of the encounter, the cultures of these Eastern societies were more fully developed and more sophisticated than were their contemporary cultures of the West. Moreover, these oriental societies possessed their own highly evolved religions, particularly Hinduism and Buddhism. In contrast to the religions of Model One societies, the precepts of these religions had been committed to writing and embodied in canonical scriptures. The presence of an elite literate class, usually a priestly caste, constituted a core of resistance to the acceptance of the Christian teachings and Christian customs that were exported by the West.

When commercial contacts were succeeded by political domination and Western imperialism was reinforced by the technological developments of the nineteenth and twentieth centuries, the influence of Western culture and Western religion upon oriental societies became more pronounced. These influences have been and still are highly complex. They have differed from one oriental civilization to another and also in different periods of time.

The Buddhist religion in Burma, as in other Southeast Asian countries, was confronted by Western Christianity and colonialism.[23] Colonial governments not only encouraged Christian missions but also, on occasion, interfered with the organization of the Buddhist Order, confiscated much monastic property, curtailed the independent jurisdiction of monastic courts, and put to death monks who protested against colonial rule. Among Southeast Asian countries, only Thailand retained her monarchy and, with it, her religious independence. Therefore, it was not surprising that the Buddhist religion, and, more especially, the Buddhist Order, should constitute a hard core of resistance both to Christianity and to Western domination.

Christian missions were successful among certain minority groups, in Burma particularly among the Karens and some other hill peoples. Moreover, the graduates of missionary schools added to the numbers of a relatively small Westernized elite who, by finding favor and jobs with the colonialists, exercised an influence greater than their numbers would suggest. Paradoxically, however, contact with the Christian West served in part to reactivate Buddhism as well as to supersede and suppress it. For not only did the mission schools add to the numbers of those able to read and speak English, but also at the same time Western scholars (themselves often Christians, as was Max Müller, the most influential of them) popularized the Buddhist Scriptures by having them translated into English. Since Pali, the ancient language in which the Theravada Buddhist Scriptures were written, was understood only by the more learned Buddhist monks, these English translations greatly increased the educated Burmese laity's knowledge of their Buddhist faith.

In the nineteenth century some Westerners actively assisted in the revival of Buddhism, either directly or indirectly. For instance, the American Civil War veteran Colonel Henry Steele Olcott helped to promote a Buddhist revival in Ceylon. In Thailand Christian missionaries were consulted by the learned

King Mongkut concerning his plans to reform the Buddhist Order in that country. Finally, in Burma, in this century, the English scholar Gordon Luce has by his historical research done
much to restore to the Burmese people the knowledge of the
more glorious periods of their Buddhist monarchical past.

The Case of Burma

Burma, unlike India and some of the other countries of
Southeast Asia, experienced its confrontation with the West relatively recently. Partly because Burma lay somewhat apart from
the focus of European expansion and trade, it was not until 1885,
after the capture of the capital at Mandalay and the extinction
of the line of Burmese kings, that British rule in Burma was
fully established. Burma was given her independence by peace-
ful agreement with the British in 1948. Hence the period during which she was subjected to colonial rule (1885–1948) was
relatively brief.

Burma's confrontation with the West, however, did not termi-
nate with the end of colonial rule. The latter was but an intensive episode in a continuing encounter. For Burma, in common
with other Asian countries in the postcolonial period, is faced
with the problem of developing viable political and economic
institutions in order to survive on the international scene. To
do so, she has been forced to borrow Western political and economic ideas and to accept aid, technical and financial, either
from the West or from Westernized Asian nations. Even though
Burma may attempt (as she is now doing under General Ne
Win) to evade world involvement by withdrawing into her own
boundaries, she cannot altogether exclude the influences of
Western techniques and political ideas.

In this encounter between Burmese society and that of the
West, has religion played a "revolutionary" role? In the following discussion the term "revolution" will be used in two distinct
but related ways. First, revolution will be understood as *revolt,*
the revolt of Burmese society against British—and Japanese—

colonial rule. In paving the way for this successful revolt, Burmese Buddhism will be seen as having played an active, revolutionary part. But with respect to the second connotation of revolution, namely, the social revolution consequent upon the more or less rapid transformation of a traditional society into a "modern" society, Burmese religion will be seen as mainly hampering, rather than furthering, the revolution of modernization.

Any assessment of the nature and extent of the revolutionary role played by Buddhism in Burma must take into account two complementary aspects of Burmese Buddhism. On one hand, Buddhism was (and still is) an integral part of Burmese culture, while on the other hand, it was (and still is) represented by a powerful and specialized social organization, namely the *Sangha,* or Buddhist Order of Monks. In the resistance to colonial domination both the cultural and the organizational aspects of Buddhism have played distinctive parts.

Buddhism, in its Theravada form, has been indigenous to Burma for almost a thousand years. How a person spent his substance, ordered his family life, celebrated his holidays, and occupied his leisure time was connected in one way or another with his being a Buddhist. By the time of the British occupation Buddhism had become part and parcel of Burmese national culture. More than 85 percent of Burma's population is Buddhist; in fact, being a Buddhist still is, culturally speaking, simply another way of being a patriotic Burmese. As one of my Rangoon acquaintances expressed it, "Squeeze a Burman like an orange and Buddhism will come out of his veins." [24] It is not surprising, therefore, that, except among the non-Buddhist *Karens* and some other hill peoples on the periphery of Burma proper, Christian missions met with little success.

The most important aspect of Burmese Buddhism, from the point of view of *social structure,* was—and still is—the powerful organization of the *Sangha,* the Order of Buddhist Monks. The monks enjoyed more prestige and respect than any other group of people in Burma; the Burmese word for monk is "pongyi," meaning "great glory." Burmese laymen considered it a privilege, as well as a means of gaining "merit," to contribute to the monks' support. This high regard in which they were held by the people greatly increased the monks' power. The main wielders of this power were those "career" monks who spent their entire lives as members of the Order and who dominated the affairs of the important monasteries in and around Mandalay. But even "temporary" monks (the Burmese Buddhist Order did not insist on a man's taking life-long vows) could acquire many privileges through wearing the Yellow Robe.

Burmese monks, however, were not sharply separated from the laity. Every day they collected their food from the villagers, and twice every month, on Buddhist Sabbath days, the laity, in festive attire, flocked to the local monasteries to celebrate the holiday and to bring gifts and pay respects to the resident monks.[25] Furthermore, every village boy went to a monastic school to learn the elements of Buddhism and of literacy. All Burmese boys sometime between the ages of seven and twenty were initiated as boy novices. Usually after their initiation they spent some weeks in a monastery, learning the monastic discipline, studying the Pali Scriptures, and helping the monks with their daily chores.[26] In these ways the gulf between monks and laity was bridged.

The capture of Mandalay in 1885 and the destruction of the royal palace was a great shock to the Burmese. It posed a threat both to Buddhism as Burmese culture and also to the social structure of Buddhism as embodied in the Order of Monks. For the Order the extinction of the kingship was a disaster, since it also involved the extinction of the office of the *Sangharaj,* the primate of monasticism in Burma. As a consequence of losing its official head, the monastic hierarchy was dislocated and the discipline of the monks seriously declined.

Burmese Buddhist culture also suffered a severe blow. During the colonial period the monastic schools, which had previously maintained a creditable standard of literacy and Buddhist education, began to deteriorate. A new English-speaking elite, who were educated in missionary and in government schools, found the monastic schools old-fashioned and the monks' learning use-less for the advancement of their secular careers. Hence Burmese Buddhist morale grew weaker among a growing number of the urban educated classes. A Rangoon resident, recalling British colonial days, put the matter thus: "Our Burmese Buddhist spirits withered under the imported sunshine of British colonial culture."

The first active protest against British rule came from young and militant members of the Buddhist Order. As early as the second decade of the twentieth century, some of the educated Buddhist laity had founded the Young Men's Buddhist Association as an organization to revitalize Buddhism. But the real thrust of the resistance movement came in the 1920s and 1930s from revolutionary monks such as U Ottama, U Wisera and Saya San. Even though the monastic rule forbade monks to take part in politics, these monks toured the country protesting against British behavior (such as walking in sacred pagoda precincts without removing their shoes) that was felt by Burmese people to dishonor Buddhism. Everywhere they went, they stirred up the populace to resist British rule.

These rebellious monks felt they had little to lose from their anti-British stance. As monks they had no jobs in jeopardy, and in any case the British were progressively undermining the posi-tion of the Order. On the other hand, they and the Order stood to gain from the tremendous support they were able to elicit from the mass of the people. The awakening of the hitherto suppressed nationalistic fervor of the common people gave strong encouragement to their attempts to instigate popular revolt. Although the monks did not, in the final showdown, secure Burma's independence, they nevertheless paved the way for it. To this day a statue of one of them, U Wisera, stands in Rangoon as a witness to the honor in which his countrymen still hold him for the part he played in their early struggles for liberation.

The Burmese finally gained their independence at the end of World War II in return for the military help they gave the British in driving the Japanese out of Burma. The "founding fathers" of Burmese independence were a group of comrades known as the Thakins.* They were secular revolutionaries who drew much of their inspiration from Western ideologies. Some were communists of various brands, others were noncommunist Marxists, and some were democratic socialists in the style of the British Labor party in power at that time. The leader of the group was General Aung San, a popular hero who became the first Premier of the newly independent Union of Burma. The new constitution provided for a secular state, with toleration for all religions but no religious establishment. The new state and its Premier were dedicated to the promotion of the material welfare of the people.[27]

From the very first there were divergent factions among the leaders and ethnic and ideological divisions in the war-torn country. Aung San, had he lived, might perhaps have welded these discordant elements into some semblance of a united nation. But he was assassinated by a political rival after only a few months in office. Thakin U Nu, a Marxist and a devout Buddhist, succeeded him to the Premiership.

Under Premier U Nu, Burma began a fourteen-year period in which the Buddhist religion played a major role in both her domestic and her foreign policy. To a great extent during this period, Burmese politics were Buddhist politics.[28] U Nu, a charismatic personality, tried desperately to reconcile his Marxism with his Buddhism, but as the years went on he turned more and more to the latter, hoping in this way to unify his divided and devastated country and to boost its morale. U Nu looked to Buddhism to play a consolidating rather than a revolutionary role, and he aimed at making religious unity a basis for political unity. Casting himself in the role of the ancient Burmese kings, he attempted to exploit in all sincerity, but also for political purposes, the Buddhist allegiance of the great majority of the Burmese people. He tried to create the impression of a revival of ancient Burmese Buddhist glory, which, hopefully, would

---

* The title "Thakin" was originally a term of respect given to the British. It was appropriated by Burmese rebel leaders as a sign of their ambition for independence.

stimulate all parties to rally around his government. He created a ministry of Buddhist affairs, encouraged Buddhist education, organized Buddhist missions, and, in 1954, invited all the Buddhist organizations of the world to send representatives to Rangoon to attend a grand Buddhist council to celebrate the twenty-fifth centennial of the foundation of the Buddhist faith. Finally, in 1961, he took the decisive step of making Buddhism the state religion.

Unfortunately for Premier U Nu, his Buddhist policy failed to consolidate the new nation and succeeded rather in stimulating a temporary euphoria that had little or no foundation in political reality. Furthermore, as will be seen, this preoccupation with Buddhism hampered rather than furthered the revolution of modernization.

Nevertheless, some of U Nu's earlier projects, such as the Buddhist Council, did have some effect in putting Burma on the map and in giving her a definite identity in the United Nations and in the world. At home, too, Burmans could be proud of their Buddhism. As one of them expressed it to me, "Without her Buddhism Burma is less than an ant among the nations of the world. But with her Buddhism she need not be afraid of great populous nations like India and China. They cannot swallow a country like Burma. She is too tough for them." However, some of Burma's more pragmatically minded political leaders felt that U Nu was spending resources on the promotion of Buddhism that the nation could ill afford and that his Buddhist enthusiasm was causing him to lose touch with political reality. He failed to take a firm hand with the various insurgent groups and was likely to be found at a meditation center with some of his ministers when rebels were burning up the countryside. He was also inept in his handling of economic affairs. When he made Buddhism the state religion in 1961, he succeeded in arousing the fears and the hostilities of both ethnic and religious minorities.[29] At the same time he called for a cessation of business on numerous Buddhist holy days, a work stoppage that interfered seriously with productivity. When, in 1962, he requested his countrymen to build sixty thousand sand pagodas to help stave off political disaster, many Burmans, including some pious Buddhists, thought it was time for a change.

Quite apart from U Nu's policies, it should be stressed that Burmese Buddhism includes some beliefs and practices that seemingly militate against the modernization of Burma's economic life. The practice of a man's donating a substantial proportion of his life savings to building a pagoda prevented the accumulation of the savings necessary for investment in economic development. Indeed, the habit of building *new* pagodas when many old ones were in decay and when public buildings and dwelling houses were allowed to fall into disrepair, was from a Western point of view the sheerest waste of economic resources. In addition, the desire of most Buddhists to gain merit toward the improvement of their lot in future existences by the support of some hundred thousand monks who mostly led lives of unproductive idleness, was, again from the viewpoint of Western-style modernizers, merely an expensive way of condoning passivity and lack of enterprise. Furthermore, the whole notion of *karma,* insofar as the main stress was laid on the influence of past actions on contemporary events, rather than on the human ability to create new *karma* in the present, was seen to have a paralyzing effect on present activities to improve social conditions here and now.

It is possible, although not yet certain, that Burmese Buddhism is open to reinterpretation in ways that would render it more suited to the pressing political needs of the new nation, and to the revolution of modern times. Indeed, some of the younger and more "practical" Burmese Buddhists have attempted to interpret it so. For instance, they have suggested that as much religious merit should accrue to those who give donations to build schools, libraries, and hospitals as to more traditional donors who give to support monks or to build pagodas. They have stressed present *karma* rather than past *karma,* thereby discounting fatalism and emphasizing every individual's responsibility to create his own *karma* by his choice of activity in the present. They have viewed meditation not primarily as a means to gain Nirvana but rather as a practical way of increasing concentration and possibly contributing to efficiency in business, in the army, and in government service. The desire to be efficient in order to be of practical use to her country was expressed by one young Buddhist woman thus: "I don't want to become a pious 'orthodox' person; I want to do something useful for my country. Too much time spent in meditation makes people lazy and pessimistic, neglecting worldly affairs, thus causing my people to be poor and backward." This point of view, held by a considerable number of younger people, may be an indication that some sort of an equivalent of Weber's Protestant Ethic is beginning to develop in Burma. Indeed, Manning Nash has predicted that "a more austere and practical element will come to mark Burmese Buddhism and that the quest of a 'remote' Nirvana will become less important." [30]

Premier U Nu's Buddhist policies were less "modern" than many educated Burmese Buddhists would have wished. He gave a blanket endorsement to the culture of popular Buddhism at the level of its lowest common denominator. Needless to say, the Premier needed the political support of the great majority of Burmese who lived in the villages. Nevertheless, when he gave his official blessing to *nat* (spirit) worship and propitiation —practices that were not strictly Buddhistic but that were followed by most village Buddhists—some Burmese felt that he was going too far. In effect U Nu was giving his approval to some of the more irrational and wasteful aspects of popular Buddhism, aspects of very doubtful utility in cultivating the kind of attitudes likely to further the emergence of Burma as a "modern" state.

In his dealings with the Buddhist Order—that is, with Buddhism in its organizational aspect—Premier U Nu also endorsed the status quo. He bent over backwards to pay respect to the Order and even adopted the practice of consulting with some of the leaders of the Order on matters of national policy. This practice not only infuriated and frustrated some of his more secular-minded governmental colleagues, but, ironically enough, it backfired on him. The leaders of the Order had no conception of the political and economic needs of the new nation. Such political insight as they had was almost entirely confined to the internal affairs of their own organization. They exploited the favored position they enjoyed under U Nu to foment political and ethnic factions and to apply pressure to gain additional privileges for themselves. When the idleness and rapacity of the monks in Rangoon became a public scandal, U Nu did attempt to revive the ancient right of the Burmese monarchs to restore discipline. As a preliminary step he required the registration of all monks.[31] This effort was met by violent resistance, especially by the younger monks, and had to be abandoned.

Premier U Nu's fall from power early in 1962 and the "takeover" of the government by General Ne Win, a former ally of U Nu in the independence struggle, ended the attempt to use Buddhism as an instrument of national policy. U Nu and his ministerial colleagues were placed under arrest, and General Ne Win set out to establish "Burmese socialism" in a purely secular state. He governed the country as a military dictator with the help of a "Revolutionary Council," composed of army officers. Buddhism was no longer established as the state religion, and no special favors were given to the Buddhist Order.

General Ne Win's military dictatorship has encountered its own difficulties, which need not concern us here. Insurgency continues and Burma's economic situation continues to deteriorate. Apparently army officers have not been able to solve many of the problems that baffled U Nu and his advisers. The military dictatorship has not, of course, extinguished Buddhism in Burma, nor has it attempted to do so. It is doubtful that any government attacking Buddhism directly could hope to survive. Ne Win's government has had to move circumspectly in regard to Buddhist affairs. It is possible that in the future the General may have to pay more attention to enlisting the support of religious forces. Meanwhile Burma has largely withdrawn from her encounter with the West and is attempting to consolidate her revolt from colonialism with her own resources and within her own boundaries.

CONCLUSION

In this chapter religion has been viewed as playing both contributory and inhibiting roles with respect to revolution in both the senses in which we have used that term. When revolution was considered as revolt against Western colonialism, it was seen that in both the African Congo (a Model One society) and in Burma (largely a Model Two society) religion, in some of its aspects, played a significant contributory role, particularly in the early stages of anti-Western movements of revolt. In the African Congo Christianity—an imported religion propagated by the efforts of Christian missionaries who also introduced numerous Western ideas and techniques along with their religious teaching —frequently fomented African resistance to Western domination, an unintended result of missionary endeavor. In Burma, on the other hand, an indigenous religion, namely, Theravada Buddhism, played a similar contributory, although a more calculated, role in stimulating anti-Western nationalism.

When, however, revolution was considered in the sense of modernization, the record was somewhat different, although again religion both contributed to *and* inhibited "revolutionary" efforts to modernize newly independent countries. Christianity, by virtue of the fact that its propagation was usually accompanied by the introduction of a certain amount of Western education and technology, has on the whole furthered modernization. Both in the Congo and in Burma the Christian populations have, by and large, been the chief agents of modernization. Buddhism, on the other hand, was seen to contain both magical and religious elements that inhibited modernization. In spite of efforts by members of the younger Burmese generation to minimize magic and to reinterpret Buddhist doctrines to give religious sanction to hard work and efficiency in this present worldly life, traditional Buddhism has remained strong enough to impede attempts to modernize Burma's political and economic life.

REFERENCES

1. Some sociologists are already working in this field. See Robert N. Bellah (ed.), *Religion and Progress in Modern Asia* (New York: Free Press, 1965); also Ivan Vallier, "Church Development in Latin America," *Institute of International Studies Bulletin* (Berkeley: University of California Press, 1967).

2. Arnold J. Toynbee, *The World and the West* (New York: Oxford University Press, 1953).

3. The stress on the "error" of indigenous faiths and the wish to displace them completely is more characteristic of nineteenth-century and pre-World War II missionaries than of missionaries today. This change in emphasis can be clearly traced in missionary journals such as the *International Review of Missions*.

4. See Kaj Baajo, "The Problem of Post-Colonial Missions," *International Review of Missions*, July 1966, pp. 322–332. Baajo, then a professor of church history at the University of Bangalore, India, denies the necessity of conversion in the conventional missionary sense. He would rather aim at the *permeation* of faiths such as Hinduism and Buddhism with the *spirit* of Christ. His views, however, are contested in some missionary circles.

5. See Baajo, *op. cit.*, for an even stronger statement of a similar view; for example, he writes: "The traditional missionary outlook was filled to the brim with Western colonialism and imperialism" (p. 327). Many modern missionaries would agree with him.

6. *Ibid.*, p. 327. Baajo claims that Christian missions have not met other religions with *Christ* but rather with the Christian *religion*, complete with Western-based organization and cultural accretions. He claims that in such a confrontation the result will be a clash of cultures rather than a meeting with Christ.

7. Somerset Maugham's Sadie Thompson in "Rain" is, of course, a caricature of a missionary's wife, and is exceptional. There is little doubt, however, that Western mores have been advocated by some missionaries with little or no regard to either the intrinsic requirements of Gospel teaching or to local conditions.

8. See Thich Hnat Hanh, *Vietnam: Lotus in a Sea of Fire* (New York: Hill and Wang, 1964), pp. 17–21. Thich Hnat Hanh, a Vietnamese Buddhist monk and a college professor, emphasizes the alienating effects of Roman Catholic missions on their Vietnamese converts. These converts were alienated from their own compatriots and, in turn, became distrusted by the latter.

9. Cited on the cover of Vittorio Lanternari's *Religions of the Oppressed: A Study of Modern Messianic Cults*, trans. Lisa Sergio (New York: New American Library, Mentor Book, 1965).

10. See Gonzalo Castillo-Cardenas, "Christians and the Struggle for a New Social Order in Latin America," in Donald R. Cutler (ed.), *The Religious Situation, 1968* (Boston: Beacon Press, 1968), p. 507, for the following citation from the writings of Father Camilo Torres:

> I have left the privileges and duties of the clergy, but I have not left the priesthood. I believe that I have devoted myself to the revolution out of love for my neighbor. I will not say the mass, but I will realize this love of my neighbor in the temporal, economic and social realms. When my neighbor has nothing against me, when I have realized the revolution I will then say the holy Mass again. Thus, I believe I will be able to obey Christ's command, "if you are offering your gift at the altar, and there remember that your neighbor has something against you, leave your gift before the altar and go, first be reconciled to your brother, and then come and offer your gift."

Father Camilo Torres lost his life in this struggle.

11. See Emory Ross, "Impact of Christianity in Africa," *Annals of the American Academy: Contemporary African Trends and Issues*, 298 (March 1955), 165. Ross states that as of 1955 the best available figures recorded 21 million or more Christians in Africa, whereas "in all the rest of the so-called non-Christian world" there were but 20 million recorded Christians. Ross warns that these figures, particularly those for Africa, must be taken with caution, since different Christian denominations compute their membership figures in differing ways, and missionary societies are sometimes overly optimistic in counting converts.

12. See John B. Carman, "Report from South India," in *The Religious Situation, 1968, op. cit.*, p. 425. "Certainly from the beginning of Western Christian missions a large majority of converts to Christianity have been outcastes. . . . However, though the Brahmins . . . avidly took to the Western education offered by the missionaries . . . very few were at all interested in joining the Christian Church."

13. See Thomas Hodgkin, *Nationalism in Colonial Africa* (New York: New York University Press, 1957), Chapter 3.

14. See Margaret Mead, *New Lives for Old: Cultural Transformation, Manus 1928–1953* (New York: Morrow, 1956), for an account of the changes that had taken place in the Manus Islands between her two visits, twenty-five years apart; see also *Growing Up in New Guinea: A Comparative Study of Primitive Education* (New York: Morrow, 1930).

15. See Vittorio Lanternari, *op. cit.* Lanternari's book is based on field studies made by numerous anthropologists, both European and American. It has an extensive bibliography (pp. 255–268). The originality of Lanternari's contribution lies in his use of comparative materials and his stress on the world context of messianic movements.

16. *Ibid.*, p. 19. The same point is also made by Hodgkin, *op. cit.*, pp. 113–114.

17. Lanternari, *op. cit.*, p. 22. The story of the Belgian monk, cited by Lanternari, is taken from J. Cuvelier, *Relation Sur le Congo Par Pere Laurent de Lacques, 1700–1717* (Brussels: 1953), pp. 22–23.

18. Lanternari, *op. cit.*, p. 23, as taken from R. Wannijn, "Objets Anciens en Metal du Bas Congo," *Zaire,* V (1952), 391–394.

19. Lanternari, *op. cit.*, pp. 24–49. I am indebted to Lanternari for his account and interpretation of the Kimbangu (or Ngunzi) movements. See also Hodgkin, *op. cit.*, Chapter 3.

20. Lanternari, *op. cit.*, p. 28.

21. Lanternari, *op. cit.*, p. 31.

22. See Hodgkin, *op. cit.*, p. 107. Hodgkin draws attention to the "remarkable consistency in the pattern of the prophetic movements that have occurred in the regions of Africa exposed to Christian influence." He points out that the successful Congolese prophets were not drawn from the new urbanized elite but were nevertheless literate and accustomed to use their literacy mainly for Bible reading. In occupation, however, these prophets were not far removed from the masses: Kimbangu was a carpenter, Matswa an ex-soldier, and Mpadi a Salvation Army catechist.

23. See Walpola Rahula, *What the Buddha Taught* (New York: Grove Press, Evergreen Original, 1959), for a brief but scholarly account of Buddhist doctrine and philosophy. The author is a Buddhist monk of the Theravada School and was until recently a vice chancellor of the University of Ceylon.

24. This expression of opinion was elicted by the author in Rangoon in 1958. In collecting this (and other) information on Burmese attitudes toward Buddhist beliefs and practices, the author is grateful for the assistance of Sao Htun Hmat Win, Research Officer of the International Institute of Advanced Buddhistic Studies, Rangoon, Burma.

25. See Manning Nash, *The Golden Road to Modernity: Village Life in Contemporary Burma* (New York: John Wiley, 1965), pp. 291–312; and also Melford Spiro, *Burmese Supernaturalism* (Englewood Cliffs, N.J.: Prentice-Hall, 1967), pp. 25–63, for recent anthropological accounts of Burmese religion at the village level.

26. See Shwe Yoe (Sir George Scott), *The Burman: His Life and Notions* (London: Macmillan, 1882; now published in a Van Nostrand paperback); and Hall Fielding, *The Soul of a People* (London: Macmillan, 1898), for older but perceptive accounts of what monks have meant in traditional Burmese society.

27. Hugh Tinker, *The Union of Burma: A Study of the First Years of Independence* (New York: Oxford University Press, 1957), pp. 1–33 and 62–92.

28. See Donald Eugene Smith, *Religion and Politics in Burma* (Princeton, N.J.: Princeton University Press, 1965), especially Chapter V. This volume, by a political scientist, gives a cogent analysis of church-state relationships in Burma during the premiership of U Nu.

29. *Ibid.,* pp. 172–176.

30. Nash, *op. cit.,* p. 165.

31. Smith, *op. cit.,* p. 186: "Estimates of the number of Buddhist monks in Burma range from 80,000 to 120,000," says Smith. In the absence of registration it was easy for a lawless character to masquerade as a monk and claim a monk's immunity from arrest.

8
Religious Organization

THE SOCIAL AND SOCIOLOGICAL PROBLEMS OF RELIGIOUS ORGANIZATION

An inescapable dilemma confronts all social organizations designed to mold human behavior after a prescribed pattern, whether the pattern is set by religious doctrine, ethical precept, or political philosophy. [If organizations are to succeed in influencing human societies in the direction of their aims, they must be effective on a double front. On one hand, they must discipline the habits of their members in accordance with their particular ideals. On the other hand, if they also desire to influence the larger society, they must eventually expand their organization and augment their potential influence by attracting to their ranks persons of prestige and power in the world outside.] These two requirements constitute the horns of a dilemma, for success on either of these fronts usually means compromise on the other. Thus religious organization is faced with the choice of maintaining its ethical and spiritual purity at the price of limiting the sphere of its social influence or, if it is to exercise a dominant influence in a particular society, the price may be the sacrifice, in whole or in part, of its own distinctive ideals.

To characterize this situation as a dilemma involves two important assumptions. The first refers to the problem of maintaining group discipline, the assumption being that strict religious and ethical discipline is likely to be opposed to the behavior of most group members. Individuals differ in their religious capacity and interest, few being outstandingly gifted religiously or totally dedicated to religious aims. Furthermore, there can be no doubt that religious discipline, when accepted in its entirety, is exceedingly demanding. The ultimate claims of religious standards are upon the whole man. He may be asked to give up the free use of his money and time, the satisfactions of affection and family life, a secure and steady job, and the pursuit of the sensual pleasures of eating, drinking, and sexuality; moreover, he may be required to reorient his entire psychic world, his innermost thoughts and imaginings, his intimate desires and yearnings. A twenty-four-hour-a-day allegiance is asked of the totally committed adherent. No other type of organization makes such a total claim, with the significant exceptions of totalitarian political organizations, which have themselves become quasireligious.

Of course, few religions in practice make such far-reaching claims upon their members; in certain types, as we shall see, the most superficial conformity is enough. But the extremes to which the demands of religious and ethical discipline go indicate some of the difficulties, such as defection, secession, and rebellion, that may beset a religious organization if its leaders draw the disciplinary rein too tight.*

Our second assumption about the problem of influencing human conduct is that the ethical aims of religious organizations usually are not consistent with the conventional aims of society and its institutions. In other words, a basic conflict exists between the religious interest and worldly society. Religious groups can meet this situation in either of two ways. They can attempt to save their members from the wicked world by withdrawing from it as far as possible, or they can engage in active battle with the world and attempt to change it. In modern

---

* Certain severe types of discipline would seem hardly feasible for large groups of men and women in daily contact with the ordinary demands of the workaday world. It was perhaps for this reason that the Lord Buddha ordained two sets of rules, one for full-time Buddhist monks and a less stringent set for part-time lay followers. Almost two thousand years later St. Francis of Assisi developed two rules for the Franciscan Order, one for the friars who took the full vows and another for the famous Third Order of Franciscans, that is, men and women associated with the Order who continued to live out their lives in the world.

times, for example, the Plymouth Brethren have taken the former path, whereas Jehovah's Witnesses have taken the latter.* The groups that withdraw usually remain small and are likely to exercise a relatively slight influence on the larger society.** The militantly propagandist groups, on the other hand, can bring their influence to bear upon the world outside only if they expand their ranks. If this expansion is to achieve the ends of the group in question, however, it must include at least some members of power and prestige in the society concerned. Thus Christianity, which at first comprised largely obscure individuals, became the dominant religion of the Roman Empire itself, with consequent power to influence its institutions, only when it enlisted individuals of high standing, including finally the Emperor Constantine.

The dilemma lies in the fact that this expansion with its increasing capacity to influence society is achieved at the cost of dilution. In the course of its growth in numbers and power, the religious organization comes to include at least some elements that it has been combating. Thus a part, at least, of the formerly sinful world is no longer excluded but is integrated with the religious organization. Therefore the religious struggle with the world outside has to be waged not only with external foes but also within the social arena of the organization itself. As the religious organization grows in responsibility and social influence, it incorporates the entire range of worldly problems: problems of policy and of government, of leadership and ambition, and of the amassing of wealth, its use, distribution, and control. Hence religion in its organizational aspects—and here we are not

---

* We do not wish to imply, however, that withdrawing organizations, such as the medieval monasteries, have no influence on the outer world or, for that matter, that the more active group places no emphasis on the individual's salvation from the world. The difference in relative emphasis is nevertheless significant.

** Religious social action groups existing within larger, more conservative religious organizations also battle the world. There is also frequent conflict between such groups and the larger religious organization as well as with "the world."

concerned with its supernatural side—is marked by the same human problems as social life in general.[1]

Keeping in mind the limitations of all human institutions, the sociologist J. Milton Yinger has sought to find a theoretical point of maximum effectiveness for religious organizations.[2] This point would be most nearly reached when an organization had grown in numbers and power sufficiently to exert a strong social influence without having abandoned its essential ethical and religious ideals. If both these ends could be achieved fully and simultaneously, there would, of course, be no dilemma. But Yinger contends that the chances of gaining the ideal balance are increased either if a large influential organization can remain sufficiently flexible to retain a place for a variety of smaller groups that are strong in religious discipline and fervor and that act as a spiritual leaven, or if a relatively small but intensive organization can maintain its own ethical purity but at the same time devise methods to extend its influence in the world. In Yinger's opinion the Catholic Church in the thirteenth century most nearly approached maximum effectiveness by following the first alternative, whereas the twentieth-century Society of Friends approximates this goal by following the second one.

Many thoughtful and even religious-minded people feel disillusioned with the organizational side of religion; therefore this discussion of religious organization begins with a statement of its central, inescapable problem. We distinguished between religion conceived as an individual's relation to God and the ultimate objects of his faith and religion as a human institution, and we indicated that since institutional religion is human, it is subject to all the conditions that limit human organization in general. It may be noted in passing that this view, long held by sociologists, is gaining increasing acceptance among theologians and other professors in divinity schools. *Treasure in Earthen Vessels,* a recent book by James M. Gustafson of the Yale Divinity school, exemplifies this trend.[3] Furthermore, there is a growing tendency among parish priests and ministers to experiment with new and "far-out" organizational forms and to regard no particular form as "sacred" merely because it is ancient or customary.

Religion as human organization is thus subject to imperfection, change, and flux. We can look neither to the past nor to the future for the perfect religious organization that never changes and never fails. Important as religious organization has been and still is, not only as a stabilizing force in society but also as a source of security for its members, it is itself only relatively stable. The history of organized Protestant Christianity bears abundant testimony to the truth of this statement; and even the Roman Catholic Church, an organization of remarkable stability, has undergone many transformations in the course of its long history.[4]

We need not be surprised, then, that religious organization is not perfect or permanent, or disillusioned at the inevitable discrepancy between religion's lofty ethical ideals and their embodiment in human groups. The sociological knowledge that all social organizations are the result of willed human activity and that consequently there is no automatic correspondence between noble ideals and organizational forms should temper both disillusionment and defeatism. Furthermore, sociologists know that no single organization, religious or otherwise, is the only force at work in a society; hence what any one organization can accomplish depends to a great extent on the strength of other institutional structures and on the counterforces and trends of change at work. Thus the student of sociology, if he is a member of a religious organization, will be wise to limit his demands for perfection in organizational achievement. It is open to him, however, since human organizations are molded by human action, to exert whatever influence he may have to help his own church come closer to its avowed ideal. His sociological understanding of the organizational structure of which he is a part and of his own status within it should assist him in this task. These comments are not to be interpreted as a sort of Pollyanna endorsement by sociology of the imperfections of religious organization. Sociology in its scientific role is concerned neither with endorsement nor its opposite, but with accurate description and analysis. The thinking individual must take responsibility for his own course of action.

Moreover, when as students we try to understand the actual historical development of particular churches, including much evil perpetrated by them under religion's cloak, we are confronted with a strange paradox. Anti-institutional trends exist at the heart of religious organization itself. This fact derives from the circumstance that religion has other-worldly as well as this-worldly interests and concerns. Hence churches, unlike purely secular organizations, must somehow find room for both. Many great religious teachers have supplied a sort of running critique of religious organization, especially when the latter, deadened by formalism or corrupted by power, has stifled the expression of religion's other-worldly ends.

These religious leaders, such as Moses, the Buddha, Jesus, and Mohammed, or in more modern times men like St. Francis, George Fox, Roger Williams, Ralph Waldo Emerson, and Pope John XXIII, have usually had something of the mystic about them. As experienced within the consciousness of the worshiper, mysticism—that communication between the religious believer and the ultimate objects of his faith—is an aspect of religious experience that has proved highly resistant to organization. Furthermore, persons in whom the mystical other-worldly side of religion predominates have rarely proved entirely amenable to this-worldly organizational control.* It is hardly accidental that

---

* The mystic and the mystic element in religion, possibly just because they are never entirely amenable to organization, point up some of its basic problems. Mystics, however, are by no means always organizational rebels or founders of new religious movements. True, the thoroughgoing mystic is potentially an anarchist as far as organization is concerned, for in the final analysis there is for him no authority higher than his own inner light. The mystic, however, is frequently not so much against religious organization as indifferent to it. Some mystics have been hermits and solitaries, such as St. Simeon Stylites on his famous pillar. Others have formed their own independent communities. Still others have remained peacefully in the fold of established religious organizations, organizations as different as East European Jewry, the Society of Friends, and the Roman Catholic Church. However amenable they may be to organizational discipline in matters of indifference to them, yet, as an English bishop once said, "You can never quite tell where

the great religious teachers mentioned above were highly critical of the official religious organization of their times. Such leaders have at times disrupted existing institutions while providing inspiration for new ones. [In spite of the dilemma in which all religious organization is involved, one of its outstanding features is its abundant capacity to renew itself from within.] This polar tension between other-worldly and this-worldly, radical and conservative tendencies endows religious organization with its inherent vitality and, moreover, makes it a fascinating and exceedingly complicated study for the sociologist.

THE RELIGIOUS MOVEMENT AND CHANGING FORMS OF RELIGIOUS ORGANIZATION

The basic dilemma of religious organization may be seen more concretely when we consider one of its main manifestations, namely the "religious movement." A religious movement here refers to any organized attempt to spread a new religion or a new interpretation of an already existing religion. The great world religions of Buddhism, Christianity, and Islam can be regarded as the outcome of religious movements. Similarly, religious movements also develop within the framework of already established religions, for example, the Franciscan and the Protestant movements within Catholic Christianity, the Oxford Movement within Anglicanism, and Father Divine's Peace Mission within American Protestantism. Such movements typically pass through a series of rather well-defined stages and after their initial expansive phases usually become stabilized in relation to other religions. The more settled phases of such religious movements may themselves furnish the matrix from which later religious movements arise.

The first phase of a religious movement usually is dominated

you are with a person who claims to be guided by the Inner Light." A socially aroused mystic may turn into a dynamo of energy and play hob with the stabilized smugness of established religious organizations.

RELIGION: A SOCIOLOGICAL VIEW

by the personality of its founder. Whatever the quality of his religious insight, a successful founder must possess powerful *charisma*—a fascination, a compelling attraction, that draws men to him.* Although, as noted above, founders of religious movements are often critical of existing religious organization, their own religious and ethical message, however new in certain respects, inevitably owes much to the religious tradition in which the particular founder has been nurtured. Thus the teachings of Jesus are both critical of organized Judaism and yet grounded in it, and the message of the Buddha is at once a revolt against traditional Hinduism and yet deeply molded by it.

During their early formative years most religious movements have a fluid, informal primary-group character. Groups of first-followers, whether of Jesus of Nazareth, the Buddha, Mohammed, or St. Francis of Assisi, comprise small circles of individual adherents who stimulate one another, while being stimulated themselves, by face-to-face contact with their charismatic leader. This contact supplies for them both cohesion and dynamic. Moreover, such "circular" fellowships commonly generate enormous psychic and social energy.** The group is likely to resist organizational rigidity and its main problem in this innovating, creative phase is not organization as such, but rather absorbing and gaining a hearing for the new religious teachings. To be sure, as such groups begin to grow, their founders may supply them with a rule of life and conduct, such as Jesus' instructions to the twelve and to the seventy or the Buddha's enunciation of the Noble Eightfold Path. Yet matters of rules and discipline are not usually crucial at this stage. Few precise, intellectual answers are given to questions about the nature of the founder and the authority for his mission, although such questions almost always arise. Similarly, while the leader lives and his presence dominates his followers, the delegation of his authority and the

---

* As Weber used this concept (drawn from the Scriptures), it is applicable not only to religious but also to political leaders. Adolf Hitler and Mahatma Gandhi are examples of charismatic leaders.

** The small cells of both nazism and communism are good examples of the dynamic energy of such charismatically led political groups.

relative ranking of the individuals within the movement are unlikely to become divisive issues.

In the second phase of the movement the successors of the founder are forced to resolve and clarify important matters pertaining to organization, belief, and ritual that were left in abeyance during the founder's lifetime. At this stage the movement typically becomes what we now term a "church": the formal organization of a group of worshipers who share common and defined beliefs and rituals concerning the sacred objects and entities they revere. In this second phase, which is often precipitated by the advent of a second generation of believers, qualifications for membership are made more explicit and the lines of authority in the organization are more sharply drawn. Moreover, beliefs about the sacred person and mission of the founder are formulated as official theologies and creeds, and a cult of the founder involving formal acceptance of the beliefs embodied in such creeds not infrequently supersedes a more spontaneous, personal adherence to his teachings. Furthermore, religious practices, such as the Christian celebration of the Last Supper and the Hebrew Passover, gradually develop into formally prescribed rituals. This second stage is often accompanied by struggles over leadership, such as those that rent Islam after the death of Mohammed, or conflict concerning the formulation of beliefs, such as those that shook Christianity in the second and third centuries. To resolve such struggles a "second founder" is sometimes required. In such circumstances Christianity produced the organizing genius, Paul of Tarsus; Islam, the Caliph Omar; and Mormonism, Brigham Young.

If a movement successfully survives the second stage, the third is characteristically one of continued expansion and diversification. The movement becomes established and takes on a variety of organizational forms. Religious movements differ in the degree to which they expand, some remaining delimited by ethnic, class, and cultural barriers. Buddhism, Christianity, and Islam transcended these barriers and in addition made converts of individuals of outstanding political and economic power. At this stage a religious movement confronts the danger of becoming the victim of its own success and there comes face to face with the organizational dilemma discussed in the first section of this chapter.

This third stage, which may be protracted in time, poses another problem. The leaders now have the task of answering why, in spite of the movement's success in gaining followers, its original objectives, so immediate and vivid to the first disciples, have not yet been achieved in concrete fact. This problem is especially acute for those movements with an apocalyptic message, whose leaders have alerted their followers for the imminent second coming of a messiah, for the end of the world and the establishment, by supernatural means, of a heavenly kingdom on earth. With the advent of the third generation of Christians, for example, it became necessary to provide an additional interpretation of Christ's second coming—an interpretation that stressed His coming in the sacraments and His invisible presence in the hearts of the faithful. It was also found necessary to transfer the hope for establishment of God's Kingdom to a distant, other-worldly future.

With the principal exception of Judaism, which never entirely abandoned its hope for the tangible restoration of Jerusalem, few religions have held steadily as their objective the establishment of an earthly Kingdom of God.* The emphasis in modern times on what is known as the *social gospel,* and on social action among some Christian groups, is one attempt to implement this objective. But it has been left to the great so-called political religions of our own day, such as fascism, Marxism, and communism, to make the social embodiment of their particular version of heaven on earth their official, primary aim. These political-religious movements, however, have now entered their third stage, and their leaders, too, have been faced with difficult problems of reinterpreting objectives when their attainment has been unduly delayed. With these reinterpretations the leaders justify

* Judaism, of course, has always had spiritual as well as tangible objectives. There has persisted in Judaism a trend, however, strikingly exemplified in Zionism, to pin the hope of religious fulfillment to a particular people and a particular place.

both their own dominance and the continued existence of the movements. For at this third stage of their development both religious and political movements have an established interest in their own continuance, which becomes a major objective of their organizations. At this stage, the process of routinization, usually begun in the second stage, has fully set in.[5]

TYPES OF RELIGIOUS ORGANI-
ZATION AND TYPES OF SOCIETY

On various occasions earlier in this book we have had reason to refer to religious organization and to use, in a somewhat casual way, such terms as "church," "denomination," and "sect." Now we must examine these terms more closely and analyze their content.

All students of religious organization are deeply indebted to the writings of the German scholar Ernst Troeltsch, author of the monumental study *The Social Teachings of the Christian Churches*. Troeltsch distinguishes between two main types of religious group, the church and the sect.[6] We have already used the term "church" in a general sense to characterize all forms of religious group life. In the context of the present discussion, however, we shall use the term in this more restricted sense to denote an established church in distinction from the sect. Some sociologists, for the sake of clarity, have employed the Latin term *ecclesia* as a substitute for the term "church" when used in this restricted sense. For Troeltsch the church, or *ecclesia*, is a type of religious organization characteristic of a religious movement in its mature, established phase. A sect, on the other hand, marks the early dynamic stages of a movement. Troeltsch confined his studies to Christianity. Because of the wide range of organizational types that it comprises and also because Christianity is familiar to most of us, we will follow his example. On the other hand, the pioneer researches of Max Weber in ancient Judaism and in the religions of India and of China have sug-

RELIGION: A SOCIOLOGICAL VIEW

gested to some scholars that Troeltsch's typology may be capable of a wider application.

Nevertheless, in recent years this church-sect dichotomy has received considerable discussion, modification, and criticism by sociologists. There are some who feel that it may have outlived much of its usefulness. However, although in some respects it may appear to be outworn, no viable substitute for it has yet been devised. Therefore we shall continue to use it here, while indicating some of the difficulties of the distinction that have been pointed out by contemporary sociologists.

Those scholars, like H. Richard Niebuhr, who have been mainly concerned with the American scene, have modified Troeltsch's original polar dichotomy of church and sect by introducing the concept of the denomination as a middle term, between the conservative "established" church into which members are born and the more revolutionary voluntary sect that members join by conversion or conviction.[7] Other sociologists, such as the late Howard Becker, have elaborated still further on Troeltsch's original two categories, and have added a fourth, namely, the "cult."[8] The denomination, however, has appeared to both Niebuhr and Becker and to many other sociologists as the most prevalent form of American religious organization. Furthermore, they have remarked on a characteristic tendency of American sects to develop more "churchly" traits and thus become denominations. Liston Pope has shown how the stages in this development from sect to denomination may be distinguished by various definite criteria.[9] The English sociologist Bryan Wilson, however, has pointed out how the dynamic tendency of "successful" sects to become denominations is mainly a characteristic of societies that are expanding economically and of groups that he terms "conversion" sects rather than "withdrawing" sects.[10] Moreover, Benton Johnson has claimed that conceptualizations of church, sect, denomination, and cult are misleading and confusing for sociological research because they collect in one package a number of different variables that do not always cohere in any given case.[11] Finally, sociologists who have been studying religious organization in Asian and African societies have been discovering new and different organizational forms that cannot be subsumed under any of these sociological categories.

This note on terminological usage, which could be expanded considerably, may appear confusing or unimportant to the student.[12] He should keep in mind that its main intention is to drive home the fact that sociological concepts, which refer to religious and other forms of organization, are not static affairs but are continually being revised in the light of current research and of our knowledge of new organizational forms. It seems probable that some viable new sociological conceptualizations of religious organization will be devised in the near future.

Having registered a word of warning about the provisional nature of the organizational categories that students are likely to encounter in much existing sociological literature, we shall proceed to describe these categories in general terms. We shall follow Becker in adding to the polar types of church and sect the subtypes of denomination and cult.[13]

Church, Sect, Denomination, and Cult

A church stresses its universality within a given territory, either national or international. All members born within this given territory, by virtue of their residence, are considered in principle to be members of the church. Its patterns of authority are typically both formal and traditional. This authority is centralized and hierarchical and hence is relayed from top to bottom of the organization by means of a chain of command. Various kinds of leaders exist in this large, diversified organization, the most typical leader being the priest rather than the prophet. The priest is an official whose authority is sanctioned by the hierarchy. His main function—namely to administer the sacramental means of grace to the members—is both exclusive and crucial.

The church (or *ecclesia*), in marked distinction from the sect, neither withdraws from the world nor fights it. Its aim is rather to control the world in the interests of the organization. Hence there is close reciprocation between the government of the

RELIGION: A SOCIOLOGICAL VIEW

church and the secular institutions of the society, including civil government. For this reason, as Troeltsch has well put it, the church dominates the world and is itself dominated by it.

The ideal type of church—a universal world church—has, of course, never existed in any complete fashion. The Catholic Church in the thirteenth century, perhaps its nearest approximation, did not include even all of Western Christendom. Today the Roman Catholic Church still exemplifies, in theory, an international church, and similarly the Anglican and Lutheran Churches furnish examples of national churches.

The sect, in contrast, is typically a small, exclusive group whose members join voluntarily, usually as adults. Authority is exercised by virtue of personal charisma rather than hierarchical sanction; yet religious discipline is rigorous and is commonly enforced by the mutual scrutiny of the group members. Generally sects are characterized by religious and ethical fervor, their beliefs stress primitive gospel teachings, and their practices emphasize the way of life of the early Christians. Sectarian beliefs and practices sharpen the distinction between the small, closely knit group of sect members and the outside world. Indeed, sectarians are usually hostile to members of all other churches and often to those of rival sects. "Come out from among them and be ye separate" might well be the motto of the sect. Hence sects also tend to be radical in their rejection of secular government; sect members may, for instance, refuse to bear civil office, to perform military service, to take oaths, and to pay taxes.

Sects are of two main varieties: withdrawing sects and militant sects. The monastic orders were the principal withdrawing sects of medieval times, whereas in the modern world sects of this type include the Plymouth Brethren and the Old Order Amish of rural Pennsylvania. Among the militant sects may be numbered the Anabaptists of the seventeenth century and, although possibly less militant, the Jehovah's Witnesses of our own day.

A denomination is a relatively stabilized group, often of considerable size and complexity, that recruits its members largely by birthright. It is characteristically one among a number of churches within a given territory or within a number of given territories. Authority in a denomination is sometimes hierarchical in nature and sometimes stems from the elective action of local congregations. Its discipline, unlike that of the sect, is on the whole formal and conventional rather than fervid and exacting. Its priests and pastors are usually temperate in their evangelical zeal and hold themselves chiefly responsible for the welfare of their own congregations. The denomination neither withdraws from, fights, nor controls the world, but for the most part cooperates with it. As a rule it also cooperates with the civil authorities and with most other religious bodies.

Denominations are of two main kinds. They may be one-time sects, tamed and matured, that have made their peace with the world. Or they may be former churches that have been forced to accept denominational status as the condition of their survival in societies like the United States, where the Constitution prohibits an established church of any kind. The Methodist and Baptist Churches are well-known examples of denominations that have evolved from former sects, whereas the Episcopal and Lutheran Churches, which were nationally established *ecclesiae* in England and Sweden respectively, are denominations in the United States.

The cult is a small religious group in some respects similar to the sect, although, unlike the sect, its membership is largely confined to dwellers in metropolitan areas. Ancient Athens and ancient Rome were riddled with cults no less than London, New York, and Los Angeles are today. Cult members are frequently rootless urban individuals who may embrace a cult when they are confronted with loneliness and frustration in middle and later life. Thus cult members, like sect members, are voluntary joiners. But joining a cult does not imply the acceptance of group discipline. In the cult, authority is at a minimum. Members may join a cult not because they accept all of its beliefs and practices but rather because some of them happen to fit in with their own. Furthermore, membership in a cult is not exclusive and need not debar individuals from membership in other, perhaps more conventional, churches. Thus the individual's commitment to the cult is more tenuous, and the term of his membership is likely to be more transient, than in a sect. Cult organization is therefore frequently loose and amorphous.

Cult leadership is charismatic, informal, often precarious, and under metropolitan conditions of relative anonymity, sometimes corrupt. Cult beliefs frequently emphasize one particular aspect of Christian teaching, such as spiritual healing, or they may blend Christian beliefs with beliefs borrowed from other cultures, often oriental ones. Cult beliefs are usually more esoteric and mystical than the plain gospel teachings stressed by the typical sect.

Cult members as a rule neither withdraw from the world nor are likely to be in militant opposition to it. Indeed, cultists, with some notable exceptions, are unlikely to be actively concerned with broader political and social issues. The function of the cult is rather to help its members adjust as satisfactorily as possible to the world and its institutions.

There is less general agreement among sociologists as to the definition of "cult." Some have equated "cult" with the early formative stages of a sect's development. Our emphasis here, however, is on the more permissive nature of cult discipline as opposed to the ethical strictness of the sect, and on the eclectic nature of cult beliefs in comparison with the sect's "gospel" emphasis. Examples of cults are Father Divine's Peace Movement (of the Depression era) and the "I Am" movement. Some young people's groups today, such as Krishna Consciousness and the followers of Meher Baba, may also be classified as cults. The state of California is a prolific breeding ground of cults.

Affinities Between Types of Religious Organization and Types of Society

Some types of religious organization are more congenial to certain types of society than to others. Nevertheless, it is possible for several different types of religious organization to exist together in the same society.

Model One societies need hardly concern us, for in them religious organization is likely to interpenetrate the total organization of the society rather than to be separate and distinct from it.

Model Two societies have provided the social setting for the great churches of the Western world, the Roman Catholic Church and the Eastern Orthodox Church. These "universal" *ecclesiae* were, in the later stages of many Model Two societies, superseded by "national" churches, such as the Church of England, the national Lutheran Churches of Germany and Scandinavian countries, and the various national churches of the Eastern Orthodox connection. Before the rise of strong national states, an agricultural feudal society with shifting political boundaries accorded well enough with forms of religious organization that symbolized a widespread overall unity. The rise of national states shattered this unity, but these national states at first sought to strengthen themselves by a modified form of church in which religious unity reinforced national unity.

As Model Two societies began to break up, however, and the power of absolutist monarchs was challenged, the sectarian type of religious organization furnished the most viable type of organization for combating both the religious and the political establishment. Out of the struggle of the sects both with the dominant churches and with each other, a new era of religious toleration and freedom was born.

Model Three societies were the heirs of the religious freedom that had been gained by the sects. In these urbanized, heterogeneous, and individualistic societies no new churches (*ecclesiae*) have been born. The climate of opinion (as well as the social structure) of Model Three societies is, on the whole, unfavorable to "established" churches. In such societies already existing church establishments, whether universal or merely national in their claims to allegiance, have had to accept, either willingly or unwillingly, an approximately denominational status.

The denomination is the type of religious organization that seems to be most "at home" in Model Three societies. Some denominations, as suggested above, are former established churches which, within specific political boundaries, have abandoned their universalistic claims. But the great majority are "tamed" sects, whose members have improved their social and

234

economic status by utilizing the opportunities that an industrialized society offers to the industrious and fortunate. The denomination was—and is—congenial to such people. It is large and dignified enough to symbolize middle-class standing. Its type of organization is reassuringly familiar. Membership in it is voluntary, and the choice of a denominational affiliation has met a deeply felt need for self-identification as well as provided an outlet for status striving.

In spite of the dominance of denominational types of religious organization, new sects—and new cults—have continued to proliferate in Model Three societies. Not all members realize the rather general expectation of upward mobility. Those who fail to do so sometimes withdraw from the association with their more prosperous denomination-oriented fellow religionists and form a new sect. The ways in which these new sects are brought into being has been described in illuminating fashion by Liston Pope in his *Millhands and Preachers*.[14]

Another reason for the persistence of sect-type religious groups inheres in the heterogeneous nature of Model Three societies and the very different demands that life in rural and in urban areas make on those who live in them. New migrants are continually being drawn from rural hinterlands, either foreign or domestic, to live and work in large cities. These people, whether southern Negroes, Puerto Ricans, or Mexicans, have a hard struggle to adjust to impersonal, big-city living and are likely to find themselves lost and ill at ease in a large (and possibly formal) city church even though it may be a church of their own denomination. Their only effective community is their immediate neighborhood, usually a low-rent area. In such areas new "gospel" sects are frequently formed. Sect membership helps these migrants to gain social standing in their new urban environment and to recapture some of the more intimate primary group atmosphere of the church back home. The Pentecostal churches and the Churches of God are examples of religious sects that have grown up to meet this need. Such sects frequently ease the adjustment to urban ways of living and eventually facilitate social mobility. The need for such sect-like churches is likely to persist as long as cities grow larger and multiply and continue to attract needy people from rural areas.

Sects are to be found in some rural areas, too, particularly in the South, and especially in mountainous regions and in open farm lands where dwellings are scattered and cultural resources meager. The "Churches of God," of which there are several varieties, exist not only in cities but also in rural surroundings. Even predominantly Roman Catholic territory, such as rural New Mexico, has its sect-like groups, notably the *Penitentes*. Moreover, sect membership is not confined to lower-class persons. A significant number of middle-class people belong to such sectarian groups as the Pentecostals, Jehovah's Witnesses, and some others.

The cult is almost entirely a metropolitan, Model Three society phenomenon. The metropolis is typically characterized by "anomie" (a term originating with Durkheim), which implies an absence of common agreement regarding the standards (or norms) that define correct ways of behaving. The rural or small town individual, usually accustomed to regulating his behavior by such norms, hence experiences moral confusion and insecurity when encountering in the metropolis a great variety of competing and often conflicting ethical standards. Furthermore, the high degree of anonymity of much of urban life causes the individual to be very much on his own, with a minimum of group control.

In such a situation "faith" in the more conventional and orthodox religious norms is readily lost. The atomization and impersonality of life under metropolitan conditions leaves some individuals rudderless and confused. Furthermore, religious and ethical beliefs and philosophical ideas from all over the world are to be found in the metropolis. These ideas may form a basis for cult beliefs, some of which attract urban individuals whose considerable intellectual curiosity may or may not be balanced by sophisticated discrimination. Such cults as Bahaism, The Rosicrucian Order, Subud, The Order of Krishna Consciousness, the fast-growing Scientology and many others offer a haven to such questing individuals.[15] Some attract the educated, and others attract the ill-informed. Most of them give alienated and groping individuals an "in" feeling without making too many stringent ethical demands. Insofar as Model Three societies comprise a greater proportion of alienated individuals than either of our other models, it is not surprising that the cult is especially congenial to societies of this type. A glance at the Saturday "church page" of *The New York Times* or other metropolitan newspapers will demonstrate the number and variety of such cults.

Are the United States and some other Model Three societies now actually in a post–Model Three stage? This is an interesting question with an important bearing on the appropriateness of some current forms of religious organization for serving contemporary needs. We may already be experiencing life in a hypothetical Model Four society, the characteristics of which are not yet clearly defined. It has been suggested that the shift from an industrial society to a "technotronic" one, dominated ever more by technology—especially electronic communication and computers—may be as revolutionary in character as the change from an agrarian to an industrial society.[16]

If this is the case, the further question arises: Does the prevalent form of denominational organization continue to be suited to the religious and social needs of the society's members? Modern man seems destined to lead his life in an increasingly bureaucratic context. More and more he finds his identity defined in terms of *numbers*, whether he goes to the bank, to his job, or to the motor vehicle or social security office. In this situation he struggles to discover in qualitative terms his own individual identity and to assert it in discernible ways. Possibly he looks to religion and religious organization as a kind of last resort where he may perhaps experience self-discovery and self-expression. He may wish to exercise more direct control than is possible merely through membership in church-related subgroups. If such is indeed the case, he is likely to be disenchanted with large-scale denominational organization, which he cannot hope to control and in which his personal identity is lost.

Furthermore, electronic communications and business relationships are bringing religiously interested individuals in touch with the entire world and therefore with a vast variety of religions and religious organizations. Partly for these reasons and partly because of a new ecumenical spirit generated by the Second Vatican Council, some people—particularly young people—are finding conventional denominational structures too "uptight," walled-in, and self-contained.

There are many signs today that the more conventional forms of religious organization are under considerable strain. Not only are existing religious bodies themselves attempting to experiment with new organizational forms, but new independent organizations are also coming into being. These new forms will be discussed more fully below.

FORMS OF DENOMINATIONAL GOVERNMENT AND LOCAL CHURCH ORGANIZATION

So far we have been concerned with broad and general aspects of the interrelationship between the organization of religion and the organization of society. We shall now consider briefly some of the main forms of church government and their repercussions on church life on the local, congregational level. It is here, if anywhere, that the religious objectives of the organization become tangible in the lives of the membership and influence the social life of local communities.

There are generally considered to be three main types of church government: the episcopal, the presbyterian, and the congregational.[17] The differences between these types of government have often been discussed, and each of these types, in theory, involves a particular set of consequences for social relationships within the church group.

The episcopal form of government sets the tone for the relationship between the parish priest and his congregation by making his appointment dependent upon episcopal choice and sanction and by subjecting him to episcopal discipline. Again, in theory, the position of the parish priest as an officer of a centralized episcopal hierarchy, while limiting his freedom of action in some aspects, also frees him from too binding a dependence upon the wishes and whims of a local congregation. On the other hand, the autonomy of local congregations is limited by this type of arrangement. The laity in theory have the power of protest rather than the full right of initiative.

The episcopal form of government can be seen most clearly in churches of the *ecclesia* (or established) type and most clearly of all in the Roman Catholic Church.[18] The episcopal form of government, however, also obtains in some other denominations, such as the Episcopal and Lutheran Churches (which are still national churches in England and the Scandinavian countries) and also in the Methodist Church in the United States. Methodist Church government, it should be noted, is a hybrid, combining, as does the government of the United States, strong centralized authority at the top with considerable autonomy at the bottom.

The presbyterian form of organization places the main control in the hands of the presbytery, or body of preachers, which in principle is an aristocracy stressing educational competence. The endorsement of this organization enhances the authority of the preacher vis-à-vis his congregation, even though it subjects him to the control of his top-ranking colleagues. On the other hand, the congregation, which is also subject to the aristocratic control of the elders, has the right to request the appointment of a preacher, who is sometimes chosen on the basis of a kind of preaching contest.*

The congregational type of church government, as exemplified by the early Baptists and other independent congregations (such as the Unitarians and Universalists), maximizes the power of the local groups in both the choice and control of the minister and in

---

* Some readers may be familiar with the old Scottish story about the conference held by two elders who had just listened to the preaching of a ministerial candidate. "Ay, ay," said the first, "he preached a rare powerful sermon." "Ay, ay," replied the second, "But his firrrrst prayer clean damned him."

the conduct of all organizational affairs. With the power of the central organization legally nonexistent or at a minimum, the dependence of the minister, both financial and otherwise, on the members of the immediate congregation is at a maximum. The minister becomes a democratic leader of a congregation that usually exercises its considerable powers of initiative and control through a congeries of not always harmonious committees and subassociations. Lacking the possibility of citing the authority or enlisting the aid of a central organization, the local congregational minister is on his own, to sink or swim, as far as his relationships with the local church are concerned.[19]

For the sake of clarity we have described these three forms of church government as distinct types. In our contemporary society, however, all three forms have been modified to a great extent. In the episcopal churches, not excluding the Roman Catholic Church itself, since there is no sufficiency of gilt-edged endowments, the enhanced financial powers of the laity have gained for them both hearing and representation, including, particularly since the Second Vatican Council, increasing powers of initiative in other than financial affairs. In the Anglican churches in some areas committees of the laity have a limited choice, or at least a power of veto, in the selection of their priests. In part due to the influence of corresponding changes in civil government the tendency has been to democratize the episcopate and to grant a greater measure of autonomy to the local churches.

Similar tendencies have been at work to modify presbyterian forms in a democratic direction. The congregational form, on the other hand, has developed associations of local churches on a nationwide basis. This trend has also been typical of Jewish congregations, no less than of Baptist, Unitarian, and other Christian community churches. Indeed, the isolated, detached congregation appears to be ill-adapted for long-term survival in Model Three societies. Although in the associations and federations that increasingly bind these congregational churches together much care has been taken to safeguard the reserve powers of the local constituent bodies, both ministers and members feel that some degree of centralization of financial and other resources—for example, facilities for ministerial education—is of great benefit to the local churches. In this development of co-operation between a federated government and local bodies the churches are in line with nationwide trends in the joint federal-local handling of education and social welfare.

BUREAUCRATIC TRENDS IN RELIGIOUS ORGANIZATION

Although the organizational differences just described persist as part of the tradition of various denominations, the plain fact is that all sizable religious bodies in America, Protestant as well as Catholic, have either developed or are developing strong centralized bureaucracies. Thus many of the historic distinctions in regard to church government are becoming increasingly academic. A bureaucratic hierarchy has long been a recognized aspect of Roman Catholic religious organization. The organizations of the Anglican and Lutheran Churches follow a similar hierarchical pattern. In these churches centralized bureaucratic power is religiously and legally legitimated power and hence wears the mantle of sanctioned authority.* A Catholic diocesan bishop is aware that he is a bureaucrat—even though he might not like to be called a *mere* bureaucrat—and a priest working on the staff of a diocesan headquarters knows quite well that he is an "organization man." Neither has cause to apologize for his situation since he is simply exercising legitimate ecclesiastical authority. This fact has not prevented parish priests from overtly protesting episcopal and even Papal decisions, nor regional and local churches from desiring and sometimes obtaining a greater degree of autonomy. For the most part, however, con-

---

* We are using here Max Weber's distinction between power and authority. "Power" implies "the ability of a person or group to determine the actions of others without regard for their needs and desire" whereas "authority" is the legal right to exercise specifically defined powers. Hence power may exist without authority as *de facto* power, and while authority gives the right to exercise power, the power in question may or may not be exercised.

cessions are made through regular channels. Although there are occasions, of course, in which power is informally exercised by individuals and groups without authority, there does not exist *in theory* that basic conflict between authority and power that often manifests itself in the congregational type of church polity.

While the central hierarchy of the Roman Catholic Church has recently been delegating authority from above to regional and national units, which have thereby been enabled to exercise a greater degree of autonomy, in the case of the "free" churches a reverse process has been taking place.[20] The churches descended from the left-wing Calvinist tradition—notably the Baptists, the Disciples of Christ, the Congregationalists, and the Unitarians—have claimed scriptural authority for the complete autonomy of their local congregations. Throughout their history they have been, and still frequently are, extremely suspicious of centralized authority and power. Insofar as these churches have been forced through the logic of their own needs to delegate powers to a central organization, it has been a case of "authority" from below, as vested in the individual congregation, reluctantly acquiescing in the delegation of "power" to those above. For the denominational associations, nominally the creatures and servants of the churches, typically become in course of time great independent corporations that control certain of the churches' important enterprises, such as missionary work, ministerial training, publication, and religious education.[21]

How did this change come about? We mentioned earlier that the single autonomous congregation was ill-adapted for survival in Model Three societies. One reason for this is that the successful church in modern urban society is becoming more and more a multifaceted operation, supplying a variety of services that are increasingly expensive to finance and call for a considerable variety of administrative and executive skills. This circumstance has made it mandatory for individual congregations to cooperate, for the attainment of such objectives requires not only a degree of centralized financing but also the maintenance of a denominational headquarters and the recruitment of staff members with the requisite specialized skills. The recent tendency toward denominational mergers, such as those that created the United Churches of Christ, the United Methodist Church, and the Unitarian Universalist Association, has further accentuated the need for centralized administration.

It was inevitable that these headquarters staff members should develop considerable *de facto* power, since they are "on the job" all the time and "in the know" concerning many aspects of denominational affairs of which ministers occupied with local congregational matters may well be ignorant. But among those who adhere to the congregational, in contrast to the episcopal, type of church polity there exists a long and hardy tradition of distrust for centralized authority and power. This distrust may persist even when it has been "functionally necessary" for the survival and health of the denomination as a whole to grant certain powers to a headquarters staff. Such distrust has sometimes manifested itself in a reluctance to grant legal authority to those at denominational headquarters who in any case must exercise actual power.

In an attempt to meet this situation, the free churches, as mentioned earlier, have tried to devise ways to "put a fence" around this centrally exercised power. The extent to which they have succeeded is questionable. With respect to the (North) American Baptist Convention, Paul M. Harrison believes that the "fences" are largely futile and that the failure to grant full authority to those who must necessarily exercise power merely compounds organizational inefficiency and encourages the emergence of extra-official personal power.[22] Those who disagree with Harrison would regard the vesting of ultimate authority in the local congregations as an essential guarantee of their continued power to challenge headquarters' directives. In their view such authority is a condition of health in a nationwide denomination that is thus put under pressure to adapt its programs to local and regional differences. The growth, both in numbers and autonomy, of regional associations has been one concrete expression of this point of view. Furthermore, in the smaller regional associations the constituent congregations, clergy as well as laity, are better able to influence decisions.

The custom of holding annual meetings or conventions has also been regarded as one of the main checks on the exercise of centralized bureaucratic power. Local congregations elect delegates to these conventions, where the policies and allocations of funds for the following year are supposedly determined. Harrison has claimed that in the case of the American Baptist Convention the effective authority exercised by the delegates is minimal. Supporting his conclusion, he notes that most of the business has been carefully processed ahead of time by members of the headquarters staff and that many of the delegates are inexperienced and come to the business "cold." Furthermore, the denominational budget, on which the implementation of policy largely depends, is often as complex and incomprehensible to the average layman as the budgets presented by business corporation executives at an annual shareholders' meeting. In addition, the inexperienced delegate "does not know how to operate the caucuses, when to speak in the open meetings, how to gain entry to the crucial 'backroom' discussions, or how to unravel the tangle of technical reports that perplex him." Lengthy discussions of issues and an opportunity to cast a vote cannot compensate the delegate who requires longer hours of preparation to comprehend the proceedings.[23]

For some of their ineffectiveness the delegates—and the churches that elect them—have only themselves to blame. Delegates are sometimes elected with little regard for their competence, and when elected, they are poorly prepared to take part in the meetings. They are often bored by the long discussions, fail to attend the business meetings, and are not on hand to record their votes. They may regard attendance at the convention as an opportunity for meeting old friends and perhaps for gaining a little "spiritual uplift." Moreover, the denominational powers-that-be often, for their part, use the conventions and the access to the mass media that they usually facilitate as an opportunity to engage in public relations and promotional activities. Since annual meetings are largely mass meetings composed of any who care to attend, the officials of the denomination rarely encounter trouble in directing such a meeting into channels acceptable to them, although this situation is changing very considerably with the advent of "confrontation" politics.

This account is not intended to be unduly cynical. The problems that modern organized religions face as human organizations are similar to those confronting all large-scale organizations in modern industrial societies, whether industrial corporations, trade unions, or learned societies. In fact, almost exactly the same points could be written about the annual conventions of the American Sociological Association. The major problem is to reconcile efficiency with democracy. The larger the organization, the greater the tendency to centralized control and the greater the difficulty of holding those who exercise such control accountable to the membership.

CHURCH GOVERNMENT AT THE CONGREGATIONAL LEVEL

Church government at the grass roots is also becoming increasingly similar in pattern, regardless of denominational differences. The reins of government are typically in the hands of an elected governing body, which may be termed a church council, vestry, or board of trustees. Such governing bodies are commonly elected by the church membership for terms of three years, generally on a rotating basis similar to that employed by the United States Senate, so that there is never a complete turnover of members in a single year. The minister or pastor usually guides this governing body, although he does not always preside at their meetings. In many cases a lay chairman presides. Governing bodies ordinarily meet once a month and have authority to carry on routine business without the obligation to consult with the congregation as a whole. The entire congregation, however, may participate directly in church government at an annual meeting, at which the work of the past year is reviewed and the succeeding year's plans, including the budget, are set forth and new members to the governing body are often elected.

Congregational meetings vary considerably in the degree to which the ordinary member participates. In general, the smaller the congregation and the more direct the awareness of each member of his personal budgetary responsibility, the more likelihood of lively congregational participation. In some large churches congregational meetings may be very perfunctory affairs.

In most churches this central governing body is augmented by a group of committees, each charged with some particular responsibility, such as finance, plant maintenance, religious education, and the like. Although the minister is ultimately responsible for the conduct of the affairs of the church, the amount of actual power he may exercise will vary from congregation to congregation, and even in the same congregation at different periods. In general, however, the minister has a good deal to say about who is elected to the council and appointed to the various committees.

Who are the members of these congregational councils, whom do they represent, and how are they elected? Where does the real power lie, and for what purposes is it exercised? These are interesting sociological questions.[24] For answering them, we have at present some reasonably good clues, although little "hard" data. As early as 1928 Jerome Davis conducted a study on the social composition of the boards of control of 367 Protestant churches representing seven denominations.[25] He found that "on the whole the membership of the boards of control is made up overwhelmingly of the favored classes." Davis was of the opinion that such domination of church governing councils resulted in a basically conservative point of view and constituted a built-in resistance to change and innovation. Since Davis's study, no other was made until the early 1960s, when James Swift of the Survey Research Center of the University of California (Berkeley) examined the data collected in an investigation of twelve urban Lutheran churches in a way roughly comparable to that adopted by Davis. It would seem that the years since 1928 had brought relatively little change. In essentials Swift's findings reinforced those of the earlier study. He found that the leadership was primarily drawn from members who are in the professions and hold managerial positions, that their level of education is higher than that of the general membership, and that their ages tend to cluster in the forty- to fifty-year range. A further interesting finding was that in spite of the well-known fact that women are both more numerous and more active in most areas of church life than are men, very few women are members of governing bodies.[26]

Although these findings are scarcely surprising, the consequences they imply for the role of the church in society—the question Davis raised—are still highly pertinent. Social scientists generally agree that class differences and age differences are associated with different ways of looking at the world and that, more often than not, the older and more well-to-do a person is, the more satisfied he is likely to be with the world as it is.[27] On the other hand, younger and less affluent persons may see the world from a different angle, be less satisfied with what they see, and hence be more open to change. Furthermore, since middle- and upper middle-class members may have relatively little intimate contact (except as possible victims) with such social disorders as crime and juvenile delinquency, and little personal experience of racial discrimination, they may not be sensitive to the social forces contributing to such behavior. Even if they are, they may have very little idea of how the churches might help in dealing with it. It is possible that the tendency of governing bodies to view the world through middle-class, middle-aged, and white spectacles may partly account for the hesitancy of the churches to deal with the social problems of their communities.

Local Churches and their Communities

Religionists who wish to make their churches more "relevant" are currently much concerned about increasing their churches' effectiveness in helping to alleviate community problems. This is a difficult and complex matter that will require more than the complete democratization of local church-governing bodies—itself no mean task—for its solution. It is, of course, unreasonable to expect the churches, with their relatively limited resources, to do what society at large has failed to do. But in some important matters of social concern the churches are less progressive than is the secular community. For example, eleven o'clock on Sunday morning is, generally speaking, the most racially segregated hour of the week.

Some pioneering attempts, however, are being made to create religious organizations and religious communities more in harmony with the needs of our hypothetical emergent Model Four society. These new organizations are largely antibureaucratic and appeal particularly to young people and those who are alienated by what they consider the political and religious "establishment." These new experimental organizations try to maximize the personal fulfillment, self-expression, and contribution of individuals. They are characterized, in general, by their spontaneous primary-group character, their high degree of lay involvement and participation, and their ecumenical stance.

These groups are frequently situated in the heart of the inner city, in close proximity to ghetto areas. They are little concerned with denominational distinctions, ecclesiastical protocol, convention, or "respectability"; but some are much concerned with direct contact with hippies, drug addicts, draft-resisters, social dropouts, and malcontents, while others work to improve the lot of ethnic communities and to alleviate problems of poverty. They are less concerned with correcting people's "sins" than with understanding them.[28] Thus some of these groups may be regarded as unduly permissive by constituted religious authorities. Members of these groups, both clergy and laity, are ready to experiment with ritual and liturgy. As is increasingly the practice even in some of the more conventional churches, drama, jazz, rock and soul music, and many varieties of modern dance are frequently utilized as valid forms of religious expression.

Some of these new-style religious groups have grown out of "established" denominations and churches. Glide Memorial Church in San Francisco, which, among other activities, carries on an active ministry to homosexuals, happens to be a Methodist Church. Its spirit, however, is in accord with the new experiments. Other denominations, such as the Unitarian Universalists and the Society of Friends, sponsor and partially finance loosely related fellowships and social service groups to which they allow a maximum of autonomy and freedom. To many of the new Roman Catholic groups, denominational distinctions have become irrelevant, and out-and-out ecumenical communities, such as Packard Manse in Boston, have grown up.

The emergence of these experimental groups in a time of rapid social change is a striking illustration of a characteristic of religious organization mentioned at the beginning of this chapter, namely, its capacity to renew itself from within.

THE INFLUENCE OF ORGANIZED RELIGION TODAY

Earlier in this chapter we stated that in modern secular societies, churches reflect rather than mold their social surroundings. This statement should not, of course, be taken to mean that Christian churches make no attempt to influence their national and local communities in accordance with the Christian ideal. On the contrary, in pulpit pronouncements and in philanthropic and other activities much effort is expended. The question remains, however, as to just how effective these efforts are in modifying the social scene. Gerhard Lenski has expressed the view that while organizations are rarely successful, nevertheless the "daily actions of thousands [or millions] of [religious] group members whose personalities have been influenced to greater or lesser degree by their lifelong exposure to the group and its subculture" does have a very considerable, although incalculable, effect.[29] Furthermore, he declares that the ultraconservative policies of some religious associations may well be due to the influence of the religious subcommunity rather than of the religious organization proper. This opinion would appear in line with Fichter's finding that while run-of-the-mill parishioners may be extremely conservative in their views, those more involved with the parish organization, who take part in discussion groups and other more intimate church-oriented activities, tend to be more liberal.[30]

Our previous discussion of the composition of the governing bodies of churches of various mainline Protestant denominations helps us understand the nature of the impact made by the churches in modern communities. It is also helpful to examine some of the ways in which social pressures operate within individual congregations. As early as the 1930s, in a study made of opinions on social issues held by both clergy and laity in the Baltimore area, questions were asked designed to discover to what extent respondents either supported or resisted certain suggested changes in the status quo. A definite attempt was made in the questions to suggest changes that were in line with the Christian ethic. The responses of most of the clergymen to these questions showed them to be, as a group, "a little left of center." Differences between clergy in episcopal as opposed to congregational types of organization were almost negligible. The most significant differences were found to be those between clergy and laity in all types of church. Furthermore, whereas the general body of the laity tended to be only somewhat more conservative than the clerical group, the members of boards of trustees and other financial and policy-making officers of these churches were markedly more resistant to the suggested changes than were the clergy interrogated. Thus, the separation between those who favored a safe conservatism and those who desired more progressive and, presumably, more Christian social policies marked a cleavage *within* the membership of the individual local congregations.[31]

At the close of the 1960s the situation described above appeared to be even more accentuated. Such issues as Black Power and the war in Vietnam have given rise, in almost all denominations, to splits and tensions in the ranks of clergy and laity alike. The younger clergy and more radical laity have been attempting to bring pressure on the central administrative bodies of the churches—including the Roman Catholic Church—to make public statements of a progressive kind on controversial racial and social issues. They have also been urging boards of trustees to donate and invest church money in progressive social causes.*

Whether at the congregational or the central administrative level, the citadel of power in any bureaucratic organization inheres largely in the control it exercises over the budget. Those who exercise this control are particularly sensitive to the opinions of possible contributors with regard to controversial issues on which a particular denomination may wish to take a public stand. They are also likely to bear in mind the probable reaction of public opinion to church investment policies.

Whether religious organizations should deliberately manipulate their resources and investments in order to advance their moral and social aims is an interesting question. It opens the complex issue of the nature of the obligations owed by religious bodies to society on account of their collective wealth. The investment portfolios of churches run into billions of dollars. Their annual purchases of goods and services, together with their annual building construction programs, each comprise another billion dollars. Furthermore, the material assets of religious bodies receive favorable treatment as compared to those of most secular organizations insofar as they are tax-deductible. Moreover, donors to religious denominations can deduct taxes for gifts. At present almost all sizable religious bodies depend heavily for their financing not only on the relatively modest pledges of the majority of their members but on the large tax-deductible contributions of business corporations as well. Needless to say, ecclesiastical financial officers are especially concerned that there might be a decrease of these contributions. These officers fear that if churches make a common

---

* To some extent these pressures have been successful, as when the rich middle-class Presbyterian churches agreed to allocate some millions of dollars to be spent on the improvement of ghetto conditions and various other black concerns. Other churches have allocated money to provide legal help and financial aid to draft resisters. An important group of churches in 1967 voted to withhold proxies on some 30,000 shares in Eastman Kodak in order to force Kodak to reconsider its withdrawal from an earlier promise to train several hundred unskilled Negroes.

practice of using their tax-exempt income to further "advanced" causes unpopular with the business community, such a decrease might become considerable.[32]

Individual clergy, particularly Protestant clergy, who are directly dependent for their salaries on the financial support of their congregations, are most vulnerable to any threat of the withdrawal of such support. In view of the considerations mentioned above, it is not surprising that while a determined group of socially concerned clergy and laity may prevail upon a central denominational convention, or even on the National Council of Churches of Christ in the United States, to take a strong public stand on a controversial social issue, these same clergy, as lone individuals, are not likely to be able to maintain that stand face-to-face with their own congregations and boards of trustees.

A few of those clergy who favor aggressive policies in regard to the investment and use of church funds, even at the risk of losing not only tax exemption but salaried clerical jobs, are beginning to envisage a self-supporting type of ministry and priesthood. They argue that the great missionary apostle St. Paul was a tentmaker and are of the opinion that clergy who work to support themselves in the secular world will be freer to serve God and their fellowmen according to their Christian consciences. Pioneer communities of working priests have been attempting to put this philosophy into practice.* Others have been trying to find ways of earning a livelihood that would combine suitably with the exercise of ministerial and pastoral functions.[33] It remains a moot question, however, as to whether a nonsalaried clergy might not find that they had bought their freedom from the ecclesiastical bureaucracy dearly if in return they had to submit their consciences to the possibly more stringent pressures of the secular marketplace.

---

* It is an interesting fact that one of the fastest growing religious bodies in the United States, namely, the Mormon Church, does not have a salaried ministry.

REFERENCES

1. Talcott Parsons, *Religious Perspectives of College Teaching in Sociology and Social Psychology* (New Haven: Edward W. Hazen Foundation, 1951) , p. 27.
2. J. Milton Yinger, *Religion in the Struggle for Power* (Durham, N.C.: Duke University Press, 1946) , p. 23.
3. James M. Gustafson, *Treasure in Earthen Vessels* (New York: Harper & Row, 1961) .
4. Parsons, *op. cit.*, pp. 27–29.
5. See Max Weber, *The Sociology of Religion,* trans. Ephraim Fischoff (Boston: Beacon Press, 1963) , pp. 60–61, and also N. J. Demerath, III, and Phillip E. Hammond, *Religion in Social Context: Tradition and Transition* (New York: Random House, 1969) , pp. 59–69.
6. Ernst Troeltsch, *The Social Teachings of the Christian Churches,* trans. Olive Wyon. 2 vols. (New York: Harper & Row, Harper Torchbook, Cloister Library, 1960) , vol. 1, pp. 333–334.
7. See H. Richard Niebuhr, *The Social Sources of Denominationalism* (New York: Meridian, 1957) , pp. 17–25.
8. See Leopold von Wiese and Howard B. Becker, *Systematic Sociology* (New York: Wiley, 1932) , pp. 624–628.
9. See Liston Pope, *Millhands and Preachers* (New Haven: Yale University Press, 1965) , pp. 122–124.
10. See Bryan Wilson, "An Analysis of Sect Development," *American Sociological Review,* 24 (February 1959) , 3–15.
11. See Benton Johnson, "A Critical Appraisal of Church-Sect Typology," *American Sociological Review,* 22 (February 1957) , 88–92; also Benton Johnson, "On Church and Sect," *American Sociological Review,* 28 (August 1963) , 539–549.
12. See W. Seward Salisbury, *Religion in American Culture: A Sociological Interpretation* (Homewood, Ill.: Dorsey Press, 1964) , pp. 95–100, for a clear summary of various current interpretations of "church," "sect," and "denomination."
13. See von Wiese and Becker, *loc. cit.*
14. See Pope, *op. cit., passim.*
15. See Charles Braden, *These Also Believe: A Study of Modern American Cults and Minority Religious Movements* (New York: Macmillan, 1949) .
16. See, for example, Zbigniew Brzezinski, "The American Transition," *The New Republic,* December 23, 1967.

17. See Salisbury, *op. cit.*, pp. 131–134.

18. Catholic sociologists have pioneered in sociological studies of the parish. Among them may be mentioned C. J. Nuesse and Thomas Harte (eds.), *The Sociology of the Parish* (Milwaukee: Bruce Publishing Co., 1951); Joseph H. Fichter, S.J., *The Dynamics of a City Church*, Vol. I of *Southern Parish* (Chicago: University of Chicago Press, 1951), and Fichter, *Social Relations in the Urban Parish* (Chicago: University of Chicago Press, 1954). The Catholic parish, unlike the Protestant congregation, which is based on voluntary membership and is relatively loosely tied to a local area, is a territorially based unit that comprises all baptized Catholics resident in the unit. Within this area the parish priest is the primary leader of all church-related groups, including the supervision of the parochial elementary school. Although in respect to some of these groups the priest may give but little more than nominal direction and advice, in principle all lay leaders and teachers (the latter including many nuns) are responsible to him.

19. Luke M. Smith, "Clergy: Authority, Structure, Ideology, Migration," *American Sociological Review,* 18 (June 1953), 242–248.

20. See Paul M. Harrison, *Authority and Power in the Free Church Tradition* (Princeton, N.J.: Princeton University Press, 1959).

21. *Ibid.,* p. 209.

22. *Ibid.,* pp. 3–16.

23. *Ibid.,* Chap. 9, especially pp. 180–181.

24. See Charles Y. Glock, "Afterword," in Walter Kloetzli, *The City Church: Death or Renewal* (Philadelphia: Muhlenberg Press, 1961), pp. 184–188.

25. Jerome Davis, "The Social Action Pattern of the Protestant Religious Leader," *American Sociological Review,* 1 (February 1936), pp. 105–144.

26. See Glock, *op. cit.,* pp. 131–132.

27. See *ibid.,* p. 186.

28. See Malcolm Boyd (ed.), *The Underground Church* (New York: Sheed and Ward, 1968), for accounts by participants of religious groups in this newer, more informal category.

29. Gerhard Lenski, *The Religious Factor: A Sociologist's Inquiry* (Garden City, N.Y.: Doubleday, Anchor Book, 1963), p. 343.

30. Fichter, *Dynamics of a City Church, op. cit.*

31. See Yinger, *op. cit.,* pp. 155–158. See also Jeffrey K. Hadden, *The Gathering Storm in the Churches* (Garden City, N.Y.: Doubleday Anchor Book, 1970), *passim,* for recent similar findings.

32. See Jack Mendelsohn, "Commentary" to the Guild of St. Ives, "A Report on Churches and Taxation," in Donald R. Cutler (ed.), *The Religious Situation, 1968* (Boston: Beacon Press, 1968), p.

960. Dr. Mendelsohn has summed up the tax-exemption situation in relation to "progressive" investment policies in cogent terms:

Realism dictates in a social order as tax and money conscious as ours, that untaxed church wealth is tolerated partly because it is viewed as being relatively benign in the economy. If, and as, the churches become more economically partisan and aggressive, Mammon's sufferance will diminish. Clemency granted to a cross that dwells in a realm essentially different from that of the wallet can be withdrawn with startling swiftness if the cross starts behaving as though it and the wallet share a common turf. A sacred cow becomes less sacred if it turns from grazing to goring.

33. See Laile E. Bartlett, *The Vanishing Parson* (Boston: Beacon Press, 1971) , for a study of this dilemma. Some priests and ministers may drop their formal denominational affiliations yet still wish to continue an informal religious ministry. See also Laile E. Bartlett, *Bright Galaxy* (Boston: Beacon Press, 1960) , for an account of the problems of Unitarian Fellowships, which often exist without regular ministers but frequently have the assistance of volunteer "dropout" ministers.

9
Religion in American Society

INTRODUCTION

Chapter 8 on religious organization cites various illustrations drawn from the American scene. But throughout we have considered the functions, organization, and changes of religious systems in a larger social and historical framework. Sociological generalization requires this procedure—requires, that is to say, the study of various societies and cultures and diverse religions. A developed sociology of religion, it should be stressed, would demand far greater use of comparative material than a work of this size permits. However, we have been able to suggest at least some answers in sociological—not religious—terms to such questions as the following: What are religion's most important functions in society? To what extent are they modified by social change? How and why does religion play a part in situations of stress? How does religion provide moral interpretations of political, economic, and class systems? What problems inhere in religious organization itself? How far and under what conditions have religious groups exerted influence upon society?

These questions, if directed to contemporary America, to some extent could guide a sociological investigation of religion in this country. But such a study would involve additional questions. For as we move from the general to the particular—say from a view of religion as such to religion in a particular time and place —our queries necessarily become more concrete and specific. The more general and abstract formulations will greatly enhance our understanding of the particular case if they are grounded in sound research; but the specific case always has its own peculiarities and, in some measure, its own explanation. This is true, of course, of religion in the United States.

In this chapter we make no attempt to develop this theme fully.* Our goal is limited and twofold. First—and this is the more concrete aspect—we shall consider briefly the relationship between Protestant Christianity and basic American values, interconnections between religion and the class system, and those between religious organization and political democracy. We shall be concerned with functional contributions of religion to the stability of American culture and society and also with certain aspects of the dysfunctional role organized religion sometimes plays. These matters must, of course, be viewed in their specific social context. Secondly, however, we shall suggest interpretations here and there that stem from theoretical generalizations, for example, those of Max Weber, based upon studies of non-American situations.

We caution the reader that the following pages are a very limited treatment of religion in the United States. If interested in pursuing this subject, he will find available extensive historical and sociological materials, some of which are described briefly in the Selected Readings at the end of this study.

PROTESTANT CHRISTIANITY AND THE AMERICAN VALUE SYSTEM

Modern American values may seem to have little connection with religion. Yet many of those most familiar and important to us are more or less secularized versions of values of religious origin.[1] American religious tradition was set in the country's formative years, especially by the early Protestant settlers; therefore we must examine certain values emphasized

---

* For more extended treatments the reader is referred to W. Seward Salisbury, *Religion in American Culture* (Homewood, Ill.: Dorsey Press, 1964) ; and Herbert W. Schneider, *Religion in 20th Century America* (Cambridge, Mass.: Harvard University Press, 1952) . See also the more recent Robert N. Bellah (ed.) , *Religion in America* (American Academy of Arts and Sciences) (Boston: Houghton Mifflin, 1968) .

by Protestant Christianity itself. We must also bear in mind that Protestantism, in common with all Christianity, contains much that is derived from the older tradition of Judaism and from the thought of ancient Greece.

Activism, universalism, and *individualism*—three rather formidable abstractions—perhaps best summarize the secularized religious values that pervade American life.

Christianity, in common with Judaism, and in sharp contrast with Hinduism and Buddhism, ascribes a positive value to the natural material world. Although the Christian has a supreme other-worldly goal, he positively values this world, including its material aspects, as the scene of his active endeavors. This activist attitude toward the material world is especially strong in Protestant Christianity. The implication is not that the world as it is is unrelievedly good—far from it—but that it is the God-given duty of man to master, control, and improve it for the glory of God and for man's own benefit.

A second dominant characteristic of Christianity is that it views its truths as universal values. Thus Christians regard their truths as being equally true for all people, in all places, at all times. The ancient Greeks, moreover, had bequeathed to the Christian world the conception that the physical universe constitutes a challenge to the exploring intellect of man. It was only a further step to extend this universalistic attribute of Christian religious belief to assumptions about the natural world.

The concept of universal natural law is basic to modern science. Robert Merton has pointed out that it was probably no accident that the use of scientific means for the solution of human problems was initially most readily adopted in those countries influenced by Christianity, especially Protestant Christianity, with its universalistic conception of truth.[2] In spite of much modern talk about the conflict between religion and science [3] it was Newton, a deeply religious man, who furnished science with a religious vindication by claiming that the supreme task of the scientist is "to know God through His Works."

When the notion of universal law is combined with the activist approach to the material world so characteristic of Calvinistic

Protestantism, there results a powerful impetus to science and technology. Since early America was settled mainly by members of Calvinistic and independent Protestant sects who faced a natural environment that made heavy demands on their ingenuity, it is not surprising that achievements in science and technology became dominant values in American life. Science as well as religion has its missionaries; in our American tradition the Christian missionary has often set the pattern and paved the way for his scientific successor. With the Agency for International Development and Technical Assistance Programs, the Fulbright, Rockefeller, and Ford programs, the United States has a heavy interest in the spread of the technological gospel in the world today—and is aided by the fact that technology speaks a universal language.

A third trait of Christianity, one given particular emphasis by Protestantism, is its stress on the individual. Individualism stems in part from the Christian idea of the individual soul, which assigns a sacred value to each human being. Although Christianity has at times valued the ethereal soul at the expense of the earthly body, the belief that the body is the temple of the soul enables the value imputed to the soul to be extended to the totality of the individual. This concept of the supreme worth of the individual human being became a cornerstone of American democratic thought. Moreover, Protestant Christianity in particular emphasized the responsibility of each individual to take at least some independent initiative with respect to the salvation of his own soul.

Generally, the values of activism, universalism, and individualism have exercised a positive function in American society, helping to shape a tradition that has contributed considerably to the unity, coherence, and stability of a society composed of diverse peoples. In spite of our many differences, these shared values increase our awareness of how we are expected to act toward one another as fellow Americans. This fact has been, and still is, of major importance for the maintenance of our society.

But to state that these values have a positive function in American society is by no means to claim perfection for them. Different sets of values may perform positive functions for different kinds of societies. Moreover, any cultural values are likely to have some negative, dysfunctional consequences in the society in which they prevail. For example, the American policy of active individualism in the material world has led to much exploitation and waste of both material and human resources, a staggering waste of which our society is only belatedly becoming aware. The right of individualistic private commercial enterprise to cut down our forests, dam our rivers, destroy natural beauty, pollute our water supply and the very air we breathe is but one aspect of this waste. Furthermore, individualistic and unregulated patterns of real estate development are largely responsible for the extreme human wastage that may be seen in the slums and ghettoes of American cities.

RELIGION AND THE AMERICAN CLASS SYSTEM

The ranking scale of any society is always closely related to those values that the society in question esteems most highly. American society is no exception. The high premium placed on successful individual achievement is fully in keeping with the values we have just discussed. In the semi-open class society that emerged in the United States during the process of developing a new continent, individual success, as manifested by wealth and occupation, largely took the place of the Old World emphasis on family and inherited land as the principal requirements for high social standing. Hence the self-made man became a person not only of economic consequence but also of social prestige.

But it was also necessary to justify the self-made man. Religion has played an important part in this justification and has thereby helped to moralize our entire class system. In the same manner that religion has aided the Hindus to interpret the rigidities of their caste system, religion has provided moral justification to Americans for certain aspects of the competitive class system, particularly the high premium placed on success and the consequent penalization of failure. Without this interpretation the successful might feel guilty about their success and the unsuccessful discouraged and resentful about their failures. Furthermore, given positive attitudes to the material world, it is not enough to claim that all moral imbalances will be rectified in heaven; it is crucial to interpret success as morally right—and failure as implying moral lack—here and now. It is true, of course, that American Protestants have believed that the good are to receive their reward in heaven and the wicked their punishment in hell. But this other-worldly balancing of the moral books has been most stressed by those individuals and classes who are least privileged and presumably most in need of compensation for their lack of success, and therefore of status, in this world.[4]

We have already seen that the religious beliefs of the early Protestant settlers were well adapted to this type of interpretation, for their religion taught them that God bestowed his special favor on those individuals who strove most actively and diligently in their this-worldly activities. Success, then, could be considered as the justly deserved reward of a man's purposeful, self-denying, God-guided activity.[5] Thus the *successful* man could think of himself, and be thought of by others, as the *righteous* man. These beliefs also served to make moral sense of the plight of the so-called failures. Since religion taught that the help of an all-powerful God is equally available to all and since all men if they will can be diligent and thrifty, it is a man's own fault if he fails. Even "failures" usually accepted the moral justice of this interpretation, an interpretation, be it noted, that did not deprive them of hope. Furthermore, these religious doctrines were well suited to the circumstances of a pioneer people, mostly of humble station, who had to rely on their own resourcefulness to develop a new and potentially rich country.

Economic and social circumstances, however, have changed markedly since those early days. Today impersonal economic and political forces, often beyond the individual's control, are in part responsible for his failure or success. Yet the older religious interpretations, more suited to earlier conditions, still persist in some measure. During the mass unemployment of the 1930s, for instance, the majority of one group of both employed and unemployed when interviewed explained their respective economic situations almost entirely in individual moral terms. Most of those employed attributed their success to their own superior efforts, implying that anyone could have done as much with comparable effort. It is significant that the unemployed and those on relief generally accepted this valuation, regarding their failure as somehow their own fault.[6]

However, changed circumstances eventually modify religious interpretations of economic and class systems. The depression and its aftermath contributed to such reinterpretations in the United States. Earlier we noted two aspects of the individualism of Christianity: one is the emphasis on individual striving and initiative; the other is the supreme valuation of each individual human being. Sometimes, as during the Depression, it has seemed necessary to limit the insecurities and hardships to which some individuals are exposed even at the cost of curtailing the initiative of others. In striving to guarantee to each individual a minimal freedom from want, the proponents of social security legislation can also look to religious values for justification. Which of these two interpretations of individualism is likely to be stressed at any given time depends largely on the current state of the economy. The latter interpretation, justifying security measures, is perhaps less characteristically American, but it is nevertheless partly grounded in the Christian religion. In recent years, moreover, various Protestant (and other) denominations have taken strong stands in support of social security and welfare measures.

Religious doctrines, interpreted with considerable flexibility, have thus served to justify the economic and class system—a fact that has contributed to the persistence of the system itself. Although the imputation of righteousness to the successful man has sometimes exercised a negative function (notably in condoning hypocrisy), it has also fulfilled a positive one in putting pressure on the successful man to act as if he *were* righteous. Max Lerner

RELIGION: A SOCIOLOGICAL VIEW

has emphasized the fact that relatively few of the American business tycoons and captains of industry have lived in flamboyant fashion. The image of the wealthy playboy has not been a popular one. Indeed, the descendants of our Carnegies, Rockefellers, and Fords have usually not felt free, as have many successful capitalists in other countries, to dissipate their material gains in riotous living and what has been called "unproductive expenditure."[7] The investment of a substantial part of their gains in great foundations and other schemes for human betterment has also helped to soften some of the rigors of our competitive system and to spread its benefits, and thus indirectly to stabilize and develop our economy. Even attributing failure to lack of moral stamina, as evidenced by the absence of hard work, enterprise, and thrift, is not a counsel of despair, since such failure need not be permanent. This explanation, by encouraging quite a few of today's lower-status persons to think of themselves as tomorrow's middle class, again contributes to the continuing stability of the class system.

A "stable" class system, to be sure, carries advantages and liabilities for both individuals and society. What concerns us here, however, is that religious interpretations may break down in the face of the continued existence of an "underclass," including racial and other minorities, who may possess no viable means of social mobility. Members of such disprivileged groups are likely to experience a feeling of hopeless alienation from the larger society.[8] This persisting sense of alienation may give rise to aggressive and even revolutionary modes of expression should opportunity for advancement continue to be denied—in spite of legal regulations to the contrary—during a period of general prosperity. In the 1960s, for example, movements like Black Power[9] and other "black" and "Third World" movements were organized by deprived minorities with the avowed objective of challenging the privileges of the white middle classes and of resorting to violence when considered necessary. Even the black churches, which formerly were mainly churches of "accommodation"—that is, churches that helped Negroes to reconcile themselves to their place in the dominant white society—became more aggressive and militant. In 1968 the nonviolent "Poor Peoples' March" on Washington organized by Martin Luther King's Southern Christian Leadership Conference aimed at pressuring Congress to grant certain specific demands. More recently welfare recipients have organized into unions to strengthen their demands for increased appropriations from both state and federal governments. In both cases the objective was to equalize opportunity and so to change the status of the American underclass.

RELIGIOUS ORGANIZATION AND DEMOCRACY

From a broad historical viewpoint, it would seem that the type of religious organization that has grown up in the United States is, on the whole, compatible with our political and industrial democracy. This compatibility has been due in part to two related features of the American religious scene, both of which date from the early years of the Republic and which have been implicit in our entire discussion. The first is the separation of church and state; there is no powerfully established church, or *ecclesia*. The second is the coexistence of a plurality of different denominations and sects, no single one of which is strong enough to exercise a predominant influence on the society as a whole.[10] The variety of religious affiliations of the early settlers made expedient the toleration of people of all religious faiths, including Catholics and Jews, at an earlier date than in most European countries. In addition, the influence of French revolutionary thought upon the founders of the American Republic helped to bring the separate secular state into existence sooner in America than in any other part of the Christian world. This situation has had profound effects, both positive and permissive, upon the development of liberal democracy.

On the positive side, most Protestant groups have asserted, on religious grounds, an active faith in democracy itself. Furthermore, this Protestant faith in the destiny of America as a democratic nation has extended beyond the confines of Protestantism itself. This democratic faith has been viewed by Robert N. Bellah as an American civil religion.[11] The liberal Protestant churches in particular, with their vigorous tradition of individual independence in religion initiated in colonial times by Roger Williams and developed further by Emerson and Thoreau, have greatly helped to keep the faith in individual liberty alive. The freedom of the individual to choose and express his own religious and political beliefs without coercion has been a prime value for those churches. One of the nation's greatest glories is generally considered by these churches to be the opportunity afforded by America for people of wide religious differences to live together peacefully under the protection of a religiously neutral state. These beliefs have also helped to make our country a haven for the religiously and politically oppressed. Churches that today continue actively to hold these beliefs are sensitive about any infringement of civil as well as religious liberties. Their members join organizations to protect the rights of minorities, whether racial, ethnic, or economic, and are easily alarmed if in their view any one church attempts to gain special privileges from the state.

On the permissive side, the lack of a single, united, and socially influential religious organization has facilitated the development of the United States as an "open society," that is, one free to pioneer in techniques and in ideas.[12] We have observed on several occasions that religion can be very conservative. The same circumstances that precluded the development of an *ecclesia* also permitted wide experimentation in a number of fields exceedingly important to the character of the developing society. In all likelihood the United States could not have pushed on so fast and so far in industrial development, the application of science, the extension of free education to all ages and classes, and in the elaboration of political democracy if the cultural tone had been set by a single dominant church. Talcott Parsons has noted the contrasting case of Quebec, where for the past three hundred years the Catholic Church has been the dominant *ecclesia* and where until quite recently a society has persisted strikingly similar to that of rural France in the seventeenth century.

The absence of a dominant church has also helped to prevent American people from dividing into religious and antireligious camps.[13] Such a cleavage would have had important consequences for the political stability of American society. In this respect our political history of the last two centuries contrasts significantly with that of certain European countries, for example, France and Russia. In the latter cases the social, economic, and intellectual changes that followed the industrial revolution occurred in societies possessing established churches, that is, *ecclesia*. During the period of political upheavals ushered in by the French Revolution, the once-dominant *ecclesia* attempted to retain its influence by making common cause with the conservative vested interests and the landed classes. Hence the intellectuals and many members of the urban industrial classes became bitterly antireligious and anticlerical. In France the alignment of the antimonarchical with antireligious and anti-Catholic forces, so important during the revolutionary period, continues to set the tone of modern French radicalism. In Russia the alliance between the reactionary Czarist regime and the Orthodox Church (of which the Czar himself was the titular head) enabled communism to thrive as a violently antireligious force and thus helped to precipitate one of the greatest revolutions of our day. No comparable polarization of the population along religious and antireligious lines has taken place in the United States.

In contrast to many European countries, outright hostility to religion in the United States is rare, even though our society is highly secularized. [Marginality, or nominal religious group membership, is more typical of Americans than is hostility to organized religion.[14]] The fact that in presidential elections the candidates of both major parties are as a rule professed church members, and apparently feel that endorsement of religion in general is expected of them by the majority of all voters, suggests that American society is far from being divided along religious and antireligious lines.[15]   Furthermore, the election in 1960, with the help of many votes from non-Catholics, of the Roman Catholic John F. Kennedy to the Presidency of the United States showed that religious differences are by no means decisive in political choice.

Americans are so far from being hostile to organized religion that some 90 percent of them express a religious "preference," and 64 percent of them are members of religious bodies.[16]   This is a high figure in comparison with the record of other industrialized countries, such as England [17] or France.   Scholars differ, however, as to whether to regard the people of the United States as intrinsically more "religious," in any absolute sense, than members of other comparable industrialized societies.   Indeed, any informed view of the matter must depend not merely on statistics of church membership, church attendance, and amounts of financial support, but, as Charles Y. Glock has pointed out, on various other "dimensions of religiosity," which are extremely difficult to measure.[18]

Some sociologists, notably Herberg, have seen this rather high percentage of religious group membership in the United States as fulfilling secular rather than religious functions.[19]   Such scholars have drawn attention to the group identification function that membership in religious organization frequently performs.   They see some such means of group identification as a functional necessity in a society as large and heterogeneous as the United States where merely to designate oneself as an "American" is psychologically unrewarding.   Furthermore, at the present time Catholics and Jews have become acculturated to American society to the extent that the religions of Catholicism and Judaism, as well as Protestantism, are now regarded for the most part as acceptable, democratic, *American* religions.   Hence, self-identification in terms of religious affiliation is seen as providing a convenient and available means of self-reference.   In addition, the increasing movement of Catholic and Jewish middle-class families into suburban areas previously occupied almost entirely by Protestants has enhanced the tendency to make use of this form of identification.   Newly arrived suburbanites often find themselves in a very different environment from that of the ethnic communities of the central cities that they have left behind, and they are apt to welcome the opportunity to affiliate themselves with groups of people who share the same social, as well as religious, patterns of behavior.[20]

Nevertheless, although voluntarism and denominational pluralism in religion have been congenial to the development of a democratic and industrial society, from the standpoint of religion there is a debit side to the account. American churches have been exposed to powerful secularizing influences. The United States stands in sharp contrast with England, for example, where a modified form of state-established church has been able to utilize at least some of the government's influence in the fields of education, recreation, morals, and philanthropy. A plural system of religious organization coupled with a theoretically rigid separation of church and state weakens religion's hold on the other institutions of the society.

In the United States the public school system, the most far-reaching educational agency, is dependent on the secular government, both local and national. Largely because of religious divisions, the teaching of religion in schools is prohibited.* Similarly, the control of recreation has passed in large part to commercial agencies. The elaboration of the economic system has created such huge problems for social service and philanthropic organizations that much, although not all, of their administration has also passed into governmental hands. In the face of this situation the churches have generally reacted rather than acted. They frequently struggle to hold their members by borrowing secular techniques. They try to compete with commercialized recreation by sponsoring their own, and to this end use motion pictures, radio, television, and the like. They also compete with mass communication specialists by presenting forums and book-review sessions, and by preaching popular sermons dealing with practical life and avoiding scientifically

---

* In England, on the other hand, the furor in New York State in 1964 over the "Regent's Prayer" would not have occurred. In that country the government both accredits and supports church-related schools.

dubious dogmas. In spite of the use of such popular (and expensive) techniques, some churches have barely survived.

Walter Kloetzli has drawn attention to the moribund state of many city churches. Although the churches Kloetzli has studied are Lutheran, city churches of other denominations are undergoing comparable difficulties.[21] Furthermore, the newer suburban churches, insofar as they are flourishing organizations, have tended to specialize in the kind of secular attractions just mentioned. Protestant, Catholic, and Jewish sociologists have all drawn attention to the predominance of the secular over the religious functions performed by many suburban churches.[22]

America's churches continue to bring religious and other benefits to thousands of individuals, an achievement that should not be underestimated. Nevertheless, it must be admitted that the churches have mitigated rather than substantially modified inequitable features of the economic and class system; nor have they checked the powerful trend of national states toward war. Indeed, in the field of race relations the churches, particularly the Protestant churches, have frequently been more segregated than some other community agencies. With the exigent demands of making a living, improving social status, paying taxes, and performing military service, most Americans, whether or not they are church members, are not overly preoccupied with "intrinsically" religious matters. Although there was considerable talk of a religious "revival" in the 1950s,[23] in 1968 a Gallup Poll showed that 64 percent of those interrogated thought that religion was losing ground in American life. This 1968 figure contrasts sharply with the mere 14 percent who reportedly held a similar view in 1957. Significantly, individuals aged 21 to 29, rather than older persons, and Protestants rather than Roman Catholics, were inclined to take a pessimistic view of religion's influence.[24]

On the other hand, Gerhard Lenski, in his Detroit study *The Religious Factor,* has not limited his estimate of religion's impact on American social life to an evaluation of the direct influence of organized religious bodies. His researches have led him to conclude that the influence of religious communities on secular institutions has been underestimated since most evaluators have ignored the indirect effects of the "daily actions of thousands (or millions) of group members whose personalities have been influenced to greater or lesser degree by direct, lifelong exposure to the religious group and its subculture." [25] Nevertheless, the fact that religious organization reflects rather than sets the tone of American society is illustrated by the parallelism, pointed out by many sociologists and recently by N. J. Demerath, that denominational divisions largely follow social class lines.[26] In most American communities the churches have a rough rank order of social prestige.* In New England the Unitarian, Episcopal, and Christian Science churches are those of the "best people," followed by the Congregationalists and the Methodists, the Baptists, and other groups. In the South the Presbyterians take the place of the Unitarians, and in the Middle West the Methodists rank considerably higher. In New Orleans the Catholic descendants of the early French and Spanish settlers are among that city's leading families. One result of this social ranking of churches is the tendency of people who rise in the social scale to change their religious affiliation in the process.

Social ranking of religious denominations, to be sure, is consistent with the American open-class system. Furthermore, since

---

* Unfortunately, this brief chapter omits discussion of racial and ethnic elements, as distinct from class elements, as influences in the religious life of the United States. The case of the black churches is outstanding. To be sure, there is a class aspect of religious affiliation that is applicable to black Protestantism as well as to white. Black church members, the vast majority of whom are Protestant, are distributed among various denominations and classes. The elite churches are usually Methodist and Episcopalian, the great bulk of the middle-class churches are Baptist, while the Pentecostal churches and Churches of God comprise a mainly (but not exclusively) lower-class membership. Increasing mention is currently made, however, of *the* Black Church. While strictly speaking, for reasons mentioned above, such a reference is a misnomer, it is increasingly used by black churchmen, who claim for the Black Church a distinctive and unique religious and theological identity. This new emphasis stems no doubt in part from the growing sense of a separate identity among all black Americans and is enhanced by a greater knowledge of black church history. In addition, a rather rapid grass roots ecumenism appears to be at work among some of the membership of the black churches. This trend, if it does in fact exist, merits study by sociologists.

by their very nature Protestant congregations are rather loosely organized voluntary groups, they function best if their members feel at home with one another. This feeling of social ease is important in producing spontaneous consensus, which occurs much more readily when the members are of similar class and educational background. But a system of rank order of social prestige not only distresses sincere religionists [27] but, once established as a part of the community life, cannot be easily modified. Religious organizations whose participants experience their togetherness sacramentally more than socially, most notably in the Catholic Church, have been the most effective in bringing together members of diverse social classes. The less inclusive character of Protestant churches also extends to racial and ethnic groups.

DIFFICULTIES AND TENSIONS

The "Americanization" of Catholicism and Judaism, described in Chapter 6, has, to a large extent, lessened interfaith tensions. These tensions are likely to decrease further if, as Herberg has maintained, there is a commonly acknowledged basic unity underlying the three communities that is "rooted in the American way of life." [28] The change whereby America shifted from a Protestant-dominated single-religion society to a triple-religion society [29] undoubtedly removed many social and psychological pressures from Catholics and Jews. However, our current three-religion society has generated its own brand of tensions, which are clearly apparent in our larger cities where the three faiths are most evenly balanced. Even the recently recognized "equality" of American religious faiths, as seen by Herberg, does not preclude conflict and tension. At times, indeed, this equality may stimulate tensions, for in the new situation each of the three faiths may on occasion feel itself to be a minority. [30]

For example, the Protestants, a national majority, are currently developing a minority-group psychology. Indeed, in some metropolitan areas Protestants are actually a numerical minority. They must now adjust to the fact that they no longer wield unquestioned political and social dominance—a disconcerting situation for some. Furthermore, the Catholics, whose rise in occupational and educational standing has been a notable achievement of the last two or three decades, sometimes feel that their new class and educational status is insufficiently recognized by Protestants.[31] Hence some bitter memories linger. Similarly, Jews, less than 4 percent of the population, are often defensive; they are sometimes on the lookout for slights on their faith, and their rabbis are apprehensive about rising rates of intermarriage.[32] Studies such as that of Charles Y. Glock and Rodney Stark on *Christian Anti-Semitism,* sponsored by B'nai B'rith, document in impressive fashion the extent of underlying anti-Jewish prejudice among Christians even where overt discrimination may be absent.[33] Cooperation and understanding appear to vary with theological sophistication. As between Christians and Jews, unsophisticated Protestants and Catholics alike may still exhibit ignorance about Judaism and prejudice against Jews. Furthermore, the change from a position of subordination to one of three equally American faiths has both strengthened and weakened the internal cohesion and solidarity of Judaism. It is as yet uncertain whether strength or strain will predominate in the long run.

Many of these tensions, the sources of which are exceedingly complex, are likely to come to a focus in disputes about church and state relationships. The growth in power and influence of the Roman Catholic Church especially has stimulated problems associated with the fact that the Catholic Church is an international church, or *ecclesia,* ruled from Rome. An *ecclesia,* as we have seen, functions most harmoniously in Model Two societies, whereas modern American urban society more nearly approximates a Model Three type. Traditionally the *ecclesia* is a universal church, comprising all the members of a given society and therefore accustomed to rely on the civil governments for the endorsement of its authority. Although the central body of the Catholic Church in modern times has in practice modified this position, it has not abandoned it in principle. We know too that when Catholicism is dominant in a society, as in Spain, it tends to revert to the *ecclesia* pattern, abandon toleration of other religious groups, and assert its authority over the entire population.*

Hence the rapid growth of the Catholic Church has occasioned some fear (whether the fear is well grounded is not the issue here) that with its increased power the Church will attempt to revive its *ecclesia* tradition in the United States. This fear is not unmixed with envy on the part of the Protestants, for in fields where Protestantism is divided and weak, the Catholic Church, with its unity of command, has superior effectiveness and has, until recently, been able to retain a firmer hold on its adherents than have the more loosely organized Protestant churches. Indeed, it has often been remarked that intra-Protestant ecumenism, as seen in the mergers of major Protestant denominations, is in reality a defensive action on the part of Protestantism in the face of Catholic unity. In recent years, however, it has become abundantly clear that the Catholic Church is by no means a monolithic entity. Divisions among Catholics are now clearly apparent even to non-Catholics, and this fact, coupled with some of the pronouncements of the Second Vatican Council, has given encouragement to Protestants to engage in ecumenical dialogue with Catholics.[34] Meanwhile, Catholics are encouraged by the fact that, in the words of Father Gustav Weigel, "The United States is no longer white, Anglo-Saxon, and Protestant. It is a land of many religions, and Protestantism must take its chances along with others." [35] Therefore, Catholics are no longer so much "afraid" of Protestants.

Nevertheless, in spite of these more recent tension-alleviating circumstances, political differences have often combined with religious differences to accentuate tensions between religious groups. Because of the heavy concentration of Catholics in the large cities of the East, the feeling of tension has been greatest

---

* One Catholic reply to this statement is that the oppression of religious minorities is to be found in all authoritarian countries.

there, and religious issues have frequently been acute in municipal politics. Since established local elites for the most part have been Protestant,[36] and since until recently the Catholics have been preponderant in the lower-status groups, class tensions have been added to religious tensions. Moreover—and this is important in view of the leadership of the Irish in the Catholic Church in America—some of the traditional (and well-deserved) Old World hostility of the Irish toward the English may have colored American Catholic attitudes toward "Anglo-Saxon" Protestants.

Tensions may also be observed in connection with the stand taken by the Catholic Church on morals. According to Catholic religious organization and belief, the hierarchy is empowered to regulate the morals of Church members. In the United States, however, such regulation cannot always be effective without impinging on the freedom of choice of non-Catholics as well. Catholic attempts to censor the mass media are a case in point. Thus, on occasion some part of the moral code of the Church is enforced with the aid of state legislation, involving Catholics and non-Catholics alike. That Catholic voters should endeavor to introduce or to maintain legislation embodying the Church's stand on such matters as divorce and birth control is, of course, their constitutional right, a right they share with other groups. This right is not an issue here. But no sociologist can doubt that legislation maintaining the Catholic stand on divorce and birth control sets up in certain states legal standards powerfully at odds with dominant trends in the development of the American family structure, especially in large cities.[37] The fact that these laws are frequently circumvented by Catholics as well as non-Catholics emphasizes this disparity. Indeed, among Catholics themselves, since Pope Paul VI's 1968 encyclical, *Humanae Vitae,* banning all artificial methods of birth control, this moral issue has become charged with a highly divisive potential.

In view of the existence of these strains we would expect some degree of strong feeling and prejudice on the part of Catholics toward non-Catholics and vice versa. When such questions as tax aid to parochial schools or the distribution of birth control literature are under consideration, tempers are likely to get out

RELIGION: A SOCIOLOGICAL VIEW

of hand on both sides.[38]   Another inflammable issue concerns
the right to teach "religion" in public schools, and how, in a
public school context, the teaching of religion is to be defined.
The heated arguments that were exchanged during the New
York Board of Regents' prayer case (June 1962) and the June
1963 decision of the Supreme Court that forbids Bible reading
and the recital of the Lord's Prayer as "religious activities" in
public schools,[39] well illustrates the continued existence of potentially explosive controversial issues.   In general Catholics
(well aware that many of their children attend public schools)
were in favor of a modicum of religious teaching, while most
Protestants opposed all religious teaching on school premises.
The National Council of Churches of Christ (a mainly Protestant body) supported the Supreme Court ruling and declared
that "neither true religion nor good education is dependent on
the devotional use of the Bible in the public school program"
(Policy Declaration, June 6, 1963).   However, several Catholic
and Episcopal leaders opposed the Supreme Court ruling on the
ground that it "strengthened the establishment of secularism and
encouraged freedom *from* religion."   Thus the late Bishop
James A. Pike stated that "the decision *deconsecrates* not merely
the schools but the *nation. . . .*   The Supreme Court still opens
its session with '*God save the United States and this honorable
Court.*' " [40]

It is noteworthy, however, that both in this controversy and
in a subsequent one involving the decision about whether to substitute the somewhat weaker statement of the federal Constitution on the separation of church and state for a very strong
statement in the New York State Constitution, the fight was not
between a solid block of Catholics opposed to a solid block of
Protestants and Jews.   The issues involved were broader and
more complex than the simple opposition of Catholics and non-
Catholics.   There was an increased feeling among some individuals of all religious persuasions that one reason for an alarming
increase in immorality was the absence of religious education.
The spread of "religious illiteracy" was regarded by these people
as a public menace.   Because of the holding of such opinions, as

well as because of strong political pressures applied by the Catholic hierarchy, the strict interpretation of the First Amendment (separation of church and state) is not infrequently "watered down." The allocation of public funds for buses, school lunches, and textbooks for parochial schools (both Catholic and Jewish) is a case in point.

Difficulties between Jews and non-Jews are on the whole less troublesome than difficulties between Catholics and non-Catholics. For one thing, the Jews comprise but 4 percent of the total population. They do not seek to make converts and so do not constitute a threat to other religious bodies. Anti-Semitism is still to some degree based on "religious" grounds, as Glock and Stark have shown. But anti-Semitism stems far more from economic and cultural tensions, which have been the subject of extensive economic and sociological analysis; and the problem is by no means exclusively a religious one. Because of the ethnic character of Judaism, however, anti-Semitism in America is sometimes attributed to primarily religious causes. Anti-Jewish feeling among Catholics has, by and large, been more prevalent than such feeling among Protestants, with the exception of "fundamentalist" Protestants. As far as Catholics are concerned, however, the Vatican pronouncement exonerating the Jews from the sole culpability for the death of Jesus of Nazareth may mitigate somewhat Catholic-Jewish tensions.[41]

Whereas some important sources of tension between Catholics and Protestants stem from differences in religious organization, traditional Jewish patterns of religious organization accommodate themselves rather easily to the American scene. Most Jewish groups adjust readily both to denominational pluralism and to the secular state. Basic to this adjustment is the fact that Judaism has no surviving tradition of an established church, or *ecclesia,* no central hierarchy, and no proselytizing tendencies. Its vital organizational unit is the synagogue or temple, a local congregation democratically governed.* The authority of the

---

* Democratically, that is, except for the exclusion of women—in principle —from their governing bodies. The Hadassah and other women's organizations, however, are influential in the total conduct of Jewish religious affairs.

rabbi over his congregation receives considerably less institutional support than that of the Protestant minister.[42]   The rabbi's function is not essential to the conduct of the synagogue, which for prayer, worship, and study requires only the existence of a *minyan,* namely, a quorum of ten adult males who have been admitted to Bar Mitzvah.   Moreover, since the Dispersion, the Jewish people have constituted minority groups in almost every country of the world, and they have, putting it mildly, come to expect no preferential treatment from governments, particularly Christian ones.   Therefore the constitutional assurance of the benevolent neutrality of the secular state has great positive value for Jews, as well as for other groups.

In addition to organizational compatibility, from the doctrinal point of view there is little to distinguish liberal Reform Judaism from liberal Protestantism.   This fact suggests once more that tensions between Jews and non-Jews are only in small measure due to intrinsically religious differences.

Today the salient phenomenon on the American religious scene is the ferment and tension within the Roman Catholic Church.   This Catholic crisis, sparked by the Second Vatican Council, is worldwide, but it manifests itself in different ways in different national societies.   In the United States the upgrading of many Catholics educationally and occupationally has resulted in a self-confident group of middle-class laity who are rapidly emerging from what has been termed the "Catholic ghetto." This trend has been reinforced by religious directives (notably the document known as *The Church in the Modern World*) stemming from the Second Vatican Council.   In 1967 Pope Paul VI followed up this theme with the encyclical *Progressio Populorum.*   These documents constitute a mandate for church members to involve themselves actively in the problems of the modern world and in the reform of political, economic, and social institutions.   These directives, coming from the highest authority, authorize Catholics to turn to the world and to find Christ in the service of humanity rather than to focus exclusively on their own internal churchly affairs and their own private salvation. Furthermore, these directives were associated with a new conception of the meaning of the Church itself, and the relationship of its members to it. No longer was the established hierarchy conceived as the central value, with the members bound to it simply by obedience. The Church was rather conceived of as a pilgrim church, in which hierarchy, priesthood, and laity were all enjoined to play active roles.[43]

Although the restlessness engendered by these potent new ideas spread throughout the Catholic world, the unrest they gave rise to has been especially strong in the United States. Relative to European countries, such as France or Holland, the American Catholic hierarchy—and American Catholic theology—are largely conservative. Indeed, European Catholic theologians have anticipated many of the ideas and policies authorized by the Second Vatican Council. Yet with the exception of a few intellectuals, these ideas had been relatively unknown to American Catholics. Furthermore, the whole history of the Catholic Church in America—an immigrant church, whose members had been subjected to considerable prejudice and discrimination— had contributed to the development of an ingrown mentality. As long as a large majority of the members were in low-paying occupations and lived in urban ghettoes and only a small minority received higher education, it was very natural that Catholics should be willing to turn from the world and to seek, in their own religious community, a shelter from the Protestant-dominated world outside. In addition, willingness to accept ecclesiastical authority is likely to be greater in a population composed mainly of individuals of rural ancestry and little formal education.

The fact that these liberal Vatican Council and Papal pronouncements came at a time when increasing numbers of Catholic laity were improving their economic, educational, and social standing gave a powerful boost to the liberal views that were beginning to be popular with a minority of the more articulate Catholic laity. These laity were, in actual fact, merging with the "outside" world not only in politics but also in business, professional, and social life. After the Second Vatican Council they could claim the highest ecclesiastical sanction for doing "more of the same." Furthermore, this authorization coincided with a time when socially concerned Americans of all faiths were searching for effective ways in which they might further such causes as civil rights, urban renewal, ghetto education, and the termination of the Vietnam war.

Nevertheless, the conservative forces in the American Catholic Church are powerful and are deeply entrenched. Their conservative views and conservative policies, both in the parishes and in the dioceses, continue to find many supporters among those who still live in immigrant ghettoes or retain a ghetto mentality. In spite of the ferment following the Second Vatican Council, an important segment of the Catholic hierarchy and the parochial clergy are slow to implement reforms and to promote Catholic "renewal" at the grassroots.

Hence in the last five years there has been a growing impatience among a good many Catholics at the slowness of church "renewal" in the United States. At times this impatience is very near to outright revolt, and what has been termed a "revolution" of the laity may be taking place. To an ever greater extent, active lay members and many of the younger priests (especially those who are not in administrative positions) are no longer content to wait until "renewal" policies are initiated by the bishops and the hierarchy. As one priest put it, "We have found that Committee methods are too slow. We don't want just 're-newal' any more, we want the whole set-up changed. The quickest way is to take matters into our own hands." [44]

One aspect of this growing revolt, which has been accentuated since the promulgation of the encyclical *Humanae Vitae,* is the proliferation of an "underground church." Theologian Michael Novak has put it as follows:

> All across the country—in the staid and wealthy St.
> Louis suburb of Webster Groves; in prosperous Montclair,
> New Jersey; in Rochester, New York, and in at least
> twenty locations in Los Angeles and dozens in Chicago—
> Catholics are forming their own religious communities.
> They seek to worship their Lord in their own way, and

ignoring the traditions of culture, to bring new joy and
vitality to Catholic practices. In rare instances these
"underground" groups are supported by bishops, but more
typically the bishops are ignorant of their existence or
unhappy about them. Yet, more and more younger
priests—nearly all those ordained within the last ten years,
according to some estimates—are willing to celebrate the
new "illegal" Masses to small groups, meeting in secret.[45]

Many of these groups are ecumenical in character and, after some
experimentation with new liturgical forms, their members are
likely to become involved in political action of a "progressive"
character. Priests and nuns, moreover, are, in increasing numbers leaving their orders for the purpose of carrying out what
they believe to be their Christian commitment *in the world.*

Whether these recent stirrings will change the face of American Catholicism or whether there will be a major split within
the American Catholic Church, it is yet too early to tell. For the
most part the hierarchy remains conservative and is giving the
new movements little encouragement.

The current Catholic crisis is, however, not only of concern
to the Catholic Church itself. The movement of American Catholics, who constitute more than a quarter of all American church
members, from relatively low status to a central position on the
religious and social scene is likely to have important consequences not only for other American religious bodies but for
secular institutions as well. Ivan Vallier and Rocco Caporale
have described the present posture of the American Catholic
Church as that of "The good neighbor who, after living behind
his hedge for many years, cut it down one morning (just as he
got the house painted) and stands on the fence line waiting for
the other neighbor to invite him in for coffee. The goal problem of the corporate church is how to merge with society or de-
ghettoize, while at the same time gaining a leadership role, and
without losing the solid religious bank roll of lay commitments
and loyalties in the process." [46]

It is doubtful, however, that such a posture could be maintained successfully without the active participation of a large number of the articulate laity. Some observers are of the opinion that the active loyalty of American Catholics is likely to depend on the extent of the decision-making roles that the hierarchy is prepared to grant them. According to these observers a considerable segment of the concerned laity are prepared to be "loyal" only if they are "allowed to help run the Church in the same way" as they now "help to run the (secular) society." [47] If these concerned lay Catholics do in fact remain loyal, it is possible that the Catholic Church in America may become exceedingly strong and influential in both religious and secular affairs. But even granting this possibility, there is still uncertainty as to how the numerous non-Catholic religious bodies in the United States will respond to this new stance of the American Catholic Church.

In the absence of historical perspective, an objective estimate of the extent to which these cleavages and strains between these three major religious groups are functional or dysfunctional for our society is impossible. On the other hand, some of their consequences may be seen in the area of municipal politics and government. Decisions in this field are made too often, not on the objective merits of the persons or issues involved, but rather with a view to their possible effect on Catholic, Jewish, or Protestant interests, or with an eye to maintaining a balance between the different religious groups.

On the positive side, however, strains and disharmonies in the social structure may serve as stimuli for creative adaptations that may enable the structure to encompass a wider range of variations. There is evidence that to some extent this has already taken place in the United States and that the long-continued effort to achieve unity in diversity and order with freedom has been favorable to useful social and political experimentation. The tensions we have just described need not lead to disaster. If we can keep our social system sufficiently flexible and dynamic, we retain the possibility of absorbing these strains. Thus we may hope to preserve the most cherished values of our society.

REFERENCES

1. See Robin Williams, *American Society: A Sociological Interpretation* (New York: Knopf, 1960), pp. 323–371, especially Chapter VIII.
2. See Robert K. Merton, *Technology and Society in Seventeenth Century England,* Osiris Studies in the History and Philosophy of Science (Bruges, Belgium: St. Catherine Press, 1938).
3. For a recent interpretation of the "conflict between religion and science," see Charles Y. Glock, *Religion and Society in Tension* (Chicago: Rand McNally, 1965), pp. 362–366. Glock's evaluation of the present status of the conflict is well worth reading. His opinion that the conflict persists rests on a traditionalistic supernatural interpretation of religion. He is not concerned with humanistic ethically based religion.

   See also Herbert Feigl, "The Scientific Outlook and Naturalism," in Herbert Feigl and May Brodbeck (eds.), *Readings in the Philosophy of Science* (New York: Appleton-Century-Crofts, 1953), p. 16:

   If by religion one refers to an explanation of the universe and a derivation of moral norms from theological premises, then indeed there is a logical incompatibility with the results, methods and general outlook of science. But if religion means an attitude of sincere devotion to human values, such as justice, peace, relief from suffering, there is not only no conflict between religion and science but rather a need for mutual supplementation.

4. See H. Richard Niebuhr, *The Social Sources of Denominationalism* (New York: Meridian Books, 1957), pp. 29–33.
5. See Max Weber, *The Protestant Ethic and the Spirit of Capitalism,* trans. Talcott Parsons (New York: Scribner, 1958), pp. 176–177; see also Max Weber, "The Protestant Sects and the Spirit of Capitalism" in *From Max Weber: Essays in Sociology,* trans. Hans H. Gerth and C. Wright Mills (New York: Oxford University Press, 1946), pp. 302–306, in which Weber described (in a light vein) how in America, membership in a religious sect or denomination, such as the Baptists or Methodists, had come to be regarded (circ. 1900) as in itself a guarantee of financial responsibility. According to Max Weber, the Calvinist ethic was especially important in ascribing this meaning to worldly success. However, some American historians who agree in part with Weber contend that the independent Congregational, rather than the Calvinist, sects were the

main exponents of this ethic. Still other historians consider that the conditions of American pioneer life, combined with the lowly origin of most of the settlers, gave rise to the ethic, rather than vice versa. These controversies need not concern us since it is sufficient for our purposes that religion played a part, and there is no doubt that the religious ethic of the Protestant settlers was consistent with, even congenial to, the actual conditions that they encountered.

See also Scott Miyakawa, *Protestants and Pioneers* (Chicago: University of Chicago Press, 1964), Chapter 1. Miyakawa has made the point that the active individualism of the frontier was not always the "lone" individualism of popular imagination. The Protestant sects acted as important socializing agencies.

6. Clinch Calkins, *Some Folks Won't Work* (New York: Harcourt, Brace, 1930), especially pp. 7–22.

7. Max Lerner, *America as a Civilization,* vol. 1 (New York: Simon & Shuster, 1957), pp. 280–284.

8. See, for example, Michael Harrington, *The Other America: Poverty in the United States* (New York: Macmillan, 1964).

9. See Vincent Harding, "The Religion of Black Power" in Donald R. Cutler (ed.), *The Religious Situation: 1968* (Boston: Beacon Press, 1968), pp. 3–39 for an explication of the *religious* aspects of the Black Power movement. Thus, on page 31:

> . . . few adherents of Black Power deny their need for religious moorings, and, though no clear pattern has yet emerged, it must be evident by now that for many persons it is likely to become as fully a "church" as the earlier phase [Martin Luther King's Southern Christian Leadership Conference] was for others. Not only does it begin to fill the need for personal commitment and a sense of fellowship with other similarly committed black persons; it also embodies impressive social concern, a call for ultimate justice, and a search to be present with the sufferers of society. Gladly identifying with the oppressed beyond national borders, this church increasingly seeks to glorify at least that part of God which may reside in black folk.

10. Two hundred fifty religious bodies are listed in the 1966 *Yearbook of the American Churches.* Of a total 123,307,449 members of these bodies, 68,299,478 were Protestants; 45,640,619 were Catholics; and 5,600,000 were Jews. The other 3,657,387 persons were members of various Eastern churches. Since the Protestants are divided into numerous denominations and sects, the Roman Catholic Church, comprising some 36 percent, is the largest single religious group. See *Yearbook of the American Churches,* ed. B. Y. Landis (New York: National Council of Churches of Christ in the U.S.A., 1966).

11. See Robert N. Bellah, "Civil Religion in America," *Daedalus,* 96, 1 (Winter 1967), 1–19. Bellah presents a case for the existence of a

"civil religion" broader in scope than Protestantism, although related to it. This civil religion of America exists alongside of the churches but is rather clearly differentiated from them (p. 1). Bellah sees this civil religion as

never anti-clerical or militantly secular but as having borrowed selectively from the religious tradition in such a way that the average American saw no conflict between the two. In this way civil religion was able to build up without any bitter struggle with the church powerful symbols of national solidarity and to mobilize deep levels of personal motivation for the attainment of national goals [p. 13].

Bellah believes that this "civil religion" is still very much alive.

12. See Talcott Parsons, *Religious Perspectives in College Teaching of Sociology and Social Psychology* (New Haven: Edward W. Hazen Foundation, 1951), p. 35.
13. *Ibid.*, p. 36.
14. See John F. Cuber, "Marginal Church Participants," *Sociology and Social Research,* 25 (September–October 1940), 57–62.
15. See Bellah, *op. cit.*, p. 3. Bellah cites Kennedy's inaugural address and points out how Kennedy's references to God and to religion were in the spirit of what he has called the "civil religion of America" and not in terms of Kennedy's own personal commitment to the Roman Catholic faith.
16. See *Yearbook of the American Churches,* 1966, *op. cit.* In 1966 approximately 90 percent of the population expressed a religious "preference" even though they were not enrolled on the books of any religious body. However, only some 45 percent—less than half —of those who expressed a preference were regular in church attendance. However, all statistics of religious membership must be viewed with considerable caution, in part because the units recorded are not the same for all denominations; for example, while most denominations record individual memberships, Jews count *families* and Christian Scientists refrain from "numbering the people." See W. Seward Salisbury, *Religion in American Culture: A Sociological Interpretation* (Homewood, Ill.: Dorsey Press, 1964), pp. 73–93, for a clear, brief account of trends in American religious statistics.
17. See David Martin, *A Sociology of English Religion* (New York: Basic Book, 1967), pp. 34–51, for statistics on the distribution of church membership and attendance in England and the United Kingdom.
18. See Charles Y. Glock and Rodney Stark, *Religion and Society in Tension* (Chicago: Rand McNally, 1965), pp. 18–38. Some of the "dimensions" considered are the experiential, ideological, ritualistic, intellectual, and consequential. See also Gerhard Lenski, *The*

Religious Factor: A Sociologist's Inquiry (Garden City, N.Y.: Doubleday, Anchor Book, 1963). Lenski has been mainly concerned with the consequential dimension of religious affiliation, namely, its consequences for behavior. His study does, however, suggest some other "dimensions."

19. See Will Herberg, *Protestant, Catholic, Jew* (Garden City, N.Y.: Doubleday, Anchor Book, 1960), pp. 62–63.
20. See Marshall Sklare, *Conservative Judaism: An American Religious Movement* (Glencoe, Ill.: Free Press, 1955); and Albert I. Gordon, *Jews in Suburbia* (Boston: Beacon Press, 1959).
21. See Walter Kloetzli, *The City Church: Death or Renewal* (Philadelphia: Muhlenberg Press, 1961); and Robert Lee (ed.), *Cities and Churches* (Philadelphia: Westminster Press, 1962).
22. See, for example, Gibson Winter, *The Suburban Captivity of the Churches* (Garden City, N.Y.: Doubleday, Anchor Book, 1961); Andrew M. Greeley, *The Church and the Suburb* (New York: Sheed and Ward, 1959), in which Greeley discusses changes in emphasis brought about in the suburbanization of the Catholic Church; Gordon, *op. cit.*; and Peter Berger, *The Noise of Their Solemn Assemblies: The Christian Establishment in America* (Garden City, N.Y.: Doubleday, 1961).
23. See S. M. Lipset, "Religion in America: What Religious Revival?" *Columbia University Forum*, 2 (1958–1959), pp. 17–21.
24. See *The New York Times*, May 25, 1968.
25. Lenski, *op. cit.*, pp. 342–343.
26. See N. J. Demerath, III, *Social Class in American Protestantism* (Chicago: Rand McNally, 1965), especially pp. 1–4. Demerath includes the following table of social class profiles of American religious groups:

Denomination	Upper	Class Middle	Lower	N [*]
Christian Scientist	24.8%	36.5%	38.7%	(137)
Episcopal	24.1	33.7	42.2	(590)
Congregational	23.9	42.6	33.5	(376)
Presbyterian	21.9	40.0	38.1	(961)
Jewish	21.8	32.0	46.2	(537)
Reformed	19.1	31.3	49.6	(131)
Methodist	12.7	35.6	51.7	(2100)
Lutheran	10.9	36.1	53.0	(723)
Christian	10.0	35.4	54.6	(370)
Protestant (small bodies)	10.0	27.3	62.7	(888)
Roman Catholic	8.7	24.7	66.6	(2390)
Baptist	8.0	24.0	68.0	(1381)
Mormon	5.1	28.6	66.3	(175)

Denomination	Upper	Class Middle	Lower	N [*]
No preference	13.3	26.0	60.7	(466)
Protestant (undesignated)	12.4	24.1	63.5	(460)
Atheist, Agnostic	33.3	46.7	20.0	(15)
No Answer or Don't Know	11.0	29.5	59.5	(319)

[* N = number of cases in the sample.]

From Herbert Schneider, *Religion in 20th Century America* (Cambridge, Mass.: Harvard University Press, 1952), Appendix, p. 228. Reprinted by permission.

Demerath is careful to point out that this national picture is modified by regional differences. Furthermore, important status differences exist between individuals (and between local congregations) within each of the major denominational groups.

27. See Niebuhr, *op. cit.*, pp. 21–25.

28. Herberg, *op. cit.*, p. 231.

29. This triple-religion society has been found to be associated with three religious intermarriage "pools"; hence the United States is viewed as having comprised a triple rather than a single melting pot. See Ruby Jo Reeves Kennedy, "Single or Triple Melting Pot? Intermarriage Trends in New Haven, 1870–1940," *American Journal of Sociology*, 49 (January 1944), pp. 331–339.

Gerhard Lenski has hazarded an educated guess that the triple melting pot will remain triple and that the separateness of religious communities will even be gradually accentuated until the United States is a "compartmentalized" society, not unlike Holland or Lebanon, in which "most of the major institutional systems are obliged to take account of socio-religious distinctions." See Lenski, *op. cit.*, p. 365. This writer, however, is doubtful that Lenski's projection of the future will be verified.

There is at present no unanimity among sociologists as to whether this triple melting pot is likely to be a permanent feature of the American scene or whether, after all, it is merely a way station on the road to more generalized mixing. Trends in interreligious group marriage rates are currently being studied in order to furnish some clues as to what might be expected. See Salisbury, *op. cit.*, pp. 415–425 for a brief discussion of mixed-marriage studies. Devout religionists of all three groups are less likely to intermarry than those who take their religion more lightly. Jews are less likely to intermarry than are either Protestants or Catholics; yet Jewish interfaith marriage rates are also rising. Erich Rosenthal, *American Jewish Yearbook, 1963* (Philadelphia: American Jewish Publication Society), found in his sample that first-generation (foreign-born) Jews had an intermarriage rate of 1.4 percent; second-generation Jews, 10.2 percent; and third-generation Jews, 17.9 percent. Rosenthal also found, however, that where the Jewish community was large and could organize the marriage "market," the intermarriage rate was lower than in smaller and "unorganized" Jewish communities. American rabbis are disturbed about the rising intermarriage rates; since the Jewish community is small and has a low birthrate, they fear the weakening of Judaism. See Albert I. Gordon, *Intermarriage: Interfaith, Interracial, Interethnic* (Boston: Beacon Press, 1964).

30. Herberg, *op. cit.*, pp. 211–230.
31. See Charles F. Westoff, "Catholic Education, Economic Values and Achievement," *American Journal of Sociology*, 69 (November 1963), 225–233; and Andrew Greeley, "Influence of the 'Religious Factor' on Career Plans and Occupational Values of College Graduates," *American Journal of Sociology*, 68 (May 1963), 658–671. Westoff and Greeley take issue with Lenski, who viewed the Catholic stress on large families and family solidarity as inhibiting the upward mobility of Catholics in Detroit (see Lenski, *op. cit.*, pp. 83 and 345). Lenski's critics pointed out that his Detroit sample contained an unusually large proportion of fairly new Polish immigrants. It is noteworthy that Catholic scholars have been concerned to raise the intellectual level of Catholic education; see, for example, John Tracy Ellis, S.J., *American Catholicism* (Chicago: University of Chicago Press, 1956), pp. 146–148; and Thomas F. O'Dea, *American Catholic Dilemma* (New York: New American Library, Mentor Omega Book, 1962), *passim*.
32. See Gordon, *Intermarriage, op. cit., passim*.
33. See Charles Y. Glock and Rodney Stark, *Christian Anti-Semitism* (New York: Harper and Row, 1966).
34. See Robert McAfee Brown and Gustave Weigel, S.J., *An American Dialogue: A Protestant Looks at Catholicism and a Catholic Looks at Protestantism* (Garden City, N.Y.: Doubleday, Anchor Book, 1960). Weigel is of the further opinion that "The Protestant wants to be a Catholic but not a Roman Catholic."
35. Gustave Weigel, S.J. "Catholic and Protestant: End of a War?" in *Thought*, 33 (Autumn 1958), 390.
36. See Digby Baltzell, *The Protestant Establishment* (New York: Random House, Vintage Book, 1964) for an excellent sociohistorical account of Protestant elites in the United States.
37. Kenneth Underwood, *Protestant and Catholic* (Boston: Beacon Press, 1957). Underwood made an intensive study of Catholic-Protestant relations over the issue of the right to teach birth con-

trol in Holyoke, Massachusetts, during a period when the majority of the population was shifting from Protestant to Catholic.

38. This problem is particularly acute in states like Connecticut and Massachusetts, which have passed state laws forbidding the free distribution of birth control information.

39. The cases on which the Supreme Court rendered this pronouncement were *Murray v. The Baltimore School Board* and *Schempp v. The Town of Abingdon, Pennsylvania.*

40. See Herbert W. Schneider, *Religion in 20th Century America* (New York: Atheneum, 1964), p. 42.

41. See the "Declaration on Relations of the Church with Non-Christian Religions," a Papal encyclical.

42. See Sklare, *op. cit.,* pp. 168–198, for a discussion of the institutional role of the rabbi and the limitation on his authority.

43. See Sister Marie Augusta Neal, "Catholicism in America," in Robert N. Bellah (ed.), *Religion in America* (American Academy of Arts and Sciences) (Boston: Houghton Mifflin, 1968), pp. 312–336.

44. See Michael Novak, "The Underground Church," *Saturday Evening Post,* December 1968–January 1969, and Theodore M. Steeman, "The Underground Church: The Forms and Dynamics of Change in Contemporary Catholicism," in Donald R. Cutler (ed.), *The Religious Situation: 1969* (Boston: Beacon Press, 1969), pp. 713–747.

45. *Ibid.*

46. Ivan Vallier and Rocco Caporale, "The Roman Catholic Laity in France, Chile, and the United States: Cleavages and Developments" (University of California, *Institute of International Studies Bulletin,* 1968), pp. 11–12.

47. *Ibid.,* p. 11.

Appendix
Theoretical Approaches and Types of Research in the Sociology of Religion

Fifteen years have passed since the earlier and much shorter *Religion and Society* appeared. During those years much work has been done by sociologists in the field of religion. A number of textbooks have appeared, a few significant theoretical essays, and a great number of empirical studies. Reports of such studies of religion may be found in an increasing number of professional journals, such as *The Review of Religious Research* (begun in 1959), and *The Journal for the Scientific Study of Religion* (begun in 1961), as well as in general sociological journals, for example, the *American Sociological Review, The American Journal of Sociology, Sociological Analysis* (the journal of the American Catholic Sociological Society), and *Commentary,* a journal devoted in part to Jewish life and thought. Whether or not there has been a religious revival in the United States—a debatable point—there has certainly been a revival of scholarly interest in religion. This interest concerns not only religion per se, but more important it includes also the relationship of religion to the organization of society and to social behavior in general.

Religious professionals and laity alike have become increasingly preoccupied with the social consequences of religious commitment; and theologians and religionists have become more aware of the potential contribution of sociology to an understanding of their ultimate concerns. At the same time, sociologists have become more conscious of their need for a closer acquaintance with the actual content of religious experience. It has become apparent that a familiarity with religion's formal and institutional aspects is, in and of itself, insufficient to provide realistic understanding of the societal aspect of religion that is the proper concern of sociology. This realization today constitutes a major challenge to the development of the sociology of religion as a serious discipline.

How can we account for this upsurge of interest in the sociology of religion? The existence of worldwide crisis and confusion provides, to be sure, part of the answer. The decline of compelling faith in the more traditional supernatural aspects of religion is, we suspect, another part of it. Furthermore, increasingly frequent encounters between members of different faiths—Hindu, Buddhist, Christian, Jewish, Islamic—as fellow students, professional colleagues, visiting diplomats, and business associates, have stimulated interest both in the content of their various religions and in the role their religions play in their respective societies. Perhaps most importantly, the ecumenical spirit abroad in today's world, in spite of powerful counterinfluences of religious nationalism, has made it mandatory that men take a closer look at the organizational as well as the creedal and liturgical aspects of their religious divisions. The influence of Pope John XXIII in particular, and the concern he expressed at the Second Vatican Council that religion should be "relevant" to modern social conditions and that "updating" (*aggiornamento*) was therefore essential, has also served to turn men's minds to the relationship between religion and society.

Looking back over the history of the sociology of religion, we can discern interesting and revealing fluctuations in both its popularity and productivity. The so-called "golden age"—that of Durkheim, Troeltsch, Weber, and Simmel at the turn of the century—was one in which the sociology of religion was part of the mainstream of sociological thought and its development. In that period were produced great seminal works that are still influential today. However, the second and third decades of the present century were a rather dull and unproductive period, during which the study of religion was shunted into a sociological backwater. This period of neglect was in part due to a lingering heritage of positivistic ideas, coupled with Marxian influences, but it also stemmed from the intense preoccupation of American sociologists of that time with the problems of our rapidly growing cities, the shift from rural to urban ways of life, and all the implications of these changes for society. Sociologists of that period were keenly aware of the impact of economic and political factors and attributed little imporance to religion and its institutions, which in the cities then seemed fragmented and weak; hence they devoted little time and energy to studying them. Gerhard Lenski has pointed out, furthermore, that those sociologists did not really consider religion apart from organized religious bodies, that is, churches, denominations, and sects. They did not fully envisage the influence exerted by the more broadly cultural aspects of religion, an influence that, as recognized now, often transcends organizational boundaries. They were, for the most part, blind to the fact that people sharing the same religious tradition, even if not active members of organized religious groups, constitute religiously oriented cultural communities that exert a powerful influence on behavior and on the transmission of moral norms.* Jewish ethical norms (to take one outstanding example) may be as effectively inculcated in the coffee-klatch as in the temple or synagogue.

The beginning of sociologists' new interest in religion, which started in the 1930s, was largely due to the work of Pitirim Sorokin and, more particularly, Talcott Parsons who, through his 1930 English translation of Weber's *Protestant Ethic and the Spirit of Capitalism* and through several of his own writings, popularized Durkheim's and Weber's work in American sociological circles. The revival of interest thus initiated has continued to grow.

---

* Gerhard Lenski, *The Religious Factor: A Sociologist's Inquiry* (Garden City, N.Y.: Doubleday, 1961), pp. 11–13, has called this informal religious-cultural influence the *communal* aspect of religion as distinct from the formal ritual and belief practices of organized religious bodies. The latter he has termed "associational."

WAYS IN WHICH SOCIOLOGISTS
HAVE STUDIED RELIGION

The revived vitality of the sociological study of religion invites a closer inspection of the ways in which sociologists have studied religion both today and in times past. There are two main and interrelated ways in which sociologists have gone to work: first, through the formulation of theoretical approaches to the analysis of socioreligious data; and second, by means of empirical study and collection of relevant data for analysis. Ideally speaking, these two ways of study should go hand in hand, since the most valuable theoretical studies are those related to a substantial body of relevant data and the most valuable empirical studies are those meaningfully related to a significant theoretical approach. Hence the distinction between "theoretical approaches" and "empirical studies" in the following discussion should be regarded as largely one of convenience. Nevertheless, from a historical standpoint a distinction in emphasis can—and should—be made.

On one hand, the nineteenth-century pioneers of the sociology of religion were theorists in the grand manner. The data they used in support of their theories and hypotheses were largely culled from history, anthropology, and general observation. However, some sociologists today do not consider such data strictly "empirical"; they restrict this term to contemporary data gathered systematically at first hand. Even early twentieth-century sociologists of the stature of Émile Durkheim and Max Weber were far from possessing our modern means of gathering and processing vast quantities of data. Since they lacked modern means and methods of research, they were forced to rely on written anthropological and historical sources supplemented by the rudimentary statistics then collected by governments. Although they used a more sophisticated critical technique than did their predecessors, in analyzing this data their interpretations were of necessity still limited by the limitations of their data sources.

Nevertheless, carefully authenticated historical evidence also furnishes valid "empirical" data, a fact that the collectors of firsthand contemporary statistics are sometimes prone to overlook.

Contemporary sociological research, on the other hand, is relatively weak on theory and strong on empirical data. Although the data collected are used as evidence for hypotheses and generalizations, the conclusions thus supported are frequently rather narrowly circumscribed and limited in their application.

Today's emphasis on firsthand data collection has been made possible and almost inevitable by the recent great advances in statistical techniques and the precise and sophisticated methods of data collection and processing that the computer has made readily available. These technical advances in part explain the retreat of most contemporary sociologists, including sociologists of religion, from the more ambitious types of general theorizing. They are well content, as a rule, if they can aim at what Robert Merton has called "theories of the middle range"; many content themselves with considerably less. This current emphasis on firsthand data collection, however, may be viewed in the main as a healthy reaction to the armchair, or "library," approach of much of the earlier sociological theorizing about religion. Modern empirical studies rightly aim to establish their generalizations, no matter how modest, on the basis of sound evidence methodically gathered and tested. There is, of course, the danger that this empirical emphasis may result in an overly narrow preoccupation with an endless gathering of "facts" that superficially describe what people say or do or think but do not really illuminate what is going on or give the kinds of generalizations which able scholars and scientists aim to reach. There is some indication, however, that sociologists interested in the field of religion and society are becoming increasingly aware of this danger.

THEORETICAL APPROACHES

The Functional Approach

A functional approach to religion assumes a holistic view of society; it considers religion one part of a social whole in which there is mutual interaction among the parts. In this sense, as brought out in Chapters 3, 4, and 5, religion is a set of beliefs and practices through which men seek to adjust themselves to their environment. All religions seem to possess certain universal functions: to explain evil, death, injustice, suffering; to sanction social norms; to provide superempirical answers to men's ultimate questions; and to help allay stresses produced both by man's failure completely to control his environment and also by his capacity to anticipate the future and imagine ideal states. Functional theory aims at providing a rationale for the exploration of those functions of religion within the framework of "total" societies.

Such a broad functional approach is central to this volume, and although functionalism has come in for considerable criticism and modification in recent years, we have not seen fit to abandon it. In the first place, functionalism, in a general sense, is basic to all sociological analysis, which is of necessity concerned with the roles played by social institutions and the interrelationships among them. In the second place, no viable alternative approach of equal comprehensiveness and significance is at present available.

Evolutionary Theories

Functional theories, however, are neither the only nor the earliest theories that sociologists of religion have used. Auguste Comte, who gave a name, if not a content, to sociology, saw mankind's earliest evolutionary stage as a *theological* one and his potentially most evolved stage as a *positivistic* one. Comte, in common with many early social evolutionists, equated evolution with progress, and to him progress meant the emergence of a scientific or "positive" religion. Other evolutionists, such as Herbert Spencer, theorized that man and his institutions, including his religious institutions, evolved from initially simple to progressively more complex forms.

The influence of these early evolutionists on the sociological study of religion declined for two main reasons. First, later anthropological findings undermined an important assumption on which their theories were based; namely, that all societies of necessity passed through a graded series of evolutionary stages. This assumption had made possible their various predictions as to the next stage in the development of any society that was being studied. Second, as the influence of positivism declined, it became increasingly apparent to sociologists that theories about the future role of religion in human societies were largely based on wishful thinking, supported by biased selections from historical data. Even more important, these theories, in the form then stated, could not be subjected to empirical testing. Some theorists, however, such as Oswald Spengler, L. T. Hobhouse and, in our own day, P. R. Sorokin, never stopped theorizing about the evolution of religion and society in the grand manner, but their theories were more philosophical than sociological.

Some sociologists have attempted to make a modified evolutionary approach not merely a matter of philosophical speculation but also a "testable" hypothesis. Robert M. MacIver, for instance, taking off from Spencer, found it useful to theorize about social and religious institutions in terms of the development from simple and homogeneous to more complex and highly differentiated forms. For him such a theory merely furnished a yardstick to be tested against empirical sociological materials. MacIver, moreover, was careful not to equate increase in institutional complexity with inevitable "progress." More recently, too, sociologists have shown a revived interest in a more sophisticated evolutionary approach. In 1964 almost the entire June issue (vol. 29, no. 3) of the *American Sociological Review* was devoted to a discussion of evolutionism, to which Robert N. Bellah contributed a highly stimulating, if admittedly speculative, article viewing the whole history of man's religious development in an evolutionary framework.

The influence of the evolutionary approach survives in a more restricted form as a *developmental* approach. Talcott Parsons, for instance, views religious movements as going through certain typical developmental stages; at each stage certain typical problem situations, as he views the matter, must be faced and solved if the movement in question is to survive. Developmental theories have also been used in a more limited way in the study of changes in the forms of religious organization. H. R. Niebuhr's well-known *Social Sources of Denominationalism* (1929) propounded a theory of the development of American religious sects into denominations, and this work, as noted in Chapter 8, has greatly influenced much of the research into the changes in religious organization in the United States. Liston Pope's *Millhands and Preachers* (1942), an analysis of sect development among textile workers in Gastonia, Georgia, is an excellent example of a study inspired by Niebuhr's theoretical approach.

Historical and Typological Approaches

We have seen how the early revolutionary theorists used historical data in a more or less selective manner to give support to their somewhat grandiose theories. At the turn of the century the German school of "historical" sociologists, which included Max Weber and Ernst Troeltsch, also utilized the data of history but in a much more disciplined way. They abandoned the search for universal theories in societal development and confined their efforts to testing more limited hypotheses concerning religion's role in specific periods of history or concerning the development of particular forms of religious organization. For instance, Weber's famous research into the origins of Western industrial capitalism, *The Protestant Ethic and the Spirit of*

Capitalism, involved the testing of such a hypothesis; namely, that Calvinistic religion played an independent and creative (although not exclusive) role in the emergence of the modern capitalistic order in seventeenth-century Europe.

Professional historians sometimes tend to look askance at the way sociologists, even of Weber's stature, have often used historical data. Sociologists, however, by the very nature of their discipline, are compelled to use such data in a rather different way from that of historians. The sociologist wants to find out whether certain *kinds* of historical situations are "typically" accompanied or followed by some other "typical" situation or situations. He is not interested to the same extent as the historian in a detailed elaboration of a particular situation per se, even though in some cases crucial details may have great importance for sociological study. Both Weber and Troeltsch, therefore, were impelled to construct "typologies" on the basis of their studies of history. Weber's ideal types of "capitalism" and of the "Protestant Ethic," as he stressed, were both mental constructs based on a familiarity with a wealth of actual historical instances but corresponding at all points with no *one* of them. In a similar manner Troeltsch, in his classic work *The Social Teachings of the Christian Churches,* constructed his well-known "sect types" and "church types" as representative of distinct and opposing patterns of religious organization. Such type constructs may thus become useful as yardsticks for the interpretation of still more data. For the sociologist *does* seek to uncover a pattern in history. The hazard is that he may impose his own pattern and distort history in the process.

It should be emphasized that the sociologist's use of history to construct typologies involves a serious commitment to historical scholarship and research. As a mode of sociological study it makes great demands on its practitioners. In part, perhaps, for this reason, and in part because most sociologists today prefer to work with contemporary data gathered for their own particular purposes and capable of analysis by modern techniques, the historical dimension of sociological research has been largely neglected until very recent years.*   However, although the use of historical material by sociologists has been neglected, the construction of "types" has not.   Type and model construction is currently popular among sociologists and other social scientists, although these models are usually based on contemporary rather than historical data.

Comparative Approaches

Comparative modes of study are valuable as a check on the ever-present danger of constructing generalizations, whether about typologies of religious organization or about developmental sequences, on too narrow a cultural base.   Such generalizations can hamper research if they are then superimposed on noncomparable data in such a way as to distort or obscure their meaning.

Max Weber engaged in extensive comparative studies.   In order to substantiate the creative role of the Protestant Ethic in the formation of industrial capitalism in the West, Weber set out to use the comparative method to prove the "negative case." His vast studies on the religions of India and China were designed to investigate comparatively the religious ethic of these two great oriental civilizations to see whether they contained similarities to the Protestant Ethic that Weber viewed as a crucial factor in the formation of modern capitalism in the West.   Needless to say, a negative finding would strengthen his own hypothesis.   Following in the Weberian tradition, Robert Bellah has investigated the religion of Japan—the one Asian country that by the beginning of the twentieth century had successfully developed a system of industrial capitalism.   Bellah's comparative sociohistorical study *Tokugawa Religion* (1957) aimed at demonstrating the existence of a Japanese religious ethic, operative in the period immediately preceding industrialization, that was, in his view, analogous to Weber's Protestant Ethic.

---

* For example, much of the work of Reinhard Bendix, Seymour M. Lipset, Kai Erikson, Barrington Moore, Guy E. Swanson and Robert Nisbet has been grounded in history.

Both Weber and Bellah made comparative studies of religion's influence on the economic life of oriental societies in contrast to occidental ones. Their comparisons involved societies far removed from one another in both space and time. Comparative studies may, however, involve mainly the time element and compare religion's role in the same, or similar, societies in different centuries. For instance, one of the important objectives of Gerhard Lenski's *The Religious Factor* (1961) was to find out whether adherence to the Protestant Ethic in Detroit in the mid-twentieth century had consequences for economic behavior comparable to those that Weber claimed for it in Europe in the seventeenth century.

Cross-cultural comparisons are enormously facilitated today since both anthropologists and sociologists are fanning out into almost all parts of the world and are making firsthand studies of religion's role in a great variety of societies. Furthermore, international organizations of sociologists, including sociologists interested in religion, are increasingly providing meeting places that facilitate the exchange of information about religion in numerous societies.

EMPIRICAL STUDIES

Although the use of historical or anthropological data collected by others is an entirely legitimate method of sociological research and "empirical" in the broader sense, the term "empirical studies" more narrowly used denotes research studies in which data are gathered systematically at first hand for use as evidence for a particular hypothesis. The methods used by those conducting such studies cover the entire spectrum of the methods used by sociologists in general. Such methods include community study, participant observation, the use of official statistics, case study, interviews, content analysis, schedules and questionnaires, sample surveys, and so on. It would not be wide of the mark to claim that at any one time the predominant methods of research in the sociology of religion follow rather closely those methods most often used in the field of sociology as a whole. In recent years the sample survey (together with some specially constructed instrument in the form of schedule or questionnaire) has been the most common method of data collection used by sociologists, including those concerned with sociological aspects of religion.

Most "objective" studies of religion in its societal aspects have not attempted to study religion or religious experience in and of itself but rather, as Allan Eister has expressed it, "the social and cultural distillate or manifestations of religion—the precipitates of religious experience." [1] It is the overt behavior or at least the objectively describable attitudes and opinions and *not* the vital experience of religious persons per se that have been the main concern of sociologists. These precipitates, or consequences of religious behavior, characterized by Charles Y. Glock as the "consequential dimension" of religion,[2] together with the institutional and organizational aspects of religion, have been viewed by sociologists as the main focus for empirical research. Furthermore, the major emphasis of this research has been on the behavior and attitudes of people who regard themselves, and are regarded by others, as being "religious."

An unfortunate limitation of empirical sociological studies of religion is that, relative to such fields as rural or medical sociology, religious sociology can count on no large-scale governmental financing of its research, nor do the very large foundations invest substantially in projects in this area. Much of the empirical research carried on in the United States is commissioned by the religious organizations themselves, or perhaps, in a few cases, by an association of religious bodies, such as the National Council of the Churches of Christ in the United States. The religious denominations, to be sure, show an increasing tendency to entrust the actual work of research to established university research institutes, such as Columbia University's Bureau of Social Research, the University of Chicago's National Opinion Research Council (NORC), and Berkeley's Bureau of Survey and Research. Unfortunately, however, even when university research agencies are used, the very fact that a particular piece of research is commissioned and financed by a specific religious body tends to limit the wider applicability of the results obtained. It is a relatively rare occasion when sociological research in the religious field—such as that reported by Glock and Stark in *Christian Beliefs and Anti-Semitism,* a study conducted at Berkeley and sponsored by B'nai B'rith—can be expanded to cover a wide interdenominational spectrum. Although research limited to specific religious bodies has definite uses, perhaps it is not too much to hope that the growth of ecumenical cooperation for social action in America may be accompanied by a corresponding growth in the ecumenical financing of research.

Furthermore, in common with much other research in sociology, many empirical researches in the field of religious sociology are undertaken by teaching professors and Ph.D. candidates mainly on their own time and at their own expense. These researchers are often obliged to utilize the most readily available subjects—frequently students or residents in the immediate neighborhood. Hence the samples involved may be too small and too localized to be significantly representative. Increased coordination and teamwork in research might help to counteract this disadvantage, but to date, much empirical research is atomistic and does less than it might otherwise to further generalized knowledge.

Types of Empirical Studies

In view of the increasing proliferation of empirical studies in the field, how is the sociological student of religion to find his way among them? Are there any significant ways in which they may be grouped or classified?

We group such investigations into four main categories. First, there is a large category of studies of specific behavior traits or attitudes that are thought to be linked with some particular religious trait or characteristic of the larger population. The religious trait selected might be, for instance, religious group affiliation, frequency or regularity of prayer, regularity of church attendance, degree of belief in or acceptance of religious doctrine, or any of a number of other characteristics that may be measured or counted in some way. The aim of such studies is to test hypothetical claims that such religious traits (or variables) are positively or negatively correlated with certain other general behavioral traits (or dependent variables), such as occupational preference, need for achievement, probability of marrying within (or outside) one's own faith group, political preference, educational aspiration and achievement, fertility rates, and use of artificial methods of contraception.

The second category comprises studies of religious groups and their development, particularly with reference to their organizational structure. This type of research includes the rise and development of religious movements, and that of sects and denominations of various kinds. It is hardly surprising that sociologists have chosen to make many such investigations; these studies are concerned with a rather clearly defined body of data, and they lie squarely within the sociological field. The third category, much smaller than either of the first two, comprises role studies of religious personnel, particularly of ministers, priests, and rabbis. Finally, a very small number of studies are concerned with the content of the religious beliefs of individuals as distinct from the official creedal pronouncements of religious bodies.

Statistical Correlation Studies

Empirical studies designed to link specific religious traits with particular social attitudes or behavior—our first category—cover, as indicated above, a wide range of topics. The titles of a few of them may serve to suggest their variety and range: "Religious Affiliation and Political Economic Activities"; "The Factor of Religion in the Selection of Marriage Mates"; "Church Involvement and Attitudes Towards Race"; "Fertility Planning and Fertility Rates by Religious Interest and Denomination"; "Influence of the 'Religious Factor' on Career Plans and Occupational Values of College Graduates"; "Catholic Education, Economic Values, and Achievement." Two recent important monographs that belong in this category deserve special mention, namely, Lenski's *The Religious Factor,* which relates differences in religious affiliation to specific differences in economic, familial, and political behavior, and Glock and Stark's *Christian Beliefs and Anti-Semitism,* both of which were mentioned earlier. Many sociologists have been interested in the relationship between religious affiliation and social class (some of them being of the opinion that class factors rather than religious factors are the operative causes of certain types of related behavior); N. J. Demerath's *Social Class in American Protestantism* (1965) deserves mention as a useful interpretation and theoretical critique of such studies.

Investigations such as these demand considerable ingenuity for several reasons. First, specific religious factors must be identified and defined "operationally" in such a way that they can be measured and counted and their degree of intensity ascertained. The choice of such identifiable and measurable factors or dimensions is by no means easy. Furthermore, it is only by the wise choice of such identifiable and measurable definitions of religious factors that other investigators can make comparable studies and expect to get at the same kind of facts and thus advance our general knowledge. Second, in these essentially statistical correlation studies there is always the danger that the behavior which the investigator finds to be correlated with a particular religious factor or dimension may in reality be correlated with a hidden factor that has escaped the researcher's notice. Third, since most of these investigations use an instrument (usually some sort of schedule or questionnaire) as a main means of data collection, it is important that this instrument be constructed to test relevant data without either ambiguity or "loaded" phrasing. Finally, since in most cases *samples* of the populations to be studied are utilized, much of the significance of the findings depends on the adequacy of the sample and the sampling technique.

The degree of sophistication with which these investigations are made has greatly increased in recent years. Earlier researches linking, for instance, religious affiliation with certain kinds of behavior included under a common classification all Catholics or all Jews or all Protestants. Most recent investigators, however, well aware that the influence of a merely nominal religious affiliation on certain types of behavior (for example, behavior in regard to the use of contraceptives) may well be minimal, have constructed various quantifiable yardsticks of religious involvement. Such yardsticks aim to measure the intensity of an individual's commitment to a particular kind of religious group and its principles. Joseph Fichter, by setting up criteria to designate the more and less involved—"nuclear," "modal," and "marginal" parishioners—was one of the first researchers to develop such a yardstick.[3]

More recently other investigators, notably Lenski and Glock and Stark took cognizance of the fact that there were a number of different ways in which an individual could be "religious." These were seen by Glock and Stark as the "dimensions of religiosity." For example, a person might be "religious" in the sense of attending church or temple regularly, but another person might stay at home on Sunday or Sabbath and yet spend considerable time in private prayer and devotion and feel that he had some real "experience" of the divine. Another individual might be "religious" in the sense that he subscribed fully to all the items in the official creed of his church or denomination while another might hold such creedal statements rather lightly and yet, materially, strongly "support" the church of his choice. These suggested ways of being "religious" serve to illustrate the problem involved, although they by no means exhaust the possible variations. The researcher who wishes to take into account these various "dimensions of religiosity" is then committed to finding ways to quantify the degree of involvement with respect to each "dimension" in order to form some estimate of "intensity." Needless to say, it is much easier to construct a quantifiable yardstick for such a dimension as "church attendance" than it is to do so in respect to "religious experience." Glock and Stark, however, have made a courageous attempt to measure the latter. Difficult as such yardsticks are to construct, the development of distinctions between these different ways of being religious is nevertheless extremely important for research purposes because these various dimensions are often correlated with quite different kinds of behavior. For instance, Lenski (whose study of the influence of the "religious factor" on a stratified sample of the citizens of Detroit was one of the first to emphasize such distinctions) found that subjects who scored high on "religious orthodoxy" were somewhat narrow and provincial in their social attitudes, while those who scored high on the "devotional" dimension were more likely to be broadly humanitarian.[4]

Investigations of Religious Movements and Religious Bodies

RELIGIOUS MOVEMENTS

One variety of study within this category focuses on religious movements, that is, investigations of religious bodies in their formative, dynamic stages. They are concerned with how religious organizations emerge and with uncovering the societal conditions that facilitate their growth and development. An important inquiry of this kind is Thomas O'Dea's *The Mormons* (1957). Much of the material used by O'Dea was, of course, historical and not only dealt with the social and religious situation in upper New York State in 1850 at the time that Joseph Smith, the founder of the Mormons, received his revelation, but also included the broader background of American frontier history. O'Dea also evaluated the records kept by the Mormon Church of its own history and organization, in itself no mean task. He supplemented this sociohistorical account of Mormon development with on-the-spot observation in Salt Lake City, but the major emphasis of his research was on the formative stages of the Mormon Church as a religious movement.

Such studies, however, may be contemporary, or near-contemporary, as well as historical. Eric Lincoln's monograph on the *Black Muslims in America* (1961) —a religious movement that, like the Mormons, is indigenous to the United States—is based mainly on recent information gathered by methods of firsthand observation. Lincoln was also concerned with the conditions of Negro social and religious life and in particular with the social and economic relationships between the black and white communities that had given birth to the Black Muslim movement.

He studied the nature of the emergent leadership and the means used by the leader to formulate aims and objectives that were consonant with the deep-seated desires of potential followers. Lincoln's approach, like O'Dea's, was broadly functional. He concludes the *Black Muslims* with an analysis of the functional significance of the movement for the Black Muslims themselves, for the American Negro community as a whole, and for the totality of American society.

ACCULTURATION STUDIES

The two works cited above are concerned with religious organizations indigenous to America. Other investigations of religious organization have been to an important extent *acculturation* studies—that is to say, one of their main concerns has been with the adaptation of "imported" religious organizations to the American scene, and also to the changing situation of an organization's members as they adapt themselves, in various ways, to the conditions of American life. One of the earliest of such studies was Pauline V. Young's *Pilgrims of Russian Town* (1932), an account of the acculturation of the Russian Molokans, a persecuted sect some of whose members migrated to the Los Angeles area in order to practice their religion freely. This study, carried on largely by means of participant observation and informal interviews, portrays vividly the conflicts of the Americanized second generation with the strict religious demands of their "European" parents. Similar in some respects is the present author's *Methodism and the Frontier* (1941). It shows how Methodism, imported from England as a somewhat settled religious body, became a religious movement when transplanted to America and especially when, carried by Methodist circuit riders, it followed the expanding frontier. Indeed, frontier conditions acted as a potent social solvent of European religious traditions and facilitated the Americanization of imported religious groups, both in respect to organization and to ritual and belief. *Methodism and the Frontier,* however, is largely a sociohistorical study, supplemented, as was O'Dea's work on the Mormons, with some on-the-spot observations.

More recent research has been able to "catch" the Americanization (acculturation) process closer to the time that it was actually taking place. For example, Marshall Sklare's *Conservative Judaism* (1955), which in some respects is "empirical" in the contemporary sense, bears the subtitle *An American Religious Movement*. Sklare depicts Conservative Judaism as a movement founded by American-born Jews as a religious and social response to their upward social mobility and to the changed conditions of their lives in the American environment. He is thus concerned with the way in which Orthodox Jewish beliefs and practices were modified as a result of the contact of the American-born children of Jewish immigrants with American religion and American ways. Conservative Judaism is interpreted as a movement of *accommodation* both in respect to American Protestantism and to Orthodox and Reform Judaism as well. Sklare views the Conservative movement as having survival value for the religion of many descendants of European Jews, as it has enabled them to accommodate to American life without assimilating or losing their Jewishness in the process. Since Sklare was an adherent of Conservative Judaism, he was able not only to obtain access to external documentary sources but also to utilize fully the method of participant observation and informal interviewing of laymen, rabbis, and seminary professors, thus gaining an intimate view of the group. But Sklare's study was undertaken purely for scholarly purposes and was not financed by the religious body he was investigating, a factor that no doubt helped the author to achieve an enviable objectivity.

STUDIES OF ISOLATED, CHANGE-RESISTANT GROUPS

While Sklare was concerned with the accommodation of one denomination to changes in social environment, a process that involved important ritual modifications without loss of the group's special identity, other sociologists have studied religious groups that have strongly resisted changes in their distinctive rituals and beliefs. Sometimes geographic isolation aids a conservative religious group to resist changes that would disrupt their traditional religious customs. A well-known example of such a group is the House Amish, whose rich farming acres in Lancaster County, Pennsylvania, have given them the economic independence and territorial base to resist (until quite recently) the encroachment of conventional American religious culture on the strictness of their religious discipline.

A well-documented case of religious isolationism is that of the Hasidic Jews. Although they live in the Williamsburg district of Brooklyn and many of them are to be seen riding the subways to work in Manhattan, they have to date maintained a remarkable degree of religious and psychological aloofness from American cultural influences, even those of American Orthodox Jewry. Solomon Poll's study *The Hasidic Community of Williamsburg* (1962) shows how they have skillfully channeled their economic activities to strengthen their traditional religious rites and practices.

RELIGION IN SUBURBIA

Another form of cultural influence upon religion and its organization that has received considerable attention recently is the suburb. The increasing suburbanization of the American people has been accompanied by a marked "suburbanization" of the churches and temples and a relative decay of the churches in small towns and in the inner city. The problems in religious organization that typically accompany this population shift are remarkably similar for all faiths. The suburban religious organization tends to be family-centered and community-centered. It provides a focus for group identification and, as a rule, provides a number of recreation activities, often to the neglect of wider social problems of the metropolis. Gibson Winter's *The Suburban Captivity of the Churches* (1961) analyzes this situation from a Protestant viewpoint, as does Peter Berger's *The Noise of Their Solemn Assemblies* (1961); while Andrew Greeley's *The Church and the Suburbs* (1959) and Albert I. Gordon's *Jews in Suburbia* (1959) deal respectively with Catholic and Jewish suburban communities.

Parochial Studies

An important contemporary trend in socioreligious research is the self-survey by religious bodies of their own populations. This trend marks a recent and growing rapprochement
between the churches and the sociological profession. A small
but somewhat influential group of clergy have reached the conclusion that knowledge of sociology as well as of scripture is necessary to make their churches, as human organizations, more effective in the services they render. Some of these churchmen are
themselves trained sociologists. Prominent among them is Joseph Fichter, S.J., whose pioneer sociological monographs such as
Dynamics of a City Church (1951), *Social Relations in an Urban
Parish* (1954), and *Parochial School* (1959) have blazed trails
that other researchers have followed and elaborated upon. The
Reverend Walter Kloetzli's *The Urban Church: Death or Renewal* (1961), an investigation sponsored by the National Council of Churches, is concerned with the success (or lack of success)
of eight urban Lutheran churches in adapting to various kinds of
neighborhood changes. Kloetzli describes his work as a "descriptive comparative study." He made use of congregational self-
studies, some in-depth interviews, and a membership questionnaire, yielding a combination of qualitative and quantitative
data supplemented by Kloetzli's own on-the-spot observations.

Inasmuch as such congregational and denominational self-
studies have a practical objective, they are set up and envisaged
in terms of group goals that tend to be viewed as "givens." From
a broader sociological point of view there exists the possibility
that a sociological investigator, not a member of the group under
observation, may view the situation of a particular religious
group somewhat differently from the way a priest or minister
trained in the social sciences may see a church or churches of his
own denomination. The priest or minister, however, is likely to
have a more intimate knowledge of the inner working of the organization under review.

Ecclesiastical "Bureaucracy"

Other studies go beyond the parish to inquire into the broader denominational aspects of religious organization. An interesting example of such an investigation is Paul Harrison's *Authority and Power in the Free Church Tradition* (1959). Harrison's analysis concerns the growth of a bureaucratic form of organization. This bureaucratic trend exists even in the "free churches," such as the Baptists, which have traditionally placed a premium on the autonomy of the individual congregation. Research into the Baptist organization deals with the conflict between the legality of grass-roots authority and the growth of centralized authority in actuality. He analyzes the social factors —the demands for formal ministerial training, expertise in religious education, and the like—that make the growth of a centralized bureaucratic organization inevitable, even in those churches that (unlike the Roman Catholic Church) have been traditionally opposed to centralized authority and a chain of command.

Studies of Religious Roles

Our discussion of the development of religious bureaucracy in Chapter 8 emphasized the fact that forms of religious organization in our changing society are becoming increasingly similar to such prevalent forms of secular organization as the corporation. By a somewhat analagous process religious roles, particularly those of ministers, priests, and rabbis, are, in common with those of lawyers, teachers, and medical men, becoming increasingly professionalized; that is, the decision to become a religious leader today is less likely to be experienced as a divine "calling" and more likely to be regarded as an intellectual, human decision to elect a religious "career."

Members of other professional groups have for some time conducted job analyses and updated the training of their prospective members in order to meet new role demands. Similar research and indoctrination are becoming increasingly necessary in the

RELIGION: A SOCIOLOGICAL VIEW

eyes of those responsible for the selection, training, and overseeing of religious personnel. Unfortunately, the components and problems of the minister's role have received much less careful study than those, say, of the student physician. Those sociologists who have analyzed the organization of religious bodies, such as Glock, Sklare, and Kloetzli, have been well aware of the conflicting pressures and ambiguities that presently inhere in many religious roles, and how needed changes in these roles may be impeded by the conservatism of both clergy and laity. Nevertheless, few serious inquiries have been made into the roles of religious professionals until quite recently.

However, a significant beginning has been made with Fichter's *Religion as an Occupation: A Study of the Sociology of the Religious Professions* (1961) and Philip E. Hammond's *The Campus Clergyman* (1966). The publication of the findings of Sister Marie Augusta Neal's nationwide survey of Catholic women's religious communities should soon add to our knowledge of the varied roles of such women.

Some earlier investigations have been useful trailblazers, such as Samuel Blizzard's research survey of the Protestant minister, "The Minister's Dilemma" [5] and Jerome F. Carlin and Saul R. Mendlovitz's "The American Rabbi: A Religious Specialist Responds to Loss of Authority." [6] Such studies reveal not only that there are a number of different roles played by religious specialists, but also that, as in other occupations, the same person may play a number of different roles, not all of them readily reconcilable, as Bryan R. Wilson has pointed out in his essay on the Pentecostal minister.[7] Sometimes these differences are signaled by differences in clothing, as when a Catholic priest wears vestments for celebrating Mass, a clerical "dog collar" for his traditional parochial duties, a business suit with collar and tie when teaching in a university, and a sports outfit when coaching the parochial club.

Popular Religion

Charles Y. Glock wrote in 1959 that most studies in religion do not tell us very much about the religion of the common man.[8] Unfortunately this is in large measure still true. Recently sociologists have become more interested in the content of popular religious belief since they have become more aware of how little they really know about it. The conviction has been gaining ground that the operative beliefs held by many Americans, whether they are church members or not, bear little resemblance to the official creeds of organized religious bodies.

How to "get at" the content of popular belief poses a rather difficult problem. On one hand, it is possible to make national surveys, in the manner of public opinion polls, of religious belief. A schedule or questionnaire, however, although valuable in collecting extensive data, is not a very pliable instrument for obtaining information about often half-articulate beliefs and attitudes; it is too likely to suggest answers and to fail to elicit new and unexpected information. At the opposite extreme, one can gain such information by conducting in-depth interviews with relatively few individuals; in an interview situation interviewees have time to express their half-formed ideas about religion, including ways in which their ideas have developed and changed. This method has the merit of not suggesting answers, but, if the interviewees are obtained by asking for volunteers, there is a likelihood that the material may be gathered from a skewed sampling of the population. Moreover, both questionnaires and interviews have the disadvantage of seeming to invite informants to verbalize opinions and attitudes that they feel to be appropriate to the situation. How, then, can sociologists tap expressions of religious belief without obtruding themselves or their research instruments too much, and—hopefully—without the subjects' knowing that social investigators are "listening"?

An interesting attempt to solve these knotty problems has been made by Louis Schneider and Sanford M. Dornbusch in *Popular Religion* (1958), with the use of content analysis of best-selling religious books. They regarded their study as one of religious mass culture, in this case the religious culture of middle-class people who would pay at that time from three to five dollars for a hard-cover edition of a religious book. Forty-six books were selected for analysis, the majority of them having been published in the 1940s and 1950s. Prominent among those selected were works by Norman Vincent Peale, Emmet Fox, Henry C. Link, Joshua Liebman, Glenn Clark, and Bishop Sheen. Schneider and Dornbusch found that the content of this "popular religion" largely bypassed denominationalism and gave scant attention to theological doctrine or to the "truth" or "falsity" of particular religious beliefs. In general it was a religion that looked to a benevolent God rather than to a God who would be a judge of one's actions. It was a religion that provided balm for typical middle-class anxieties—individualistic, optimistic, therapeutic, and, above all, instrumental. The religious emphasis would appear to have shifted from believing because it is *true* to believing because it is *useful*.

Conclusion

This review of theoretical approaches and types of research indicates the very considerable diversity of approaches and methods used. In the sociology of religion, as in the study of all important social and cultural phenomena, it is inevitable that there should be diverse approaches and diverse methods, each with its advantages and limitations. An informed awareness of this situation on the part of the student should help him to select the particular approaches and methods that are most appropriate to the tasks he chooses to undertake.

REFERENCES

1. Allan W. Eister, "Research Methods in the Sociology of Religion," *Review of Religious Research*, 6, no. 3 (Spring 1965), 125–130.
2. Charles Y. Glock and Rodney Stark, *Religion and Society in Tension* (Chicago: Rand McNally, 1965), p. 21–23.

3. Joseph H. Fichter, S.J., *Social Relations in the Urban Parish* (Chicago: University of Chicago Press, 1954), pp. 9–78, for an exposition of Fichter's typology of degrees of religious commitment.
4. Gerhard Lenski, *The Religious Factor: A Sociologist's Inquiry* (Garden City, N.Y.: Doubleday, 1961), pp. 18–26, and N. J. Demerath, III and Philip E. Hammond, *Religion in Social Context* (New York: Random House, 1969), pp. 148–151, make the point that the creation of "dimensions of religiosity" can be multiplied indefinitely and so degenerate into a mere taxonomic exercise.
5. Samuel Blizzard, "The Minister's Dilemma," *Christian Century*, 73 (April 25, 1956), 508–510.
6. Jerome P. Carlin and Saul R. Mendlovitz, "The American Rabbi: A Religious Specialist Responds to Loss of Authority," in Marshall Sklare (ed.), *The Jews: Social Patterns of an American Group* (Glencoe, Ill.: Free Press, 1958).
7. See Bryan R. Wilson, "The Pentecostal Minister: Role Conflicts and Contradictions of Status," in Bryan R. Wilson (ed.), *Patterns of Sectarianism* (London: Heinemann, 1967), pp. 138–157.
8. Glock, "The Sociology of Religion" in Robert K. Merton, Leonard Broom, and Leonard S. Cottrell, Jr. (eds.), *Sociology Today* (New York: Basic Books, 1959), p. 164.

SELECTED READINGS

GENERAL WORKS

Allport, Gordon W. *The Individual and His Religion*. New York: Macmillan, 1950. This discussion of the psychology of religion includes a number of functions religion may serve for the individual personality.

Bellah, Robert N. "Religious Evolution," *American Sociological Review*, 29 (June 1964). Bellah uses a neoevolutionary approach in an insightful and stimulating discussion of societal and accompanying religious changes.

Berger, Peter L. *The Sacred Canopy*. Garden City, N.Y.: Doubleday, 1967. Berger discusses the functions of religion from the perspective of the psychology of meaning and describes and analyzes the effects of secularization on traditional religion in the West.

Birnbaum, Norman and Gertrud Lenzer, eds. *Sociology and Religion*. Englewood Cliffs, N.J.: Prentice-Hall, 1969. This fine collection of readings, both "classical" and contemporary, includes excerpts from Hume, Hegel, Comte, Marx, Nietzche, and so on; and also from Adorno, Berger, Bellah, Erikson, Berger, Parsons, and other contemporaries.

Demerath, N. J., III, and Philip E. Hammond. *Religion in Social Context*. New York: Random House, 1969. This work provides a perceptive analysis of the most important and challenging sociological works in the field.

Merton, Robert K. *Social Theory and Social Structure*. 2nd ed. Glencoe, Ill.: Free Press, 1957. Merton's central theme is the functional analysis of social structures. Chapter 1, "Manifest and Latent Functions," is one of the few systematic statements of the theoretical foundations and framework of functional sociology. Chapters 14 and 15 treat the historical interconnection between religion and science.

Parsons, Talcott. *The Structure of Social Action*. New York: McGraw-Hill, 1937. This book contains a detailed analysis of the views of Max Weber and Émile Durkheim, among others.

———. *Religious Perspectives of College Teaching in Sociology and Social Psychology*. New Haven: Edward W. Hazen Foundation,

1951. This work is an outstanding essay in the sociology of religion.

———. *The Social System*. Glencoe, Ill.: Free Press, 1951. In this book Parsons lays down the main outlines of a conceptual scheme for the analysis of the structure and process of social systems. Chapters 8 and 9 discuss the role of belief systems and symbol systems in society.

Schneider, Louis, ed. *Religion, Culture, and Society: A Reader in the Sociology of Religion*. New York: John Wiley, 1964. Schneider provides a wide range of readings from modern as well as classical sources.

Wallace, Anthony F. C. *Religion: An Anthropological View*. New York: Random House, 1966. An anthropologist gives his insights into the meaning of religious behavior among both primitive and sophisticated peoples.

Yinger, J. Milton. *Religion, Society, and the Individual*. New York: Macmillan, 1957. This excellent textbook also includes a good selection of readings and an extensive bibliography.

LANDMARK STUDIES IN THE SOCIOLOGY OF RELIGION

Durkheim, Émile. *The Elementary Forms of the Religious Life*. Translated by Joseph Ward Swain. New York: Macmillan, 1915. Reprint. Glencoe, Ill.: Free Press, 1947. Originally published in 1902, this volume, based in part on Spencer and Gillen's study of an Australian tribe, is the outstanding pioneer work on the social aspects of religious beliefs and practices.

Freud, Sigmund. *The Future of an Illusion*. 1928. Reprint. Garden City, N.Y.: Doubleday, Anchor Book, 1964. This classic is a challenging and controversial essay on the future of religion.

James, William. *The Varieties of Religious Experience*. 1902. Reprint. Garden City, N.Y.: Doubleday, Dolphin Book, no date. This is a "classic" portrayal by a famous psychologist of the different ways in which individuals have experienced religion. Although James conceived of religion as an individual psychological experience, his delineation of the social contexts of the experiences he observed and recorded are nevertheless of great interest to sociologists. His book makes fascinating reading, and his focus on the experiences of individuals is a useful complement to the group emphasis of most sociologists.

Malinowski, Bronislaw. *Magic, Science, and Religion*. 1925. Reprint.

Glencoe, Ill.: Free Press, 1948. Reprint. Garden City, N.Y.: Doubleday, Anchor Book, 1954. The first part of this volume is a brilliant essay on magic, science, and religion, drawing on illustrations from the Trobrianders, so thoroughly studied by Malinowski.

Niebuhr, H. Richard. *The Social Sources of Denominationalism.* New York: Henry Holt, 1929. Reprint. New York: Meridian, Living Age Book, 1957. This important sociological study of the divisions within Christianity is written by a noted theologian who sees the perennial problem of religion as the relationship between transcendental doctrine and the necessities of organizing a religious community. The author contrasts "lower class" religion with "middle class" religion and sees the denomination as the most characteristic religious organization of the middle class.

Samuelsson, Kurt. *Religion and Economic Action: A Critique of Max Weber.* New York: Harper & Row, Harper Torchbook, 1964. Although perhaps not in its own right a "landmark study," this book is nevertheless a brief but devastating critique of one of the most influential books of all—namely, Weber's study regarding the role of the Protestant Ethic in the rise of modern capitalism.

Tawney, R. H. *Religion and the Rise of Capitalism.* New York: Harcourt, Brace, 1936. Reprint. New York: New American Library, Mentor Book, 1948. This close study of the development of Protestant thinking on economic issues is an essential complement to Weber's study of the relations between capitalism and Protestantism.

Troeltsch, Ernst. *The Social Teaching of the Christian Churches,* 1911 (published in German). London: Allen & Unwin, 1931. Reprint. 2 vols. Translated by Olive Wyon. New York: Harper & Row, Harper Torchbook, Cloister Library, 1960. A learned study of many varieties of Christian organization from the days of the early Christian Church to near-modern times. Troeltsch was the elaborator (see Vol. I, Chapter 9) of the well-known distinction between church and sect types of religious organization. The distinction itself was first made by Max Weber.

Weber, Max. *The Protestant Ethic and the Spirit of Capitalism.* Translated by Talcott Parsons. 1930. Reprint. New York: Scribner, 1958. This book is a classic research and analysis of historical relations between Protestantism and modern capitalism.

———. *From Max Weber: Essays in Sociology.* 1946. Reprint.

Translated and edited by Hans H. Gerth and C. Wright Mills. New York: Oxford University Press, Galaxy Book, 1958. Parts 3 and 4 of this work contain further material on Weber's well-known thesis.

————. *The Sociology of Religion.* 1922 (published in German). Reprint. Translated by Ephraim Fischoff. Boston: Beacon, 1963. This rewarding although rather difficult book contains Weber's mature thinking on many aspects of the sociology of religion.

RELIGION IN PRIMITIVE SOCIETIES

Freud, Sigmund. *Totem and Taboo.* 1913 (published in German). Reprint. Translated by James Strachey. New York: Norton, 1952. This is Freud's celebrated and disputed hypothesis about the origins of religion and culture.

Goode, W. J. *Religion Among the Primitives.* Glencoe, Ill.: Free Press, 1951. This work is a detailed functional analysis of comparative materials drawn from cultural anthropology.

Howells, William. *The Heathens: Primitive Man and His Religions.* Garden City, N.Y.: Doubleday, 1948. This exceedingly readable book explores such topics as the nature of religion, mana, taboo, and magic in its various forms.

Lanternari, Vittorio. *The Religions of the Oppressed: A Study of Modern Messianic Cults.* Translated by Lisa Sergio. New York: New American Library, Mentor Book, 1965. Utilizing a wealth of anthropological material, the author examines the role of messianic cults (largely among preliterate peoples) as a form of resistance to Western colonial rule.

Norbeck, Edward. *Religion in Primitive Society.* New York: Harper & Row, 1961. A good summary of many ethnographic accounts of religion in preliterate societies.

Swanson, Guy E. *The Birth of the Gods: The Origin of Primitive Beliefs.* Ann Arbor: University of Michigan Press, 1960. On the basis of a statistical analysis of anthropological data on fifty primitive societies, the author propounds an interesting theory about the relationship of deistic beliefs and social structure.

Turnbull, Colin. *The Forest People.* New York: Simon and Schuster, 1961. An anthropologist's account of his sojourn with an African Pygmy tribe, whose entire life pattern was permeated by their religion; delightful reading.

RELIGION IN TRADITIONAL AND MODERN SOCIETIES

Bellah, Robert N. *Tokugawa Religion: The Values of Pre-Industrial Japan.* Glencoe, Ill.: Free Press, 1957. The author explores the social and religious history of preindustrial Japan in order to discover why Japan was able to industrialize sooner than any other Asian country. This work is a trailblazing investigation into the sociology of Japanese religion.

Dator, James Allen. *Sōka Gakkai: Builders of the Third Civilization.* Seattle: University of Washington Press, 1969. An examination of the social functions of a fast-growing Japanese religious movement, involving both Japanese and American participants.

Geertz, Clifford. *The Religion of Java.* Glencoe, Ill.: Free Press, 1960. This important anthropological research report of the changing role of Islam in a contemporary Javanese village shows the conflict and accommodation between conservative and modernizing elements.

Martin, David. *A Sociology of English Religion.* New York: Basic Books, 1967. The first book on the subject of the sociology of religion *(in toto)* in the United Kingdom, this work is more useful for its descriptive qualities than for the depth of its sociological analysis. The author claims that religion in Britain plays a more important role than is generally realized.

Smith, Huston. *The Religions of Man.* New York: Harper & Row, Perennial Library, 1965. Although only one of several good summary descriptions of the world's religions, Smith's is a very readable, perceptive, and short treatment.

Swanson, Guy E. *Religion and Regime: A Sociological Account of the Reformation.* Ann Arbor: University of Michigan Press, 1967. Swanson analyzes and characterizes the forms of government in some forty European states in the fifteenth century (and after) in order to establish a relationship between types of regime and types of theology adopted by those states at the time of the Reformation. An original, detailed, and thought-provoking study.

Watt, William Montgomery. *Islam and the Integration of Society.* Evanston, Ill.: Northwestern University Press, 1961. Watt provides a historical and sociological analysis of the conditions underlying the rise of Islam.

Weber, Max. *The Religion of India: The Sociology of Hinduism and*

Buddhism. Translated and edited by Hans H. Gerth and Don Martindale. Glencoe, Ill.: Free Press, 1958. Weber stresses the other-worldly emphases of both Hinduism and Buddhism. He sees their failure to ascribe a religious value to rational, this-worldly endeavor as inhibiting capitalistic development.

————. *The Religion of China: Confucianism and Taoism.* Translated and edited by Hans H. Gerth. Glencoe, Ill.: Free Press, 1951. Weber views the impact of Confucianism and Taoism on Chinese society as reinforcing traditionalism because of the conservative, humanistic character of China's main culture-bearers, the *literati.* Weber sees traditionalism as a major deterrent to capitalistic development.

————. *Ancient Judaism.* Translated and edited by Hans H. Gerth and Don Martindale. Glencoe, Ill.: Free Press, 1952. Weber argues that Ancient Judaism was the religion of a pariah people. Their ethical-religious legitimation of rational profit-making applied only to their dealings with outsiders. Their ritualism and religiously sanctioned in-group relationships militated, in Weber's view, against the development of capitalism. His thesis has been contested by scholars, particularly by Werner Sombart. This and the two above volumes form a trilogy. In each volume Weber analyzes the impact of its religion on a society that had not developed a capitalistic economy. His conclusions, based on sources now somewhat outmoded, still provoke scholarly controversy. (The three volumes were all first published before 1920.)

Wilson, Bryan R., ed. *Patterns of Sectarianism: Organization and Ideology in Social and Religious Movements.* London: Heinemann, 1967. This work contains sociohistorical sketches, by various authors, of a number of religious groups in England, such as the Salvation Army, the Pentecostals, the Quakers, the Plymouth Brethren, the Churches of God. It also includes (pp. 22–45) Wilson's article "Analysis of Sect Development," which first appeared in the *American Sociological Review,* 24 (February 1959), 3–15.

RELIGION AND THE AMERICAN SCENE

Brown, Robert McAfee, and Gustave Weigel, S.J. *An American Dialogue: A Protestant Looks at Catholicism and a Catholic Looks at Protestantism.* Garden City, N.Y.: Doubleday, Anchor Book, 1960. This work is two essays: in one an eminent Catholic theologian describes American Protestantism as seen through Catholic eyes, and in the other a well-known Protestant divine does the reverse for Catholicism.

Cox, Harvey. *The Secular City.* New York: Macmillan, 1965. Using both theological and sociological approaches, a sociologically sophisticated theologian examines the rise of urban civilization and the collapse of traditional religion. Cox distinguishes between "secularity" and "secularism" and maintains that the former should be accepted and understood, rather than deplored.

Demerath, N. J., III. *Social Class in American Protestantism.* Chicago: Rand McNally, 1965. Demerath provides a statistical investigation of the relation between various aspects of Protestant religion and social class, together with an interpretation and a critique of previous research.

Ellis, John Tracy, S.J. *American Catholicism.* Chicago: University of Chicago Press, 1956. An outstanding Catholic historian surveys the development of the Catholic Church from the days of the colonial missions to the present.

Fichter, Joseph H., S.J. *Social Relations in the Urban Parish.* Chicago: University of Chicago Press, 1954. This work is a close study by a Catholic priest and sociologist of religious behavior and social relations among Catholics in a Southern urban area. The author develops a yardstick for measuring an individual's degree of "involvement" in the religious life of the parish.

————. *Religion as an Occupation: A Study of the Sociology of Professions.* Notre Dame, Ind.: University of Notre Dame Press, 1961. This book is one of the few distinguished large-scale discussions of religious professionals, although most of the materials are restricted to Roman Catholicism.

Frazier, Franklyn E. *The Negro Church in America.* New York: Schocken Books, 1963. A distinguished black sociologist gives a historical and sociological account of the development and function of Negro churches in the U.S. The title is somewhat of a misnomer; there is no single Negro church in America; a variety of churches represent the entire religious spectrum.

Glazer, Nathan. *American Judaism.* Chicago: University of Chicago Press, 1957. This sociologically sophisticated account of the evolution of Judaism in the United States is brief, interesting, and readable.

Glock, Charles Y., and Rodney Stark. *Religion and Society in Tension.* Chicago: Rand McNally, 1965. This collection of essays deals with some of the current anomalies of church government and administration and Glock's conception of a continuing conflict between religion and science. Chapter 2,

"The Dimensions of Religiosity," contains a useful analysis of the different ways in which people can be "religious."

Greeley, Andrew M., and Peter H. Rossi. *The Education of Catholic Americans*. Chicago: Aldine, 1966. This work is a rigorous investigation of the effects of Catholic versus non-Catholic schooling on such variables as secular achievement and aspiration.

Herberg, Will. *Protestant, Catholic, Jew*. Garden City, N.Y.: Doubleday, Anchor Book, 1960. In this influential essay concerning the state of religion in American society in the 1950s, Herberg attempts to reconcile the apparent paradox of an increase in religious affiliation coincident with the growing secularity of the society as a whole. Herberg argues that the three religious groups have moved closer together, serving now as alternative ways of "being American."

Lenski, Gerhard. *The Religious Factor: A Sociologist's Inquiry*. 1961. Reprint. Garden City, N.Y.: Doubleday, Anchor Book, 1963. This widely acclaimed empirical study (based on data collected in Detroit) discusses the extent to which differences in religious affiliation are related to differences in everyday economic, political, and familial behavior.

Lincoln, C. Eric. *The Black Muslims*. Boston: Beacon Press, 1963. A black sociologist gives an account of the structure and functions of a black American religious movement. Lincoln views the Black Muslims as an essentially political movement utilizing a religious vehicle.

O'Dea, Thomas F. *The Mormons*. Chicago: University of Chicago Press, 1957. This study by a sociologist covers the history and doctrine of Mormonism and, incidentally, of present-day Mormons. O'Dea considers the strengths and weaknesses of the Mormon Church and the role it has played in the United States.

Poll, Solomon. *The Hasidic Community of Williamsburg*. Glencoe, Ill.: Free Press, 1962. Poll gives a perceptive, analytic account of the persistence within a "secular society" of an ultrareligious group. The reinforcement of the religious group life by means of the economic activities of its members is especially interesting.

Pope, Liston. *Millhands and Preachers*. 1942. Reprint. New Haven: Yale University Press, 1965. This fascinating study of religion in a Southern mill town throws a great deal of light on the nature of religious sects and their relationship to economic institutions. It shows how former "sects" were transformed into "denominations" and points up a number of criteria that distinguish denominations from sects.

Religion in America. Daedalus, Vol. 96, no. 1 (Winter 1967). A collection of articles by a group of modern authorities on various aspects of religion in America. Especially valuable is Robert N. Bellah's "Civil Religion in America." Bellah cites historical and contemporary sources in making a persuasive argument for the existence of a system of "religious" beliefs and rituals connected with the federal government of the United States.

Salisbury, W. Seward. *Religion in American Culture: A Sociological Interpretation.* Homewood, Ill.: Dorsey Press, 1964. This comprehensive text contains some useful factual material on American religious movements, sects, and denominations; it has an extensive bibliography.

Schneider, Louis, and Sanford M. Dornbusch. *Popular Religion: Inspirational Books in America.* Chicago: University of Chicago Press, 1958. On the assumption that people tend to "believe" what they pay good money to read about, the authors have analyzed thematically a selected sample of best-selling religious books in order to discover the "operative" beliefs of middle-class Americans.

Sklare, Marshall. *Conservative Judaism: An American Religious Movement.* Glencoe, Ill.: Free Press, 1955. Sklare gives a historical and sociological analysis of the emergence of a movement that attempted to adapt a traditional religion to modern American society. Its perception of the role of generations of immigrants in modifying traditional religion anticipated Herberg's account.

Underwood, Kenneth. *Protestant and Catholic.* Boston: Beacon Press, 1957. This work is an intensive study of Catholic-Protestant relations in Holyoke, Massachusetts, during a period in which the majority of the population was shifting from Protestant to Catholic.

Watts, Alan W. *The Way of Zen.* New York: Pantheon, 1957. Alan Watts is a well-known interpreter of Eastern religion to modern Americans; his writings have been influential in molding the religious thinking of many persons in the "under-thirty" generation. This book is one of the most readable introductions to Far Eastern thought.

———. *This Is It, and Other Essays on Zen and Spiritual Experience.* New York: Pantheon, 1960. This work includes essays on the role of Zen in American life, on spirituality and sensuality, and on the use and abuse of L.S.D. and other drugs.

Winter, Gibson. *The Suburban Captivity of the Churches.* Garden City, N.Y.: Doubleday, 1961. A Protestant minister and sociologist analyzes the causes and consequences of the exodus of middle-class Protestant churches from the central cities to the suburbs.

Yinger, J. Milton. *Religion in the Struggle for Power.* Durham, N.C.: Duke University Press, 1946. Yinger provides an insightful analysis of the paradoxes confronting religion as it is organized to further many aims, including the aim of influencing society.

INDEX

Political conflict, *see* Church and
state; Religion
Polygamy, 188, 199
"Poor Peoples March," 57, 264
See also Negroes; United States
Pope John XXIII, 172, 223
Pope Paul VI, 177, 274, 277
Prayer, 72, 92, 101, 104–105, 150, 201,
277
Predestination, 115, 158, 163
Presbyterian denomination, 173, 270
Presbyterian government, *see*
Churches
Prophets, 147–162, 199–202
Protestant ethic, 69, 144, 154, 161, 211
Protestant religions, 43, 46, 48, 72,
156–161, 173–178, 187–192, 197–
204, 211, 222, 224, 241, 246, 250,
252, 257–259, 261–262, 264–265,
269–278
Psychology, Approach to study of re-
ligion, 5–6, 98, 106
Puerto Ricans, 51, 175, 235
Punishments and rewards, *see* Value
systems
Puritans, 158

Racial attitudes, 127–128, 187–190,
197–198, 251
Ras Tafari cult, 125
Reincarnation, 115, 130
Religion
communication, influence of, 50,
149, 164–165, 183–185, 192
community involvement, 42, 247–
251
and cosmologies, 17, 102, 105, 172
as cultural tool, 13, 34, 37–40, 43–45
definitions of, 9–12, 56
dysfunctional role, 67, 91, 94, 102,
105–106, 189, 262
and economics, 40, 69, 103, 118–119,
124–125, 132–135, 152, 155, 158–
160, 163–165, 174, 184
education, influence on, 40, 42, 47,
189–191, 213
experimental churches, 247–249

Religion (*continued*)
group aspects, 3, 33–34, 63–64, 83,
93, 98, 114, 238–239, 241, 248,
250, 267–269
individual aspects, 3–4, 34, 36, 39–
49, 59, 64, 66, 71–72, 76–78, 80–
82, 84–85, 90–91, 95–96, 104–106,
109–114, 130–132, 157–159, 168,
221–222, 226, 236, 238, 242, 245–
248, 252, 259–263, 268
innovating role, 39–40, 42, 66–68,
150, 152–153, 169, 247–250, 264–
265, 277–281
Mormons, 252
origins of, 10–13
participation mystique, 33
and politics, 69, 118–119, 123–125,
132–135, 154, 158–159, 174, 184,
208–212, 225n, 234, 266, 272–274
and psychiatry, 105–107
and science, 96–100, 103–106
secular, 3, 25–27, 35–46, 51, 102–
103, 105, 118, 120, 137, 143, 183,
208, 225, 227
sociological approach, 3–21
stabilizing influence, 34, 39, 56–60,
65–66, 68, 76–102, 153, 162, 172,
234, 259, 262–263, 278
status, influence on, 40
Syncretism, 193, 197, 199–201
and technology, 40–41, 50, 79, 89,
105, 184–185, 190, 195, 213, 237,
259
universality of, 7–9, 39, 121
vocations, influence on, 40, 130,
158, 203
women as leaders, 197–198, 247
Religious education, 47, 268, 274–276
Religious solitaries, 36
See also Monasticism
Revivalism, 174
See also United States
Ritual and liturgy, 15, 17–18, 83–87,
131, 168, 173–174, 225, 247–249
Roman Catholic religion, 16–17, 42–
43, 46, 68, 101, 142, 157, 159–161,
164, 172–177, 186, 190, 192, 200,
221–222, 223n, 224, 231, 234, 236,

Professor Elizabeth K. Nottingham received her B.A. and her M.A. from Cambridge University and her Ph.D. from Columbia University. She has taught at Wheaton College (Massachusetts) , Sophie Newcomb College of Tulane University, and was until 1968 Professor of Sociology at Queens College of the City University of New York. Professor Nottingham has also been a Fulbright Exchange Professor in Rangoon, Burma, and a Resident Scholar at the Center for Study of World Religions at Harvard University. Her writings include *The Making of an Evangelist: A Study of John Wesley's Early Years, Methodism and the Frontier: Indiana Proving Ground,* and *Religion and Society,* and contributions to the *American Sociological Review, American Journal of Sociology,* and *Journal for the Scientific Study of Religion.* Currently Professor Nottingham is associated with the Department of Sociology at the University of California at Berkeley.